THE S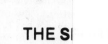

PRICE GUIDE

NO. 4

By
DR. JAMES BECKETT
AND
DENNIS W. ECKES

ISBN 0-937424-13-7

ACKNOWLEDGEMENTS

While they have always been major contributors, several collectors have provided exception
assistance in the preparation of the fourth edition of the Price Guide. CHRIS BENJAMIN worked si
by side with the authors during the final stages of the manuscript and provided many of the s
descriptions for the new issues added in this edition. He also interviewed and wrote the article
hobby pioneer John Wagner contained herin. LEW LIPSET provided illustrative material, including t
color section, on the 19th Century material contained within for the first time this year. He al
wrote the article on the 1933 Goudey set, a highlight of this issue. JACK POLLARD, one of t
true veteran collectors in the hobby, provided much of the scarce issue illustrative materi
corroborated many obscure checklists, and clarified many of the questions the authors posed duri
the preparation of the book. While Sport Americana issues no awards for contributions to the hob
in this yearly publication, if it did, JOHN WAGNER would certainly be one of the first recipients.
thank John for allowing us to interview him and for contributing so much over the years to the hobb

Major contributions — in the form of set descriptions, checklists, price input and a vast amount
personal time and energy — were unselfishly made to us by: Mike Aronstein, Buck Barker, M
Cramer, Bill and Diane Dodge, Rich Egan, Doak Ewing, Gervise Ford, Larry and Jeff Fritsch, Mike a
Howie Gordon, Bill Haber, Jim Horne, Don McPherson, Paul Marchant, Stanley McClure, B.A. Mur
Jim Nicewander, Ralph Nozaki, Tom Pfirrmann, Andrew Pywowarczuk, Pat Quinn, Tom Reid, D
Reuss, Owen Ricker, Gavin Riley, Randall Root, John Rumierz, Elwood Scharf, Don Steinbach, a
John Sterling.

In addition, significant contributions were made by: Frank and Vivian Barning, Ken Blazek, Br
Boston, George Callahan, Dan Dischley, Wayne Grove, Barry Halper, Bill Heitmann, Dave and Ro
Jones, Larry Kelley, Arlyn Kirkeide, Jim Kovacs, Don Lepore, Irv Lerner, Howie Levy, George Lyo
Stan Martucci, Michael Marz, Bill Mastro, Jim McLean, Frank Nagy, Clay and Nancy Pasternack, D
Ring, Bill Rothney, Geoff Sindelar, John Stommen, Wayne Varner, Sal Visalli, Tom Webb, M
Wheat, Bill Zekus, and Bill Zimpleman.

Many others have contributed in the form of price input, error corrections, and picture donations,
should like to thank them: Jeff Alcorn, Scott Alsobrooks, Paul Ault, Shawn Aultman, Mike Berk
Dan Bernstein, Ed Berry, Mark Bowers, Frank Bricker, Steve Brunner, Jack Byrd, Dwight Chap
Tom Charlton, Mark Christensen, Todd Churley, Charles Ciani, Jerry Clark, Wayne Clark, E
Clineschmidt, Mike Cokenour, Tony Colatruglio, Kevin Collins, Charles Comas, Empire Comics, T
Coslar, Anthony Curtis, Jay Darnell, Gordon Dean, John Dieroff, Larry Dluhy, Larry Dockum, M
Drabowski, M.W. Driskell, Dan DuByne, Larry Duquette, Mark Eckblad, John Esch, Anthony Fie
Don Frascone, Phil Gelso, Edward George, Larry Gladstone, Jeff Goldstein, Jack Goodman, D
Gordon, G. Richard Green, Bill Hall, Charley Hall, Gary Hamilton, John Hamilton, Joe Hamma
Trae Hancock, Kent Havens, Bill Henderson, Don Hicks, Mark Hogan, Derek Holmes, Dave Hou
Henry Janeski, Mike Jennings, Jerry Johnson, Gary Kaplan, Frank Keetz, Steve Kessinger, J
Kilgore, Rock Koepke, Greg Lawton, Dan Madden, Roy Maiwurm, Mike Mayko, Chuck MacBr
James McCoy, James McElroy, Stephen Markler, Dick Miller, Dick Millerd, Chuck Mitchell, W
Moore, Tom and Betty Notestine, Michael Olenick, Ron Parker, Greg Payne, Carroll Plunk,
Podnar, Bob Rathgeber, James Rogers, Stephen Roman, Joseph Rosadini, Bruce Rosenberg,
Ruhrig, Marcus Rutt, Nord Sahagrian, Peter Schneider, Joe Sencay, Larry Shane, J.C. Shannon, N
Shoff, Joel Sneed, Nick Snider, Mel Solomon, Bob Turner, Edwin Ulvila, Ernest Unrath, Paul Vag
George Wallace, Skipper Watford, Bill Wesslund, Richard West, Bob Wilke, Michael Witkowich, D
Wood, Kit Young, Wes Young, John Zalich, Jay Zeiter, Ronnie Zell, Barry Zsigovits.

The typists who worked on the manuscript and the extensive clerical and filing system necessary f
book of this magnitude deserve both our praise and thanks: Carole Barrett, Denise Delss, Suza
Ford, Millie "Slick" Phillips, Margaret Schultz Rahm, Carollyn Roach, and Charlotte Vaugh

Special thanks are extended to the Topps Chewing Gum Company (specifically Messrs. Sy Berger
Bill Haber), The Fleer Corporation (specifically Mr. Arnold Harris) and The Donruss Comp
(specifically Mr. Steward F. Lyman and Ms. Jan Burkett) for providing 1982 checklists and v
material in order that the 1982 national issues could be included in this Price Guide.

A heartfelt thank you to Patti Beckett for her patience while her husband completed the manus
and for her unselfish help in performing many of the time consuming and unglamorous funct
associated with the production of this book. Similarly, a special thanks to Dennis William Ecke
the many nights spent alone and "down the shop" while Dad worked on "the book."

1982 BASEBALL CARDS

OUR 35TH YEAR IN CARDS-AMERICA'S MOST RELIABLE CARD DEALER

WITH OVER 30 MILLION CARDS IN STOCK ... WE HAVE AMERICA'S MOST COMPLETE STOCK OF SPORTS TRADING CARDS. All sets and singles are available ... 1948-1982. We have thousands of Pre-1948 cards available also.
SUPER SERVICE!! We have four full-time employees ready and able to process your order with the maximum of efficiency and speed ... TRY OUR SERVICE & SEE ... You'll agree ... it's the best you have ever had!!! Full Money back guarantee if you are not completely satisfied with our service and products. YOU, the customer are always NO. 1 to us!!!
To receive Super Service it is necessary to send a POSTAL MONEY ORDER with your order. (all personal checks are held 15 days for clearance).

TOPPS
1. Complete set (792 cards) only $22.00 + $1.75 shipping.
2. 1.000 mint cards in never before opened boxes $18.00 + $2.00 shipping.
3. Team sets—$3.50 each ppd.

Brewers, Dodgers, Orioles, Phillies, Pirates, Reds, Red Sox, Royals, Yankees $5.00 each ppd.

RON LeFLORE

FLEER
1. Complete set (660 cards) only $20.00 + $1.75 shipping.
2. Team sets — $3.00 each ppd.

Brewers, Dodgers, Orioles, Phillies, Pirates, Reds, Red Sox, Royals, Yankees $4.50 each ppd.

DONRUSS
1. Complete set (660 cards) only $16.75 + $1.75 shipping.
2. Team sets — $3.25 each ppd.

Brewers, Dodgers, Orioles, Phillies, Pirates, Reds, Red Sox, Royals, Yankees $4.75 each ppd.

ROSS BAUMGARTEN

PARTIAL LIST OF SETS AVAILABLE

(All sets are in mint condition)

All sets are shipped in numerical order, postpaid, via UPS, in damage-free boxes.

BASEBALL SETS

1980 Topps (726)	$26.50
1979 Topps (726) (Wills-Rangers)	37.50
1979 Topps (726) (Wills-Blue Jays)	30.00
1978 Topps (726)	42.00
1977 Topps (660)	55.00
1976 Topps (660)	70.00
1975 Topps (660)	130.00
1974 Topps (660)	150.00
1973 Topps (660)	200.00
1981 Topps Super Stars (117)	52.50
1981 Topps Stickers w/album (262)	35.00
1980 Topps Super Stars (Gray) (60)	23.50
1979 Topps Comics (33)	14.00
1977 Topps Cloth Patches & Cl. (73)	35.00
1976 Topps Traded (44)	6.00
1974 Topps Traded (44)	7.00
1974 Topps Washington (11)	65.00
1970 Topps Super (63)	80.00
1970 Topps Super (41) w/o no. 38	72.50
1981 Kelloggs 3D (66)	12.00
1980 Kelloggs 3D (60)	15.00
1979 Kelloggs 3D (60)	25.00
1978 Kelloggs 3D (57)	35.00
1977 Kelloggs 3D (57)	50.00
1974 Kelloggs 3D (54)	75.00
1973 Kelloggs 3D (54)	90.00
1972 Kelloggs 3D (54)	30.00
1972 Kelloggs 3D Baseball Greats (15)	30.00
1981 Fleer All Star Stickers (128)	10.00
1971 Fleer World Series (68)	32.50
1970 Fleer World Series (66)	35.00
1959 Fleer Ted Williams (79) w/o no. 68	100.00
1976 Sports Stars (630)	15.00

FOOTBALL SETS

1981 Topps (528)	$20.50
1981 Topps Stickers w/album (262)	30.00
1981 Topps Stickers—Red Border—Test (28)	10.50
1980 Topps (528)	23.00
1980 Topps Super Stars (30)	12.50
1979 Topps (528)	30.00
1978 Topps (528)	32.50
1977 Topps (528)	35.00
1976 Topps (528)	40.00
1975 Topps (528)	45.00
1974 Topps (528)	45.00
1973 Topps (528)	60.00
1972 Topps (351)	55.00
1971 Topps (263)	70.00
1970 Topps (263)	72.50
1970 Topps Super (35)	60.00
1969 Topps nos. 89-176)	66.50
1976 Wonder Bread (24)	9.00
1975 Wonder Bread (24)	10.00
1974 Wonder Bread (30)	12.00
1981 Topps NFL in Action (88)	10.00
1980 Fleer NFL in Action (88)	11.50
1979 Fleer NFL in Action (69)	12.50
1978 Fleer NFL in Action (68)	16.50
1977 Fleer NFL in Action (67)	22.50
1974 Fleer Hall of Fame (50)	8.50
1960 Fleer AFL	75.00
1972 Canadian League (132)	22.50
1971 Canadian League (132)	25.00
1970 Kelloggs 3D (60)	32.50
1974 Nabisco Pro Faces (25)	10.00
1972 DX-Sunoco Stamps w/album (624)	15.00
1969 Tresler-Comet Bengals (19)	25.00

BASKETBALL SETS

1981-82 Topps (198)	$12.00
1980-81 Topps (88)	7.00
1979-80 Topps (132)	10.00
1978-79 Topps (132)	13.00
1977-78 Topps (132)	16.50
1976-77 Topps (144)—Large	22.00
1975-76 Topps (330)	37.50
1974-75 Topps (264)	30.00
1973-74 Topps (264)	35.00
1972-73 Topps (264)	45.00
1971-72 Topps (233)	47.50
1970-71 Topps (175)	60.00
1969-70 Topps (99)	POR
1970-71 Topps Pin Ups (24)	49.50
1969-70 Topps Pin Ups (23)	13.50

HOCKEY SETS

1981-82 Topps (198)	11.95
1980-81 Topps (264)	10.50
1979-80 Topps (264)	14.00
1978-79 Topps (264)	17.50
1977-78 Topps (264)	20.00
1977-78 Topps Glossy Photos (22)	14.00
1976-77 Topps (264)	22.00
1976-77 Topps Glossy Photos (22)	15.00
1975-76 Topps (330)	32.50
1974-75 Topps (264)	28.00
1973-74 Topps (198)	32.00
1972-73 Topps (176)	40.00
1971-72 Topps (132)	50.00
1968-69 Topps (132)	75.00
1974-75 O-Pee-Chee-WHA (66)	17.50

All above prices are postpaid in U.S. Funds. CANADA CUSTOMERS: Please send Postal Money Orders in U.S. Funds and an additional $6.00 per set for sets over 250 cards. $3.00 per set for sets under 250 cards for shipping your sets. ALASKA, HAWAII, APO, FPO & P.O. BOX CUSTOMERS: Add an additional $4.00 per set for sets over 250 cards and $2.50 per set for sets under 250 cards for shipping your sets.

BASEBALL CARD CHECKLIST BOOK

- The new BASEBALL CARD CHECKLIST BOOK is available now for immediate shipment. Illustrated checklists of all regular issue baseball cards of Topps, Bowman, Fleer and Leaf from 1948 through 1980 including the 1964, 1969-71 Super sets! It has over 18,000 players names listed.

- The new BASEBALL CARD CHECKLIST BOOK lists the card number and name of every player issued in the above sets, plus the varieties in each set. A card of each year and manufacturer is illustrated to help you identify the cards you have.

NEW FEATURE! This book has a plastic binder which allows for adding of new pages each year as the new baseball sets are issued. These pages can be purchased each year to keep your checklist book up-to-date. No need to buy the entire book each year! Your checklist book is always current.

A MUST FOR ANY CARD COLLECTOR . . . $8.50 Postpaid $10.00 Air Mail

THE ALL NEW BASEBALL CARD TEAM CHECKLIST is here!!!

- This new book lists all Bowman, Topps, Fleer and Donruss regular issues by team!!

- Contains 130 pages of fully illustrated team lists along with a list of all the wrong pictures printed by Topps and Bowman.

- The BASEBALL CARD TEAM CHECKLIST is printed on high quality, glossy paper with a removable binding to allow the addition of the current pages as they come out every year!!!

- With the BASEBALL CARD TEAM CHECKLIST it will not be necessary to page through regular checklist books or alpha books to find players on your favorite team—find them at a GLANCE!!!

$8.00 Postpaid $9.50 1st Class

FINEST QUALITY PLASTIC SHEETS

FEATURING
- NON-MIGRATING PLASTIC IN ALL SHEETS
- PLASTIC THAT DOES NOT STICK TOGETHER
- STIFFNESS TO PREVENT CARD CURLING
- INTELLIGENT DESIGN
- RESISTANCE TO CRACKING
- FULL COVERAGE OF CARDS, PHOTOS & POSTCARDS

SHEETS FIT ANY 3 RING BINDER
• Minimum order 4 sheets.

ORDER TODAY!
Get your cards protected!
SHEETS FIT ANY 3 RING BINDER

STILL AVAILABLE! 1981 Baseball Cards

1981 Topps set (726 cards)	$24.50 ppd.
1981 Topps set (858 cards) (includes scarce "Traded set")	47.50 ppd.
1981 Donruss set (605 cards)	20.00 ppd.
1981 Donruss 1st printing error set	40.00 ppd.
1981 Donruss Error cards (36)	25.00 ppd.
1981 Fleer set (660 cards)	22.00 ppd.
1981 Fleer 1st printing error sets	
With "C" Nettles	60.00 ppd.
With "G" Nettles	40.00 ppd.

TOPPS

BRODERICK PERKINS FIRST BASE
DONRUSS

DAN SPILLNER PITCHER
FLEER

48-PAGE CATALOG

LARRY FRITSCH CARDS PRESENTS (OUR 48 PAGE CATALOG)
Read by over 40,000 sports collectors!

With the great number of cards and other sports memorabilia we have in stock, it is impossible to list all of the items we have available. If you would like a complete listing of the items we have available for sale please send $1.00 to receive the next 3 big issues of our 48 page catalog (Larry Fritsch Cards Presents). The catalog includes listings of SETS & SINGLE CARDS covering: baseball 1909-1982, football 1948-1982, (basketball 1948-1982, and hockey 1955-1982). NON-SPORT CARDS (sets & singles 1948-1974), BASEBALL & FOOTBALL TEAM SETS (1948-1982), MAGAZINES (Sporting News, Sports Illustrated, SPORT Magazine, Baseball Digest & others 1954-1982). All indications are that the next L.F.C.P. will be BIGGER and BETTER THAN EVER BEFORE.

(Canada residents—$1.00 per issue, shipped 1st class)

1982 BASEBALL CREDIT CARDS

All New!! 1982 set (24 cards) $29.95 ppd.

Still Available:
1981 Superstars (32 cards)	$37.50 ppd.
1981 All Stars (18 cards)	26.50 ppd.

JOHNNY BENCH CATCHER CINCINNATI

BUYING CARDS!!! Top prices paid for cards issued prior to 1968. Please send list.

(Also buying APBA Baseball playing cards (complete sets, loose singles, or sample cards from 1950 to 1970.)

 MasterCard

LARRY FRITSCH

 VISA

(Charge Orders Add 5% To Total)

DEPT 560   735 OLD WAUSAU ROAD   STEVENS POINT, WIS. 54481

SPORT AMERICANA BASEBALL CARD
PRICE GUIDE
TABLE OF CONTENTS

SPORT AMERICANA BASEBALL CARD
PRICE GUIDE
TABLE OF CONTENTS

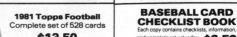

PREFACE

Sports memorabilia collecting in general and baseball card collecting in particular are popular. We've read on numerous occasions that sports collecting is the third most popular hobby in the country; whether it is or not is irrelevant. We collect baseball cards because we enjoy collecting them, not because the hobby is popular. That others also enjoy our hobby gives us the opportunity to find new and interesting hobby material and meet new and interesting people with similar interests to ours. Who could ask for more from one's hobby?

During the first three years that this Price Guide has been published, the baseball card collecting hobby has grown by leaps and bounds; prices have fluctuated upward and downward; new card sets have been produced in unprecedented amounts. Our National Pastime went through a traumatic 1981 with the infamous 50-day players' strike. While there might be a temptation to alter the purpose or format of this fourth edition of the Price Guide, in retrospect, the purpose of the book is the same as it was for the first edition, even though the size of the book has more than doubled. The format has proven useful and workable; therefore, the authors see no reason to change it.

The prime purpose of this Price Guide is to provide a functional tool to the hobbyist, not to entertain as would a novel. The Guide is about baseball cards, not the personalities pictured on them, albeit the value of a card is determined to a great extent by who is pictured on the card. However, while the prime purpose of the Guide is not to entertain, we do hope you find it interesting and useful.

The Sport Americana Baseball Card Price Guide has been successful when other attempts have failed because of its completeness, currentness, and validity. This Price Guide contains three prices, by condition, for all baseball cards in the issues which account for almost all of the baseball cards that exist today. Not only does it list prices for the so-called common player cards in each issue, but also it distinguishes the common player cards from the high value cards (Star, Superstar, Team and Special cards). These high value cards form the foundation upon which the price structure of the baseball card collecting hobby is currently based. The Guide is current; prices were added to the card lists in 1982, just prior to printing. And, the prices are valid. The prices reflect not the authors' opinions or desires but the "going" retail prices for each card based on the marketplace—hobby papers, sports memorabilia conventions, local club meetings, and dealers' catalogues and price lists.

To facilitate your use of this book, please read the "How to Use The Price Guide" and "Glossary" sections before going to the pricing data.

Sincerely,
Jim Beckett
Denny Eckes

1

INTRODUCTION

This fourth edition of the Sport Americana Baseball Card Price Guide has been expanded to include most of the pre-1900 N-card sets, the 1981 Topps, Fleer and Donruss supplemental issues and, of course the 1982 Topps, Fleer, and Donruss and their supplemental issues available at the time of printing. Collector issues have again been omitted. All prices have, of course, been revised to reflect the 1982 market value.

As more information has become available concerning errors and variations, double and triple card printing frequencies, scarcities and anomalies, and other interesting card-associated data, they have been incorporated into the Guide. New, and the authors believe interesting, articles have been added, as have different and unusual baseball card samples and uncut sheets. Features such as "Last Year in Brief" and "What's New for This Year" have been retained.

Illustrations for sets checklisted are almost all at 57% of original size. Several illustrations in the listed sets are at 50% or less, reductions necessary to accommodate the illustration to the page size. Illustrations for cards not in listed sets are normally at 50% of original sizes; however, here again some further reduction was necessary for some of these illustrations (e.g., uncut sheets) to accommodate the page size.

The authors would like to overemphasize some points mentioned at different spots later in the book, but which are so important as to deserve specific reference here:

This book is a guide. It is not the "for sale" list of anyone. The prices are not the thoughts or desires of the authors, publisher, distributors or advertisers. They are what the market place, through the law of supply and demand, has determined. Throughout the year prices on "any" card might increase or decrease. You and you alone are the final judge as to whether you should or should not buy or sell a particular card at a particular price.

Prices vary widely on many of the higher priced cards—particularly the truly scarce cards of which there are very few available for purchase (T206 Wagner and Plank; 1951 Topps current stars Roberts, Konstanty and Stanky; 1933 Goudey Lajoie) and the speculator cards which are reasonably plentiful but for which there is a large demand (e.g., 1952 Topps Mantle, 1967 Brooks Robinson, 1970 Topps Johnny Bench, 1954 Aaron, recent superstar and error cards).

HISTORY OF CARD COLLECTING

The current version of the baseball card, with its full color front and statistic laden back, is a far cry from its earliest ancestors issued nearly a century ago. The mid 1800's gave birth to the institution of the baseball card, presumably because the mood of the American public turned against the "risque" cards of actresses and entertainers then being packed with cigarettes. As to actually which was the first baseball card, the issue is cloudy. These early issues were generally printed on heavy cardboard, with the quality of photography, drawing and printing being quite poor.

Goodwin & Co., of New York, makers of Gypsy Queen, Old Judge, and other cigarette brands is usually considered to be among, if not the, first issuers of baseball cards. Their issues, predominately in the 1 1/2" X 2 1/2" size, generally consisted of photographs of baseball players, boxers, wrestlers and non-sport subjects mounted on stiff cardboard stock. Over 2000 different photos of baseball players alone have been identified. The "Old Judges", a collective name commonly used for the Goodwin & Co. cards, were issued from 1886-1890 and are treasured parts of many collections. Among the other cigarette companies issuing baseball cards which still command attention today are Allen & Ginter, D. Buchner & Co. (Gold Coin Chewing Tobacco), and P. H. Mayo & Brother. The first two issued colored line drawing cards while the Mayo's are sepia photographs on black cardboard. In addition to the small sized cards from this era, several tobacco companies issued cabinet sized baseball cards. These "cabinets" were considerably larger than the small cards, usually about 4 1/4" X 6 1/2", and were printed on heavy stock. Goodwin & Co's Old Judge cabinets and the National Tobacco Works' "Newsboy" baseball photos are two that remain popular today.

The American Tobacco Company, formed in 1890, so dominated the tobacco industry that by 1895 baseball card inserts to cigarette packages (actually slide boxes in those days) were discontinued. The lack of competition in the then burgeoning cigarette market had made "freebie" inserts unnecessary. The end of the first era of the baseball card had come.

The dawn of the twentieth century saw a few scattered baseball cards issued; however, it remained for the cigarette companies, particularly the American Tobacco Co., and, to a lesser extent, the candy and gum makers to revive the baseball card. The period from 1909 to 1915 saw the bulk of these T cards (American Card Catalog, designated hereinafter as ACC, for the Twentieth Century Tobacco issues) and E cards (ACC for Early Candy and Gum issues) released. This era, probably the most romantic if not the most popular (other than today) period of baseball card collecting gave use the fabled T-206 Honus Wagner card, card collecting's most prized treasure; the T-206 Plank card, long the second most valuable baseball card (recently relinquishing its number two position to the more distinctive and aesthetically pleasing Napoleon Lajoie card from the 1933 (34) Goudey Gum series); and the T-206 Magee error card (Magee misspelled Magie on the card), card collecting's most famous blooper card.

The ingenuity and distinctiveness of this era has yet to be surpassed. The T-202 Hassan Triple-folders, probably the best looking, certainly the most distinctive card ever issued; the durable T-201 Mecca double folders, one of the first sets with the player's records on the back; the T-3 Turkey Reds, collecting's most popular cabinet card; the E-145 Cracker Jacks, the only major set containing Federal League player cards, and the T-204 Ramlys, with their distinctive black and white oval photos and ornate gold borders, were but a few of the variety of cards issued during this period. While the American Tobacco Co. dominated the field, several other tobacco companies, clothing manufacturers, newspapers and periodicals, game makers, and companies whose identity remains anonymous did issue cards during this period before World War I. In fact, the Collins-McCarthy Candy Company, makers of the Zeenuts Pacific Coast League baseball cards remains today the manufacturer other than the Topps Chewing Gum Company with the most continuous years of baseball card issuances (1911-1938).

The coming of World War I, possibly coupled with the realization by the American Tobacco Co. that those who collected baseball card inserts to their cigarettes were youngsters, who, presumably, did not indulge in the smoking of their product (the influence of the son on Dad and Grandpa notwithstanding), meant an end to the last era of tobacco cards, although Red Man Chewing Tobacco did produce sets from 1952-1955.

The next flurry of card issues began in the roaring and prosperous 1920's. The caramel companies (National Caramel, American Caramel, York Caramel) led the way during this era of the E card; however, the strip card, a continous strip with several or many cards seperated by dotted lines or other sectioning features, did flourish. While the E cards and the strip cards are generally considered less imaginative than the T Cards or the recent candy and gum issues, they are still sought after by many advanced collectors. Another "event" of significance that occurred during the 1920's was the introduction of the arcade card or "Exhibit" as it is known, taking this designation from its issuer the Exhibit Supply Company of Chicago. The Exhibit machines, once a trademark of the penny arcades, amusement parks and county fairs across the country, dispensed for one penny a large (close to the size of a postcard) picture card on thick stock of your favorite cowboy, actor, actress, or baseball player. The Exhibit Supply or one of its associated companies produced baseball cards over a longer span of years, though discontinous, than any other manufact-urer. Its first cards were produced in 1921 while the last Exhibit issue was in 1966. In 1979 the Exhibit Supply Company was bought by a collector/dealer who has since issued other Exhibit cards, reprinted from Exhibit photos of the past.

If the T card period from 1909-1915 can be called the Golden Age of baseball card col-lecting, the period beginning at the height of the depression in 1933 and ending with the beginning of American formal involvement in World War II in 1941 can certainly be called the Silver Age. The forerunner of today's baseball bubble gum card in size, packaging, and distribution, was introduced by the Goudey Gum Company of Boston in 1933. With its Big League Gum series of 240 cards (239 issued in 1933), an extremely well done, full color, line drawing set on thick card stock, Goudey started an era in which some of the most attractive and sought after cards in the history of collecting were produced. The 1933 Goudey Big League Gum series was the largest single issue since the T-206 white border tobacco set and ranks as one of the four of five hallmark baseball card issued. The set contained over 40 Hall of Fame players, including four cards of Babe Ruth and two of Lou Gehrig. In 1934 Goudey continued its reign with a 96 card set, in color, plus the remaining card to the 1933 series—no. 106, the Napoleon Lajoie card. This rare and at-tractive card just recently passed the T-206 Plank card in value to become the second most valuable baseball card. Goudey also issued player cards in 1935, 1936, 1938, and 1941 with all but 1941 issued being well done and still quite popular.

In addition to Goudey, several other bubble gum manufacturers issued baseball cards during this era. DeLong Gum Company issued an extremely attractive set in 1933. National Chicle Company issued the largest die-cut set ever with their 192 card Batter-Up series of 1934-1936, and they also issued the extremely popular Diamond Stars series from 1934-1936. Other popular sets of this period were the Tattoo-Orbit set of 60 color cards issued in 1933 and Gum Products' 75 card Double Play set, a sepia colored set consisting of two players per card (although there were only 75 cards, each player was numbered separately giving the set numbers from 1 to 150).

In 1939, Gum, Inc., which later became Bowman Gum, issued their first of three sets, taking over from Goudey Gum as the leading producer of baseball cards. Their 1939 set of 162, entitled Play Ball-America, and their 1940 set of 240 entitled Play Ball, were both in black & white, and the latter is still considered by many to be the best looking black and white card sets ever produced. In 1941 Gum, Inc., issued their only color set, a very popular 72 card set entitled Play Ball Sports Hall of Fame. Many of the poses in this set were colored repeats of the 1940 series.

Besides regular gum cards, many manufacturers distributed "premium" issues during the 1930's. These premiums were printed on paper or photograph stock rather than card stock and were much larger in size than the regular cards. They were sold across the counter with gum (which was packaged separately from the premium) for a penny, or more often, they were redeemed at the store or through the mail in exchange for the wrappers of previously purchased gum cards, a la the proof-of-purchase box top premiums of today. The premiums are much scarcer than the card issues of the 1930's and, in most cases, no manufacturer's identification is present on the issue. Among the more common of these issues were the thin, postcard sized "fine pen" and "wide pan" premiums (called "fine" and "wide" pen depending on the boldness of the facsimile autographs on the premium); Diamond Star Gum (issued by Goudey Gum) in both sepia (4" X 6 1/4") and black and white (4 3/4" X 7 5/16"); and Diamond Star Premiums, issued anonymously by National Chicle Company.

World War II brought an end to this popular era of card collecting. Paper and rubber shortages curtailed bubble gum baseball cards until the Bowman Gum Company, the direct descendant of Gum, Inc., resurrected the baseball card in 1948, the beginning of the modern era of card collecting.

In 1948, Bowman Gum issued a 48 card black & white set available in 1c packs in which one card and one slab of gum were contained. That same year the Leaf Gum Co. also issued a set of cards in color (although rather poor color). A squabble over the rights to use players' pictures on the cards developed between Bowman and Leaf. Leaf eventually dropped out of the baseball card producing market, but not before it had left an impression on the hobby and issued some of the rarest cards in existence. Leaf's baseball card series of 1948–1949 contained 98 cards, skip numbered to no. 168 (not all numbers were printed). Of the 98 cards, 49 are relatively plentiful; however, the other 49 are rare, and quite valuable.

Bowman continued its production of cards in 1949 with a color series of 240 cards. This series remains the most difficult Bowman regular issue to complete. Its "high numbers" are both numerous and scarce. Although the set was in color and today commands quite a bit of interest because of its scarcity, aesthetically it is considered a bit inferior to the Goudey and National Chicle issues of the 1930's. In addition to the regular issue of 1949, Bowman issued a set of 36 Pacific Coast League players. While it is not a regular issue, it is still prized by collectors and has become, by far, the most valuable Bowman issue.

In 1950, Bowman's one year monopoly in the baseball card field, it began a string of excellent quality cards which it continued until its demise in 1955. The 1950 series itself contained somewhat of an oddity because the more difficult numbers to obtain were the "low numbers" rather than the traditional high numbers.

The year 1951 began the most competitive, and perhaps highest quality period of baseball card production. It was the year Topps Chewing Gum Company of Brooklyn entered the market. Topps' 1951 series consisted of two sets of 52 cards each, one set with red backs and one set with blue backs. In addition, it issued 31 insert cards, three of which (current stars Konstanty, Roberts and Stanky) remain the rarest cards of any major set. The 1951 Topps cards were quite homely and paled in comparison to the 1951 Bowman issues; however, they were successful enough for Topps to continue producing cards, which they have done every year since. In 1952 Topps issued a larger and much more attractive card. This size was to be the standard for the next five years as Bowman also began issuing larger baseball cards in 1953. This first truly major set by Topps has become, like the 1933 Goudey series and the T-206 white border series, the classic set of its era. The 407 card set is a collector's dream of scarcities, rarities, errors, and variations. It also contains the first Topps issues of Mickey Mantle and Willie Mays (in a rare and scarce series, respectively), who along with Hank Aaron and Ted Williams form card collecting's "big four" of the modern era.

As with Bowman and Leaf in the late 1940's, competition over player rights arose. Ensuing court battles between Topps and Bowman and the splitting of the market caused by stiff competition led, in January 1956, to the purchase of Bowman by Topps. From that time to 1980, Topps has remained virtually unchallenged as the leader in the production of baseball cards. Fleer Gum, with small sets in 1959, 1960, 1961 and 1963, and several cartoon sets in the 1970's, and more recently Kellogg cereal and Hostess Cakes have issued baseball cards for promotional purposes.

So, the story of major baseball card sets from 1956 through 1980 is by and large the story of Topps issues, with the single exception coming in 1976 with the issue by Sports Stars Publishing Company of a 630-card set of current players. In 1957, Topps changed the standard size of the baseball card to 3 1/2" X 2 1/2" in dimensions. That size has remained with us to the present time. In addition to their regular yearly series of current players, Topps has issued many auxiliary sets—Giant- or Super-sized cards in 1964, 1970 and 1971, die-cut stand-ups in 1964, an embossed set in 1977, a smaller version of its regular set (mini's) in 1975 and several others. From 1977-1980, Topps reprinted (a few cards contain different poses than the regular set and different numbers are on the back) several teams for use by the Burger King Restaurant Chain for promotional purposes. These auxiliary sets—many of which are called Test Sets—are also collectible and sometimes sought after fiercely.

A court decision in 1980 paved the way for two other large gum companies to enter, or re-enter, the baseball card producing arena. The Fleer Corporation, who had produced cards of current players in 1963, and the Donruss Company (a division of General Mills) secured rights to produce baseball cards of current players, and each issued major card sets in 1981 with bubble gum products. A higher court decision in 1981 revoked the earlier ruling, and it appeared that Topps had regained its position as the only major producer of current baseball cards. Undaunted by the revokation ruling, Fleer and Donruss continued to issue cards in 1982 but without bubble gum or any other edible product. Fleer issued its current player baseball cards with "team logo stickers," whereas Donruss issued their cards with a piece of a baseball jigsaw puzzle. Time alone will tell whether the baseball card collecting public can continue to support three major producers of current baseball cards, or whether, as in past history, the economics of stiff competition will eventually necessitate the withdrawal of one or more producers from the market.

What you have just read is a thumbnail sketch of card collecting from its inception in the 1880's to the present. These few pages can't begin to tell you that about which entire books have been written. If you are interested in the history of card collecting, there are many excellent books and catalogues, many of which are advertised within this Price Guide, that are available. Virtually all serious collectors subscribe to at least one of the sports collecting hobby papers. Send off for samples if you are not sure which hobby paper is appropriate for you. Also, try to attend a sport collectibles convention in your area. Card collecting is still a young and informal hobby, and the chances are good that you will run into one or more of the "experts" in the field; they're usually more than happy to share their knowledge with you.

WRITING PAD COVERS Ca. 1911

7

"ALWAYS BUYING"
Call or Write
for Quote

1113 COLUMBUS CIRCLE PG4
JANESVILLE, WISCONSIN 53545
1-608-755-0922

"ALWAYS BUYING
Call or Write
for Quote

(All Cards EX. to MINT Cond.) HI #s	COMMONS EACH	GROUP LOTS FOR SALE				
		50 Diff.	100 Diff.	300 Asst.	500 Asst.	250 G-V(
1948 BOWMAN	4.00					NOT
1949 BOWMAN	3.50					AVAILABL
50-51 BOWMAN 7.50	2.00	90.				1950-5
1952 TOPPS 45.00 & up	2.50	110.				25
1952 BOWMAN 5.00	2.00	90.				
1953 TOPPS 10.00	2.00	90.				1953-5
1953 BOWMAN 8.50	4.00	175.				
1954 TOPPS	1.25	60.	115.			16
1954 BOWMAN	1.00	50.	95.			
1955 TOPPS 3.00	.70 (150-160) 2.00		68.	200.	330.	1955-5
1955 BOWMAN 2.50-3. Umps	.50		48.	140.	225.	
1956 TOPPS	.65 (181-240) 1.00		63.	185.	305.	8
1957 TOPPS 3.00	.60 (353-407) .65		57.	165.	265.	
1958 TOPPS	.35		33.	95.	155.	1958-6
1959 TOPPS 1.25-1.50 S.N.	.35 (1-110) .45		27.	78.	125.	
1960 TOPPS 1.25-1.50 S.N.	.25 (441-506) .45		23.	67.	110.	5
1961 TOPPS 6.50-8.50 S.N.	.25		23.	67.	110.	
1962 TOPPS 1.25-3.00 RKS.	.25 (413-522) .35		23.	67.	110.	1962-6
1963 TOPPS 1.25-1.50	.20 (289-446) .30		18.	52.	85.	
1964 TOPPS 1.00	.20 (430-522) .30		18.	52.	85.	2
1965 TOPPS .50	.20 (447-506) .30		18.	52.	85.	
1966 TOPPS 2.50	.20 (447-522) .30		18.	52.	85.	1966-6
1967 TOPPS 1.50-2.50	.15 (458-533) .25		13.	35.	58.	
1968 TOPPS .40	.15		13.	35.	58.	2
1969 TOPPS	.15 (219-327) .25		13.	35.	58.	
1970 TOPPS .50	.15 (553-636) .25		13.	35.	58.	1970-7
1971 TOPPS .50	.15 (524-643) .25		13.	35.	58.	
1972 TOPPS .50	.15 (526-656) .25		13.	35.	58.	1
1973 TOPPS .50	.12		10.	28.	45.	
1974 TOPPS	.12		10.	28.	45.	
1975 TOPPS	.12		10.	28.	45.	1975-7
1976 TOPPS	.10		7.	18.	27.	
1977 TOPPS	.10		7.	18.	27.	1
1978 TOPPS	.10		6.	15.	25.	
1979 TOPPS	.10		5.	14.	20.	1979-8
1980 TOPPS	.10		5.	14.	20.	
1981 TOPPS	.10		5.	14.	18.	1
1982 TOPPS	.05		5.	14.	18.	

SPECIALS IN GD-VG
CONDITION-POSTPAID

250	54-59	$65.00
500	54-59	125.00
1000	54-59	235.00
250	60-69	35.00
500	60-69	60.00
1000	60-69	100.00
2500	60-69	230.00
250	70-76	15.00
500	70-76	28.00
1000	70-76	53.00
2500	70-76	125.00

Special 1 Different from each year 1950-82 from above $24.00 postpaid.
Special 100 Different from each year 1954-82 from above $725.00 postpaid.
Special 10 Different from each year 1954-82 from above $75.00 postpaid.
All lot groups are my choice only.
All assorted lots will contain as many different as possible.
Please list alternates whenever possible.
Send your want list and I will fill them at the above price for commons. High numbe
specials, scarce series, and stars extra.

Minimum order $7.50 - Postage and handling .50 per 100 cards (minimum $1.50
Have thousands of star and super star cards. Call or send for star list.
Also interested in purchasing your collection.
*Groups include various years of my choice.

8

HOBBY GROWTH

The year 1981 might well be remembered as the year in which more baseball cards were printed and less baseball games were played than in any previous year. We are all too familiar with the infamous 50-day baseball players' strike which plagued baseball fans during the mid-summer of last year. The less said about this matter the better. This banner year for baseball cards saw three major bubble gum producers issue 600- plus card sets of current players. In addition, another 20 to 30 other baseball card sets, some supplemental issues of Topps, Fleer, and Donruss, some promotional sets produced in conjunction with the major card producers, and some collector/dealer sets produced by hobby enthusiasts, were issued.

The year 1981 saw some major achievements and changes in the hobby media. This baseball card Price Guide soared to sales of over 100,000 copies and remained on the best-seller list of one of the largest book chains in the country for 18 weeks. A newstand magazine entitled "Baseball Cards" became the first magazine devoted entirely to our hobby to be offered for newstand and drugstore magazine rack sales. Sports Collectors Digest (SCD), founded and operated by John and Phil Stommen, changed hands during the year. Krause Publications, long a stalwart in the coin hobby, purchased SCD from the Stommens at mid-year and has maintained SCD's high standards during the ensuing months that have passed since the ownership changed. Sport Americana would like to wish Doug Watson, newly-appointed publisher of SCD, and himself an avid St. Louis Cardinals memorabilia collector, continued success with the publication. We should also like to pay tribute to John and Phil Stommen for their years of hard work and their many contributions to the hobby while at the helm of SCD.

NATIONAL CONVENTION

The second National Sport Collectors Convention was held in Plymouth, Michigan, a Detroit suburb, in mid-July of 1981. While there are sport collectors shows and conventions being held every week in some part of the country, and in fact, many hobbyists feel so many conventions are not necessary, the National Convention is a major event and deserves reporting. All things considered, the National Sport Collectors Convention has been over the past two years the highlight of the card collecting year. Whereas many conventions offer but buy and sell situations comparable to the local flea market, the national shows have been true conventions. In Plymouth, Carol and Lloyd Toerpe hosted a four-day event which included a pre-convention banquet featuring Ernie Harwell, voice of the Tigers; a discussion by a representative from the Donruss Company; and a special achievements ceremony (Gavin Riley, Steve Brunner and Mike Berkus were presented the 1981 Special Achievements to the Hobby Award both for their work in California sports collectors clubs and their efforts to provide unification in the hobby). A full course dinner was also provided. Many seminars on all phases of sports memoribilia and card collecting were presented by experts throughout the course of the show. A softball game, organized by Tim Turner of Dayton, Ohio, provided some physical activity. Collectors and dealers from almost all of the 50 states and Canada made the show truly national in scope. Special guest celebrities including Hall of Famer Al Kaline were present throughout the show. Several attempts were made to form a formal hobby organization; however, most of these activities were tabled until the 1982 show.

If you are a true card collector and a hobby enthusiast, Sport Americana recommends that you make an effort to attend the 1982 National Convention which will be held in late August of 1982 at the St. Louis Airport Marriott Hotel. Further information is presented on the inside front cover of this book.

PRICES

Post-World War II cards through cards of the 1960's continued to fall somewhat in value following a trend established during the mid and latter part of 1980. Cards of the 1970's and the early 1980's issues were the most active and witnessed the greatest percentage increase in prices. Recent superstar cards again led the way in price increases. Pre-World War II issues were basically stable during the year with slight increases or decreases noticeable in some sets.

Two trends which began in 1980 continued through 1981. The gap between mint cards, very good to excellent cards, and lesser grade cards continues to widen — a fact which points out the growing collector awareness of the condition factor. Although the sum of the individual prices of cards in almost all sets still exceeds the complete set price, the difference between these two prices is narrowing.

The apparent emphasis over the past few years on rookie cards of current superstars continues, even though almost all these cards are plentiful and readily available. Feeding this emphasis dramatically during 1981 was the fact that no longer were Topps rookie cards the only ones sought after, but Fleer and Donruss rookie cards also came into vogue. It appears that the speculatory factor is still quite prevalent in card collecting, and nowhere is it more apparent than in the issues of the past two or three years.

NEW CARD ISSUES

No year in history witnessed as many new baseball card issues as did 1981. The Topps and Kellogg's issues that we have come to expect were a mere tip of the iceberg of the new sets. The largest of the new card sets were the major issues produced by Topps, Fleer, and Donruss. Each of these sets exceeded 600 cards, and each featured the standard card size and method of distribution with bubble gum.

In addition to these major sets, Topps issued a set of small sticker cards which were actually printed in Italy. Topps also issued 5" X 7" superstar photo cards of 11 teams plus a 15-card all-star 5" X 7" photo set. In conjunction with Coca-Cola soft drink and Drake Bakeries, Topps also issued sets of current player cards. Both the Coke and Drakes sets were quite similar in appearance to the Topps regular issues of 1981. Fleer, in addition to its regular set of 660 cards, issued an attractive 128-card set of stickers. The backs of these cards were almost identical to the Fleer regular issue; however, the fronts featured one of the more attractive card faces issued during the year. Small sets were also issued by Squirt soft drinks, Granny Goose Potato Chips, and several Police/Kiwanis groups. TCMA added a Series II to its stars of the 1960's set issued a few years ago.

In September, Topps might have set a precedent for future years by issuing a full 132-card traded set consisting of players either who were missing from Topps regular issue cards or who had changed teams from the teams portrayed on the regular issue cards. The idea of a traded set is hardly novel as Topps issued small traded sets as recently as 1974 and 1976. To be sure, most cards before 1973 were issued in series, one of the main purposes of which was to update trades and portray successful but heretofore unheralded rookies. What made the 1981 Topps Traded set novel was both the method by which Topps advertised the set and the method by which they distributed the set. Before actually printing the cards, Topps established the approximate quantity that would be sold by soliciting advanced orders from hobby card dealers. Partial payment was required with the order to insure integrity. A contingency agreement allowed that if sufficient response for orders were not obtained from hobby card dealers, Topps could rescind the offer, while, of course, returning the partial payment. The distribution of these traded sets was limited to hobby card dealers only. And, to make this set even more attractive to hobby card dealers, each set was packed individually in its own traded card set box—thus eliminating the need for dealers to "sort" cards into sets. While the cards themselves mirror the Topps regular issue, they are quite interesting as they portray players on the teams for which they actually played in 1981. The real impact, however, of this traded set is in the method of solicitation and the method of distribution for which Topps might well have established a precedent.

In early 1981, a proof sheet of 12 cards bearing a remarkable resemblance to the National Chicle Diamond Star issue of 1934-36 was discovered in the Philadelphia area. Through a stroke of fate and some very quick footwork, Sport Americana acquired a full-color transparency of this proof sheet. Study of the transparency revealed that indeed the cards on the sheet were quite likely intended for release by the National Chicle Company in 1937 (players and uniforms established 1937 as the particular year). With the available data, backs were designed and biographies written to resemble that which National Chicle would probably have issued on the backs of these cards. The cards were numbered from 108 through 120 — a continuance of the National Chicle numbering sequence. At mid-year, Sport Americana released what it has entitled "The 1937 Diamond Stars" set. These cards are beautiful, full-color reproductions of the cards on the newly-discovered sheet. The cards are printed on ultra-thick stock, and a facsimile wrapper, matching in color and design an original National Chicle Diamond Star wrapper, is included with each set. The proof sheet, incidentally, is featured on one of the color pages of this book. The artwork is quite striking and definitely bears the mark of the excellent card artwork prevalent in the 1930's.

HOBBY LITERATURE

During 1981 several interesting and informative reference works were produced. As mentioned before, the third edition of this Price Guide soared to sales of over 100,000 copies. Sport Americana also produced two other reference works. The second edition of the Sport Americana Football, Hockey, Basketball and Boxing Card Price Guide was released in late October. In addition to revised prices for football and basketball cards, sport cards from the fields of boxing and hockey were added to this tome. The Sport Americana Price Guide to the Non-Sports Cards, a 300-plus page guide to tobacco and bubble gum non-sports cards, was released in early October of 1981. This volume contains over 2000 illustrations and documents over 500 non-sports card sets. Both of these aforementioned books follow the Sport Americana illustrated format and high standards of quality established in this Price Guide.

Jeff Fritsch revised and updated his team checklist book to include Topps issues over the last few years and the new Fleer and Donruss issues. The additional material could be purchased separately and added to the first edition of this book to bring it up to date. Andrew Pywowarczuk issued an update to his Hockey Card Checklist and Price Guide in late 1981. The second edition of the Even-Stommen Sport Collectors Directory, originally scheduled to be issued at mid-year, was tabled following the sale of Stommen's Sport Collectors Digest publication to Krause Publications. At the time of printing we do not know whether this book will be produced. Dick and Mark Sikes released the fourth edition of their Non-Sports Card Checklist and Price Guide late in the year.

WHAT'S IN STORE FOR 1982?

Realistically, it is apparent that the trend set last year toward many new sets of current players will be continued this year. At the time of the printing of this Guide, Topps, Fleer, and Donruss had already announced major card sets for 1982, and indeed, these sets are included in this Guide. Topps has already announced and is producing sticker cards (also included in this Guide). It is expected that Topps will issue a few more supplementary sets over the course of the year although information on them is not currently available. It is not inconceivable that Fleer and/or Donruss will also produce supplemental issues during the course of the year. Kellogg will probably issue a 60-odd card 3-D set in 1982.

In the area of collector issues at least one significant set is on the drawing boards for 1982. TCMA, of Amawalk, NY, has acquired the original artwork for 15 unpublished 1952 Bowman cards. In a manner similar to the 1937 Diamond Stars produced in 1981, TCMA will issue a full-color, 15-card "Continuation" set to this popular Bowman issue. Facts will be composed similar to those on the backs of the 1952 Bowman, and cards will be numbered 253 through 267. Collectors of early Bowman cards look forward with anticipation to the issuance of this set. No doubt other collector issues will be available during the course of the year; however, no information on them is now available.

The long-awaited Baseball Memoribilia book by Sport Americana is in production and should follow closely on the heels of this Price Guide. The formal title is The Sport Americana Baseball Memoribilia and Autograph Price Guide. A large section on autographs has been added to the original concept of this book, as no definitive autograph price guide is available, and interest in this area of collecting is considerable. In addition to the auto-graph section of this book, other sections will include yearbooks, programs, press pins, Hartland statues, gum card wrappers, commemorative envelopes, baseball coins, baseball pins, paper inserts to baseball card issues and many non-standard baseball cards and pre-miums. Look for this book at your local bookstore, or ask the many hobby card dealers who will be carrying it.

Jack Smalling and Denny Eckes will release the biennial Sport Americana Baseball Address List in May or June of this year. The autograph hunters "best friend" will provide mailing addresses and obituary data for all Hall of Famers, all big league players who began their big league careers after 1910, and many big league players who began their careers before 1910. This book is a must for the autograph collector.

With the advent and expectancy of many new card issues for 1982, most of which because of printing deadlines cannot possibly be included in this volume, Sport Americana will issue a 1982 Baseball Card Summary in early October of this year. Details are presented in an advertisement in the 1982 Topps section of this book. Briefly, this summary will include all legitimate new sets of baseball cards issued during 1982 with pricing data. Prices for the three major 1982 sets will be revised to reflect errors, variations, and "hot cards" which surface during the 1982 season. Sport Americana feels that a supplemental summary after all the 1982 sets have been issued will be a helpful addition to this Price Guide, as the current year's sets have always been of prime interest to collectors and, percentage-wise, the most sensitive towards price fluctuations during the year.

ORIGINAL ARTWORK

HOW TO COLLECT

There are no set rules on how to collect baseball cards. Card collecting is a hobby, a leisure pastime. What you collect, how much you collect, and how much time and money you spend collecting are entirely up to you. The amount of time you wish to spend, the funds you have available for collecting, and your own personal likes and dislikes determine how you collect. What will be presented here is information and ideas that might help you in your enjoyment of the hobby.

OBTAINING CARDS

Several avenues are open to you to obtain cards. You can purchase the current cards in the traditional way at the local candy, grocery, or drug store, with the bubble gum or other products included. You can purchase complete recent sets from the many mail order advertisers found in sports media publications; e.g., The Sporting News, Baseball Digest, Street & Smith's Baseball Yearbook, Baseball Magazine and others. Occasionally, a few older cards and sets are advertised in these same publications. However, most serious card collectors obtain older cards from one or more of the following three sources—other collectors or dealers, the hobby papers, and/or sports collectibles shows or conventions.

NOMENCLATURE

Each hobby has its own nomenclature to describe the collectibles that particular hobby contains. The nomenclature traditionally used for baseball cards is derived from the American Card Catalog, published in 1960 by Nostalgia Press. This catalog, written by Jefferson Burdick (who is called the Father of Card Collecting), uses letter and number descriptions for each separate set of cards. For example, the American Card Catalog (ACC) number for the popular 1933 Goudey set of 240 cards is R319.

The letter used in the ACC number refers to the generic type of card. While both sport and non-sport issues are classified in the ACC, we shall confine ourselves in this description to the sport issues which appear in The Sport Americana Price Guide. The following list defines the letters and their meanings as used by the American Card Catalog.

        T — 20th Century U.S. Tobacco
  (none) — 19th Century U.S. Tobacco
        B — Blankets
        D — Bakery Inserts
        E — Early Candy & Gum
        F — Food Inserts
        H — Advertising
        M — Periodicals
       PC— Postcards
        R — Candy & Gum Cards 1930—Present
       UO—Gas & Oil Inserts
        V — Canadian Candy & Gum
        W — Exhibits, Strip Cards, Team Issues
        N — 19th Century U.S. Tobacco (not ACC designation)

Following the letter designation and an optional hyphen is a one, two, or three digit number, i.e., 1—999.

In several cases, the ACC number is further addended by an additional hyphen and another one or two digit number, i.e., 1—99.

As an example, consider the Topps regular series baseball card issue of 1957. The ACC designation is R414—12. The "R" indicates a Candy or Gum Card produced after 1929. The "414" is the ACC designation for Topps Chewing Gum Baseball Issues; the "12" is the ACC designation for the 1957 regular issue.

As with other traditional methods of identification, there is some rhyme and reason in the system; however, serious collectors learn the ACC designation of the popular sets by rote, rather than by attempting to "figure out" what they might or should be.

With the description in the Price Guide included with the price data and checklists for each set before 1948, the ACC designation is given along with the year, maker and/or common name identification for the set.

From 1948 forward all sets are normally referred to by their year and maker, if the set is a regular issue, or by their year, maker and another distinguishing characteristic, if the set is not a regular issue or if more than one type of regular issue were issued by the same maker that year. For example, in 1964 Topps issued three distinctly different baseball card sets. The regular issue is referred to as 1964 Topps; the postcard-sized issue is referred to as 1964 Topps Giants; and the die-cut issue is referred to as 1964 Topps Stand-Ups. No ACC designations are given in the set description for regular issue sets from 1948 to the present; however, for regionals, the ACC or SCB description is mentioned.

In order to be consistent with the nomenclature used most frequently in the hobby and by the reference books used in the hobby for sets issued after 1960 (which may not have a logical ACC number), The Sport Americana Baseball Card Price Guide has opted to use the numbering system similar to that used in the 3rd edition of The Sports Collector's Bible (SCB), which uses the ACC designations as its base.

OTHER AVAILABLE LITERATURE

There have been several other more recent books which have either augmented or elaborated on material in the American Card Catalog. Among the better and more popular of these are:

> The Sport Americana Alphabetical Baseball Card Checklist
> Den's Collectors Den, Publisher
>
> The Sport Americana Football, Hockey, Basketball and Boxing
> Card Price Guide
> Den's Collectors Den, Publisher
>
> The Sport Americana Baseball Memorabilia and Autograph
> Price Guide
> Den's Collectors Den, Publisher
>
> The Sport Americana Price Guide to the Non-Sports Cards
> Den's Collectors Den, Publisher
>
> The Stirling Sport Card Catalog
> John C. Stirling, Jr., Publisher
>
> The Sports Collectors Bible
> Bobbs-Merrill, Publisher
>
> Sports Memorabilia
> Wallace-Homestead Book Co., Publisher
>
> Baseball Card Team Checklist
> Jeff Fritsch, Publisher

The Sport Americana Alphabetical Baseball Card Checklist, by Dr. James Beckett and Dennis W. Eckes, is an illustrated, alphabetical listing, by the last name of the player portrayed on the card, of all baseball cards appearing in the first issue of this Price Guide.

The 2nd edition of The Sport Americana Football, Hockey, Basketball and Boxing Card Price Guide, by Dr. James Beckett and Dennis W. Eckes, was released in late 1981 and is the definitive work for non-baseball sport card issues. American and Canadian issues are included. The illustrated format, checklists, and pricing methods are similar to this Price Guide.

The new Sport Americana Baseball Memorabilia and Autograph Price Guide was released in early 1982 and is the most definitive book on baseball memorabilia other than baseball cards. Over one year in the making, this book attempts to present in an illustrated, logical fashion information on baseball memorabilia and autographs heretofore not available to the collector.

The first edition of The Sport Americana Price Guide to the Non-Sports Cards presents checklists and current prices for American tobacco and bubble gum non-sports cards in an illustrated format similar to this Price Guide. This 300-plus page book is the definitive guide on all popular non-sports American tobacco and bubble gum cards. In addition to cards, illustrations and prices for wrappers, a growing section of the card collecting hobby, is also included.

Stirling's book, published in 1977, updates the sports issue in the American Card Catalog, including non-baseball issues. The illustrations are excellent, and although the book uses a different nomenclature, conversions to the ACC nomenclature are given. A supplemental, single price per issue list is included in this book.

The Sports Collectors Bible, 3rd edition, published in October 1979, contains sections on cards, pins, postcards, yearbooks, programs, autographs and other collectibles. Before the issuance of The Sport Americana Baseball Memorabilia and Autograph Price Guide, this book was the best available for non-card sport collectibles. It still presents the best source for non-legitimate and collector-issue baseball cards.

John Douglas's Sports Memorabilia is an extremely well-written and formatted guide to sports memorabilia collecting with an abundance of collor illustrations of cards and other collectibles. Cards, autographs, postcards, yearbooks, and other collectibles are given excellent presentations. This book is probably the best single-volume introduction to the sports collectibles hobby for the novice.

The Baseball Card Team Checklist, by Jeff Fritsch, was updated during 1981 and now includes all Topps, Bowman, Fleer, and Donruss cards, with the players portrayed on the cards listed with the teams for whom they played. This book is invaluable to the collector who specializes in an individual team as it is the most complete baseball card team checklist available.

In addition to guide books, there are several excellent standard checklist books for baseball cards. The checklist books list the producer, year issued, and each card by number (if the issue is numbered, alphabetically if not) and player portrayed. The checklist is utilized by the collector to "check off" the cards that he possesses, while the unchecked numbers become the record of which cards he does not possess.

VALUE

The value of a baseball card is determined by many factors. Among these factors are age of the card, player portrayed on the card, the amount of the card printed (initial scarcity), the attractiveness and popularity of the set in which the card is a part, and perhaps most important, the physical condition of the card.

In general, the older the card, the more renown the player on the card, the lower the quantity of the card printed, the more attractive and popular the set in which the card is a part, and the better the condition of the card, the higher the value of the card. There are exceptions (many) to all of these factors, except the condition factor. Given two of the same card, the one in the best condition always has the higher value.

So, while there are certain guidelines that establish the value of a baseball card, the exceptions and peculiarities make a simple mathematical formula to determine value impossible. But, that's why the Sport Americana Baseball Card Price Guide was written.

PRICES AND DEALERS

The prices in the Price Guide are the "retail" going rates for baseball cards as of the beginning of 1982. Dealers are profit seekers who perform the very important service of providing collectors with cards. They have overhead expenses—advertising, postage, convention fees, etc. A dealer cannot and will not buy cards at the retail rate. Normally he will pay from 30 to 70% of the retail rate, the higher rate being paid for the more popular cards that he can sell in a short period of time. Occasionally, a dealer will pay full retail for extremely scarce, popular or currently 'hot' cards, with the thought that the value of these cards is increasing rapidly, and by holding the cards for a reasonably short time, a sufficient profit can be realized.

INDIVIDUAL VS. SET PRICES

A somewhat paradoxical situation exists in the cost of a set versus the combined cost of the individual cards in the set. In nearly every case, the sum of the prices for the individual cards in the set is higher than the cost for the complete set. The reasons behind this anomaly lie in the habits of collectors and the carrying costs of dealers. Many collectors do not collect complete sets. Many collect only stars, superstars or particular teams. Because each card in the set is normally produced in the same quantity (scarcities and rare series notwithstanding) the dealer is left with a shortage of cards of certain players and an abundance of cards of many others. As a dealer, the cards that he has are intended for sale. If he cannot sell them, he can make no profit (or even recoup his costs) on these cards. Indeed, he has an expense in simply "carrying" these cards. The sale of a complete set offers the dealer a way to sell a large number of cards at a single time, any of which he might otherwise "carry" indefinitely. Therefore, he is willing to receive less than the retail for each and every individual card in the set, but benefits from the recovery of all his costs and also receives some profit on all cards in the set.

SCARCE SERIES

The term scarce series is derived from the fact that most pre-1974 card issues were made available to the public in more than one series, each of a finite number of cards, rather than all cards of the set being available for purchase at one time. At some point during the year, usually near the end of the baseball season, interest in baseball cards of that year wanes; consequently, the manufacturers produce a smaller number of these later series of cards. Nearly all national issues from the post-World War II manufacturers (1948 to 1973) can be recognized in series. For example, Bowman used 36 cards on its standard printed sheets. (While the number of cards on printed sheets is usually the same as the number of cards in a particular series, such is not always the case as will be explained below.) Topps series have been comprised of many different numbers of cards, including 55, 66, 80, 88, and others. Recently Topps has settled on what is now their standard sheet size of 132 cards.

While we have stated that the number of cards within a particular series usually has the same number of cards as the number of cards on one printed sheet, this is not always the case. As early as 1948, Bowman substituted 12 cards during later print runs of its 1948 baseball cards. Twelve of the cards from the initial sheet of 36 cards were removed and replaced by 12 different cards giving, in effect, a first series of 36 cards and a second series of 12 new cards. This replacement phenomenon in the 1948 Bowman series produced a scarcity of 24 cards in the series—the 12 cards removed from the original sheet and the 12 new cards added to the sheet. A full sheet of 1948 Bowman cards (second printing) is reproduced later in this book and one can see that card numbers 37—48 have replaced 12 of the cards on the first printing sheet. The Topps Gum Company has also created scarcities and/or excesses of certain cards in many of their sets. Topps, however, has most frequently used the double printing procedure to do this. The double printing procedure involves the act of printing more than one card of the same player and number on a particular sheet. This causes an abundance of the cards of the players who are on the sheet more than one time. During the past few years, Topps has double printed 66 cards which will likely be quite plentiful for many years to come. The Topps double printing of cards in other years is the most logical explanation for the known scarcities of particular cards in some of the Topps sets.

16

PRICE VARIATIONS IN DIFFERENT PARTS OF THE COUNTRY

Two different types of price variations exist among the sections of the country in which a card is bought or sold. The first is the general price variation on all cards bought and sold in one geographical area compared to another; the second is the specific player card price variations found in a certain geographical area and not in others.

Unlike OHIO which is high (Hi) in the middle, card prices are slightly higher on the ends, on the East and West coast, and slightly lower in the middle, in the Southwest and Midwest portions of the country. This variation is what is referred to as the general variation among different sections of the country. The specific variation in prices refers to cards with particular players portrayed on them which command a higher price in one area of the country than in all (or most all) other areas of the country. An Al Kaline card would be valued higher in Detroit than in Cincinnati because Kaline played in Detroit and the demand for an Al Kaline card is higher in Detroit than it is in Cincinnati. On the other hand, a Johnny Bench card would be priced higher in Cincinnati than in Detroit for similar reasons.

The prices in this Guide are neither East or West coast prices nor Southwest or Midwest prices but consensus prices among all sections of the country. Likewise, the prices for a particular player's cards are not the prices for that player's cards in his home team town, as even common player cards command a higher price to home town collectors, but the price of that player's cards in all other parts of the country.

An exception to this pricing policy exists with regional cards. Because regional issues are by definition released in but a limited area of the country and usually feature, to a large extent, players of the team in the area in which it is released, the preponderance of that regional are found and extensively collected only in that particular area. Therefore, Glendale prices are essentially Detroit area prices; Briggs prices are essentially Washington, D.C. area prices; and Esskay prices are essentially Baltimore area prices.

PRICES IN THE SPORT AMERICANA PRICE GUIDE

The prices in this Guide are not the "for sale" prices of the authors, the publisher, the distributors, the advertisers or any card dealers connected with the Guide. No one is in any way obligated to buy, sell or trade his or her cards based on these prices. The price listings were compiled by the authors from actual buy-sell transactions at sports conventions, buy-sell advertisements in the hobby papers, and for sale prices from dealer catalogues and price lists.

SOME INTERSTING NOTES ON CARDS AND PRICES

The numerically first card of an issue is the single card most likely to receive excessive wear; consequently, you will find the price on the number one card to be somewhat higher than its inherent status would justify. Similarly, but to a lesser extent, the numerically last card of an issue is also prone to abnormal wear. Logically, this phenomenon can be explained simply by the fact that the first and last cards are exposed to the elements (human element included) more than any other cards. They are generally end cards in any brick formations, rubber bandings, stackings on wet surfaces, and like activities.

Baseball cards have no intrinsic value. They are functionally worthless as are cancelled stamps, knick knacks, empty beer cans, the Mona Lisa and pearl earrings. The value of a baseball card, as the value of these other collectibles, can only be assessed by you and your enjoyment in viewing and possessing these cardboard swatches.

Inflation is something with which we all live. The prices in this Guide are early 1982 prices. It would be foolhearty to believe prices will stay at this level throughout the year. Baseball cards and other collectibles are hardly immune to inflation. Indeed, many investors purchase works of art, antiques, and other collectibles, including baseball cards, as a hedge against inflation. However, do not be lulled into believing prices must only go up. Last year was a case in point as many of the so-called glamor cards remained at a constant price or decreased through the course of the year.

There is no such thing as an excellent-mint (Ex-Mt) individual card; a card is either mint or not mint. However, a card could be graded very good-excellent (Vg-Ex) as two individuals could disagree on the condition (one rates very good while the other rates the card excellent) or the card may contain a mixture of attributes of excellent and very good cards. Thus a strict excellent card is more valuable than a very good-excellent card but not as valuable as a mint card— the strict excellent condition card would be valued halfway between the mint and very good-excellent prices (first and second columns of the Price Guide).

Remember, you the buyer ultimately determine the price of each baseball card. You have the supreme weapon in your ability to say NO to the price of any card. And when the cost of a baseball card, or anything else, exceeds the enjoyment or utility you will receive from that item, your answer should be "no". The authors of this Price Guide are reporters of prices. You are the ones who set the prices.

ADVERTISING IN THE PRICE GUIDE

Throughout this Price Guide you will see advertisements for sports memorabilia material, hobby paper subscriptions, upcoming sports collectibles conventions, and mail order and retail sports collectibles establishments. All advertisements were accepted in good faith based on the reputations of the advertiser: however, neither the authors, the publisher, the distributors nor the other advertisers in the Price Guide accept any responsibility for any particular advertiser not complying with the terms of his or her ad.

Should you come into contact with any of the advertisers in this Guide as a result of their advertisement herein, please mention to them this source as your contact.

CHANGES IN THIS YEAR'S PRICE GUIDE

As the card producers continue to make more and larger sets, the space requirements in this book become taxed to the limit. The authors to not want to lose the Guide's portability factor; therefore, in order to make room for the current cards and limit the book to a reasonable size, logical deletions have had to be made in this volume, and similar deletions will no doubt be made in the future. In conjunction with the new Sport Americana Memorabilia and Autograph Price Guide, which will be released on the heels of this book, we feel we can meet these space requirements while retaining all essential information within the volumes of this Price Guide and the Memorabilia and Autograph Price Guide. Because this Price Guide is directed specifically at baseball cards, all non-card issues will eventually be removed from this book and placed in the Memorabilia Price Guide. Generically, these issues include paper inserts, premiums, exhibit and arcade cards, photos, and other issues which do not coincide with the accepted concept of a trading card. Some of these issues have already been removed from this Price Guide, although they have been included in the past, and placed in the first edition of the Memorabilia Price Guide. Eventually some true trading card issue might well be alternated between this book and the Memorabilia Price Guide. Such issues will be those for which price fluctuations do not occur as rapidly as do fluctuations for recent cards. Consequently, information on price changes supplied biennially should provide the collector with sufficient information on these sets. We do hope these changes do not inconvenience you; however, we believe that such changes should be made at this time in order to maintain the major purpose and integrity of this Price Guide.

ERRATA

As in the past, we request that should you find an error in the checklist or the numbering system within this book, please drop the authors a line in care of the publisher and we will correct it in next year's issue. For the first time, we are making use of data processing equipment in this year's issue. Consequently, a few more numerical and typographical errors will be apparent than in previous issues. Future editions will no doubt be much more error free than either this edition or previous editions as all the data is now on computerized files. The authors ask your indulgence in this edition with the prospect of future issues being far superior in both format and numerical and grammatical accuracy.

HOW TO USE THE PRICE GUIDE

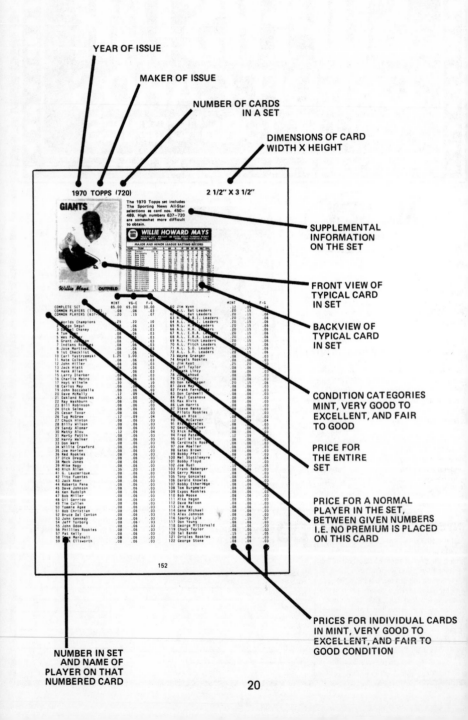

YEAR OF ISSUE

MAKER OF ISSUE

NUMBER OF CARDS IN A SET

DIMENSIONS OF CARD WIDTH X HEIGHT

1970 TOPPS (720)   2 1/2" X 3 1/2"

The 1970 Topps set includes The Sporting News All-Star selections as card nos. 450–469. High numbers 637–720 are somewhat more difficult to obtain.

SUPPLEMENTAL INFORMATION ON THE SET

FRONT VIEW OF TYPICAL CARD IN SET

BACKVIEW OF TYPICAL CARD IN SET

CONDITION CATEGORIES MINT, VERY GOOD TO EXCELLENT, AND FAIR TO GOOD

PRICE FOR THE ENTIRE SET

PRICE FOR A NORMAL PLAYER IN THE SET, BETWEEN GIVEN NUMBERS I.E. NO PREMIUM IS PLACED ON THIS CARD

PRICES FOR INDIVIDUAL CARDS IN MINT, VERY GOOD TO EXCELLENT, AND FAIR TO GOOD CONDITION

NUMBER IN SET AND NAME OF PLAYER ON THAT NUMBERED CARD

152

20

1948 BABE RUTH STORY (28)

2" X 2 1/2"

The 1948 Babe Ruth Story set of 28 black and white, numbered cards was issued by the Philadelphia Chewing Gum Company to commemorate the 1949 movie of the same name starring William Bendix. Babe Ruth himself appears on several cards. The last 12 cards (17 to 28) are more difficult to obtain than other cards in the set. The ACC designation is R421.

	MINT	VG-E	F-G
COMPLETE SET	225.00	150.00	65.00
COMMON PLAYER(1-16)	5.00	3.50	1.50
COMMON PLAYER(17-28)	12.50	8.50	3.50
1 "The Babe Ruth Story" In the Making	15.00	10.00	4.00
2 Bat Boy Becomes the Babe	5.00	3.50	1.50
3 Clair Hodgson/ Claire Trevor	5.00	3.50	1.50
4 Babe Ruth/ William Bendix; Claire Hodgson/ Claire Trevor	5.00	3.50	1.50
5 Brother Matthias/ Charles Bickford	5.00	3.50	1.50
6 Phil Conrad/ Sam Levene	5.00	3.50	1.50
7 Night Club Singer/ Gertrude Niesen	5.00	3.50	1.50
8 Baseball's Famous Deal	5.00	3.50	1.50
9 Babe Ruth/ William Bendix; Mrs. Babe Ruth/ Claire Trevor	5.00	3.50	1.50
10 Babe Ruth, Mrs. Babe Ruth, Brother Matthias/ actors	5.00	3.50	1.50
11 Babe Ruth/ William Bendix; Miller Huggins/ Fred Lightner	5.00	3.50	1.50
12 Babe Ruth/ William Bendix; Johnny Sylvester/ George Marshall	5.00	3.50	1.50
13 Mr. Sylvester, Mrs. Sylvester, Johnny Sylvester, actors	5.00	3.50	1.50
14 "When A Feller Needs A Friend"	5.00	3.50	1.50
15 Dramatic Home Run	5.00	3.50	1.50
16 The Homer That Set the Record	5.00	3.50	1.50
17 "The Slap That Started Baseball's Most Famous Career	12.50	8.50	3.50
18 The Babe Plays Santa Claus	12.50	8.50	3.50
19 Ed Barrow, Jacob Ruppert, Miller Huggins/ actors for same	12.50	8.50	3.50
20 "Broken Window Paid Off"	12.50	8.50	3.50
21 "Regardless of the Generation,Babe Ruth..."	12.50	8.50	3.50
22 Charley Grimm and William Bendix	12.50	8.50	3.50
23 Ted Lyons and William Bendix	12.50	8.50	3.50
24 Lefty Gomez, William Bendix,and Bucky Harris	12.50	8.50	3.50
25 Babe Ruth and Bill Bendix	15.00	10.00	4.00
26 Babe Ruth and William Bendix	15.00	10.00	4.00
27 Babe Ruth and Claire Trevor	15.00	10.00	4.00
28 William Bendix, Babe Ruth, Claire Trevor	15.00	10.00	4.00

1934—36 BATTER-UP (192)

2 3/8" X 3 1/4"
2 3/8" X 3"

The National Chicle Co. 1934-36 Batter-Up set, ACC designation R-318, contains die-cut cards which have been seen in tints of sepia, brown, red, purple, green, blue, or basic black & white. Numbers 1—80 are 2 3/8" X 3 1/4" in size while the higher numbers 81—192 are 2 3/8" X 3". The higher numbers are more difficult to obtain. As with other die-cut cards, if the backs have been removed, the condition of the card is at best fair.

	MINT	VG-E	F-G
COMPLETE SET	3300.00	2200.00	900.00
COMMON PLAYER(1-80)	10.00	6.00	3.00
COMMON PLAYER(81-192)	20.00	13.00	5.00
1 Berger,Wally	12.00	6.00	3.00
2 Brandt,Ed	10.00	6.00	3.00
3 Lopez,Al	13.00	9.00	4.00

	MINT	VG-E	F-G
4 Bartell,Dick	10.00	6.00	3.00
5 Hubbell,Carl	18.00	12.00	5.00
6 Terry,Bill	18.00	12.00	5.00
7 Martin,Pepper	11.50	7.50	3.50
8 Bottomley,Jim	13.00	9.00	4.00
9 Bridges,Tom	10.00	6.00	3.00
10 Ferrell,Rick	10.00	6.00	3.00

BATTER -UP (CONTINUED)

	MINT	VG-E	F-G		MINT	VG-E	F-G
11 Benge,Ray	10.00	6.00	3.00	102 Young,Pep	20.00	13.00	5.00
12 Ferrell,Wes	10.00	6.00	3.00	103 Hudlin,Willis	20.00	13.00	5.00
13 Cissell,Chalmer	10.00	6.00	3.00	104 Haslin,Mickey	20.00	13.00	5.00
14 Traynor,Pie	15.00	10.00	4.00	105 Bluege,Oswald	20.00	13.00	5.00
15 Mahaffey,Leroy	10.00	6.00	3.00	106 Andrews,Paul	20.00	13.00	5.00
16 Hafey,Chick	13.00	9.00	4.00	107 Brandt,Ed	20.00	13.00	5.00
17 Waner,Lloyd	13.00	9.00	4.00	108 Taylor,Don	20.00	13.00	5.00
18 Burns,Jack	10.00	6.00	3.00	109 Lee,Thornton	20.00	13.00	5.00
19 Myer,Buddy	10.00	6.00	3.00	110 Schumacher,Hal	20.00	13.00	5.00
20 Johnson,Bob	10.00	6.00	3.00	111 Hayes & Lyons	30.00	20.00	8.00
21 Vaughan,Arky	11.50	7.50	3.50	112 Hale,Odell	20.00	13.00	5.00
22 Rolfe,Red	11.50	7.50	3.50	113 Averill,Earl	25.00	17.00	7.50
23 Gomez,Lefty	15.00	10.00	4.00	114 Chelini,Italo	20.00	13.00	5.00
24 Averill,Earl	13.00	9.00	4.00	115 Andrews &	30.00	20.00	8.00
25 Cochrane,Mickey	18.00	12.00	5.00	Bottomley			
26 Mungo,Van	11.50	7.50	3.50	116 Walker,Bill	20.00	13.00	5.00
27 Ott,Mel	22.00	15.00	7.00	117 Dickey,Bill	45.00	30.00	12.00
28 Foxx,Jimmy	25.00	17.00	7.50	118 Walker,Gerald	20.00	13.00	5.00
29 Dykes,Jimmy	11.50	7.50	3.50	119 Lyons,Ted	30.00	20.00	8.00
30 Dickey,Bill	22.00	15.00	7.00	120 Auker,Eldon	20.00	13.00	5.00
31 Grove,Lefty	18.00	12.00	5.00	121 Hallahan,Bill	20.00	13.00	5.00
32 Cronin,Joe	18.00	12.00	5.00	122 Lindstrom,Fred	25.00	17.00	7.50
33 Frisch,Frank	18.00	12.00	5.00	123 Hildebrand,Oral	20.00	13.00	5.00
34 Simmons,Al	15.00	10.00	4.00	124 Appling,Luke	30.00	20.00	8.00
35 Hornsby,Rogers	25.00	17.00	7.50	125 Martin,Pepper	22.00	15.00	7.00
36 Lyons,Ted	13.00	9.00	4.00	126 Ferrell,Rick	20.00	13.00	5.00
37 Maranville,Rabbit	13.00	9.00	4.00	127 Goodman,Ival	20.00	13.00	5.00
38 Wilson,Jimmy	10.00	6.00	3.00	128 Kuhel,Joe	20.00	13.00	5.00
39 Kamm,Willie	10.00	6.00	3.00	129 Lombardi,Ernie	22.00	15.00	7.00
40 Hallahan,Bill	10.00	6.00	3.00	130 Gehringer,Charlie	35.00	24.00	10.00
41 Suhr,Gus	10.00	6.00	3.00	131 Mungo,Van Lingle	22.00	15.00	7.00
42 Gehringer,Charlie	15.00	10.00	4.00	132 French,Larry	20.00	13.00	5.00
43 Heving,Joe	10.00	6.00	3.00	133 Myer,Buddy	20.00	13.00	5.00
44 Comorosky,Adam	10.00	6.00	3.00	134 Harder,Mel	20.00	13.00	5.00
45 Lazzeri,Tony	11.50	7.50	3.50	135 Galan,Augie	20.00	13.00	5.00
46 Leslie,Sam	10.00	6.00	3.00	136 Hartnett,Gabby	30.00	20.00	8.00
47 Smith,Bob	10.00	6.00	3.00	137 Hack,Stan	22.00	15.00	7.00
48 Hudlin,Willis	10.00	6.00	3.00	138 Herman,Billy	25.00	17.00	7.50
49 Reynolds,Carl	10.00	6.00	3.00	139 Jurges,Bill	20.00	13.00	5.00
50 Schulte,Fred	10.00	6.00	3.00	140 Lee,Bill	20.00	13.00	5.00
51 Lavagetto,Cookie	10.00	6.00	3.00	141 Bonura,Zeke	20.00	13.00	5.00
52 Schumacher,Hal	10.00	6.00	3.00	142 Piet,Tony	20.00	13.00	5.00
53 Cramer,Roger	10.00	6.00	3.00	143 Dean,Paul	22.00	15.00	7.00
54 Johnson,Sylvester	10.00	6.00	3.00	144 Foxx,Jimmy	50.00	35.00	15.00
55 Bejma,Ollie	10.00	6.00	3.00	145 Medwick,Joe	30.00	20.00	8.00
56 Byrd,Sam	10.00	6.00	3.00	146 Collins,Rip	20.00	13.00	5.00
57 Greenberg,Hank	18.00	12.00	5.00	147 Almada,Mel	20.00	13.00	5.00
58 Knickerbocker,Bill	10.00	6.00	3.00	148 Cooke,Allan	20.00	13.00	5.00
59 Urbanski,Bill	10.00	6.00	3.00	149 Berg,Moe	20.00	13.00	5.00
60 Morgan,Eddie	10.00	6.00	3.00	150 Camilli,Dolph	20.00	13.00	5.00
61 McNair,Rabbit	10.00	6.00	3.00	151 Melillo,Oscar	20.00	13.00	5.00
62 Chapman,Ben	10.00	6.00	3.00	152 Campbell,Bruce	20.00	13.00	5.00
63 Johnson,Roy	10.00	6.00	3.00	153 Grove,Lefty	45.00	30.00	12.00
64 Dean,"Dizzy"	45.00	30.00	12.00	154 Murphy,Johnny	20.00	13.00	5.00
65 Bonura,Zeke	10.00	6.00	3.00	155 Sewell,Luke	22.00	15.00	7.00
66 Marberry,Fred	10.00	6.00	3.00	156 Durocher,Leo	25.00	17.00	7.50
67 Mancuso,Gus	10.00	6.00	3.00	157 Waner,Lloyd	30.00	20.00	8.00
68 Vosmik,Joe	10.00	6.00	3.00	158 Bush,Gus	20.00	13.00	5.00
69 Grace,Earl	10.00	6.00	3.00	159 Dykes,Jimmy	22.00	15.00	7.00
70 Piet,Tony	10.00	6.00	3.00	160 O'Neil,Steve	20.00	13.00	5.00
71 Hemsley,Rollie	10.00	6.00	3.00	161 Crowder,General	20.00	13.00	5.00
72 Fitzsimmons,Fred	10.00	6.00	3.00	162 Cascarella,Joe	20.00	13.00	5.00
73 Wilson,Jack	10.00	6.00	3.00	163 Hafey,"Bud" Daniel	22.00	15.00	7.00
74 Fullis,Chick	10.00	6.00	3.00	164 Campbell,Gilly	20.00	13.00	5.00
75 Frankhouse,Fred	10.00	6.00	3.00	165 Hayworth,Ray	20.00	13.00	5.00
76 Allen,Ethan	10.00	6.00	3.00	166 Demaree,Frank	20.00	13.00	5.00
77 Manush,Heine	13.00	9.00	4.00	167 Babich,John	20.00	13.00	5.00
78 Collins,Rip	10.00	6.00	3.00	168 Owen,Marvin	20.00	13.00	5.00
79 Cuccinello,Tony	10.00	6.00	3.00	169 Kress,Ralph	20.00	13.00	5.00
80 Kuhel,Joe	10.00	6.00	3.00	170 Haas,Mule	20.00	13.00	5.00
81 Bridges,Tom	20.00	13.00	5.00	171 Higgins,Frank	20.00	13.00	5.00
82 Brown,Clint	20.00	13.00	5.00	172 Berger,Wally	20.00	13.00	5.00
83 Blanche,Albert	20.00	13.00	5.00	173 Frisch,Frank	36.00	24.00	10.00
84 Berger,Boze	20.00	13.00	5.00	174 Ferrell,Wes	20.00	13.00	5.00
85 Goslin,Goose	30.00	20.00	8.00	175 Fox,Pete	20.00	13.00	5.00
86 Gomez,Lefty	36.00	24.00	10.00	176 Vergez,John	20.00	13.00	5.00
87 Glenn,Joe	20.00	13.00	5.00	177 Rogell,Billy	20.00	13.00	5.00
88 Blanton,Cy	20.00	13.00	5.00	178 Brennan,Don	20.00	13.00	5.00
89 Carey,Tom	20.00	13.00	5.00	179 Bottomley,Jim	30.00	20.00	8.00
90 Birkofer,Ralph	20.00	13.00	5.00	180 Jackson,Travis	20.00	13.00	5.00
91 Gabler,Fred	20.00	13.00	5.00	181 Rolfe,Red	20.00	13.00	5.00
92 Coffman,Dick	20.00	13.00	5.00	182 Crosetti,Frank	22.00	15.00	7.00
93 Bejma,Ollie	20.00	13.00	5.00	183 Cronin,Joe	30.00	20.00	8.00
94 Parmelee,Leroy	20.00	13.00	5.00	184 Rowe,Schoolboy	22.00	15.00	7.00
95 Reynolds,Carl	20.00	13.00	5.00	185 Klein,Chuck	30.00	20.00	8.00
96 Cantwell,Ben	20.00	13.00	5.00	186 Warneke,Lon	20.00	13.00	5.00
97 Davis,Curtis	20.00	13.00	5.00	187 Suhr,Gus	20.00	13.00	5.00
98 Webb & Moses	25.00	17.00	7.50	188 Chapman,Ben	20.00	13.00	5.00
99 Benge,Ray	20.00	13.00	5.00	189 Brown,Clint	20.00	13.00	5.00
100 Traynor,Pie	36.00	24.00	10.00	190 Derringer,Paul	22.00	15.00	7.00
101 Cavaretta,Phil	22.00	15.00	7.00	191 Burns,John	20.00	13.00	5.00
				192 Broaca,John	22.00	15.00	7.00

1959 BAZOOKA (23)

...e 1959 Bazooka set of 23 ...ll color, unnumbered, blank ...cked cards were issued on ...xes containing 25 individual ...eces of Bazooka gum. ...iginally, nine cards were ...ued. Later 14 more cards were issued. These later issued cards are indicated in the checklist below by an asterisk and are more difficult to obtain than the originally issued nine cards.

2 13/16" X 4 15/16"

WILLIE MAYS
OUTFIELD · SAN FRAN. GIANTS

	MINT	VG-E	F-G
COMPLETE SET	1800.00	1200.00	500.00
COMMON PLAYER	30.00	20.00	8.00
1 Hank Aaron	125.00	85.00	35.00
2 Richie Ashburn*	75.00	50.00	20.00
3 Ernie Banks*	125.00	85.00	35.00
4 Ken Boyer*	75.00	50.00	20.00
5 Orlando Cepeda	45.00	30.00	12.00
6 Bob Cerv*	60.00	40.00	16.00
7 Rocco Colavito*	75.00	50.00	20.00
8 Del Crandall	30.00	20.00	8.00
9 Jim Davenport	30.00	20.00	8.00
10 Don Drysdale*	90.00	60.00	25.00
11 Nellie Fox*	75.00	50.00	20.00
12 Jackie Jensen*	60.00	40.00	16.00
13 Harvey Kuenn*	60.00	40.00	16.00
14 Mickey Mantle	180.00	120.00	50.00
15 Willie Mays	125.00	85.00	35.00
16 Bill Mazeroski	30.00	20.00	8.00
17 Roy McMillan	30.00	20.00	8.00
18 Billy Pierce*	60.00	40.00	16.00
19 Roy Sievers*	60.00	40.00	16.00
20 Duke Snider*	125.00	85.00	35.00
21 Gus Triandos*	60.00	40.00	16.00
22 Bob Turley	30.00	20.00	8.00
23 Vic Wertz*	60.00	40.00	16.00

1960 BAZOOKA (36)

1 13/16" X 2 3/4"
2 3/4" X 5 1/2"

WARREN SPAHN
MILWAUKEE BRAVES   pitcher
NO. 19 OF 36 CARDS

HARMON KILLEBREW
WASH. SENATORS   3rd base
NO. 20 OF 36 CARDS

JACKIE JENSEN
BOSTON RED SOX   outfield
NO. 21 OF 36 CARDS

The 1960 Bazooka set of 36 full color, blanked backed, numbered cards was issued on boxes of Bazooka bubble gum. The cards were issued in panels of three cards per panel. The cards could be cut from the panel; therefore, individual cards plus full panels are in existence. The checklist below indicates prices for both individual cards and panels of three.

	AS INDIVIDUALS			AS PANELS		
	MINT	VG-E	F-G	MINT	VG-E	F-G
COMPLETE SET	135.00	90.00	40.00	200.00	130.00	55.00
COMMON PLAYER	2.50	1.70	.70	XXXXX	XXXX	XXXX
COMMON PANEL	XXXX	XXXX	XXX	12.00	8.00	3.50
1 Ernie Banks	9.00	6.00	2.50			
2 Bud Daley	2.50	1.70	.70	18.00	12.00	5.00
3 Wally Moon	2.50	1.70	.70			
4 Hank Aaron	16.50	11.00	4.50			
5 Milt Pappas	2.50	1.70	.70	27.00	18.00	8.00
6 Dick Stuart	2.50	1.70	.70			
7 Bob Clemente	11.00	7.00	3.00			
8 Yogi Berra	9.00	6.00	2.50	27.00	18.00	8.00
9 Ken Boyer	3.75	2.50	1.00			
10 Orlando Cepeda	3.75	2.50	1.00			
11 Gus Triandos	2.50	1.70	.70	12.00	8.00	3.50
12 Frank Malzone	2.50	1.70	.70			
13 Willie Mays	16.50	11.00	4.50			
14 Camilo Pascual	2.50	1.70	.70	27.00	18.00	8.00
15 Bob Cerv	2.50	1.70	.70			
16 Vic Power	2.50	1.70	.70			
17 Larry Sherry	2.50	1.70	.70	18.00	12.00	5.00
18 Al Kaline	9.00	6.00	2.50			
19 Warren Spahn	7.50	5.00	2.00			
20 Harmon Killebrew	7.50	5.00	2.00	21.00	14.00	6.00
21 Jackie Jensen	3.75	2.50	1.00			

```
1960 BAZOOKA (CONTINUED)
                      MINT    VG-E    F-G       MINT    VG-E    F-G
  22 Luis Aparicio    3.75    2.50    1.00
  23 Gil Hodges       6.00    4.00    1.60     15.00   10.00    4.00
  24 Richie Ashburn   3.75    2.50    1.00
  25 Nellie Fox       3.75    2.50    1.00
  26 Robin Roberts    6.00    4.00    1.60     15.00   10.00    4.00
  27 Joe Cunningham   2.50    1.70     .70
  28 Early Wynn       4.50    3.00    1.20
  29 Frank Robinson   7.50    5.00    2.00     18.00   12.00    5.00
  30 Rocky Colavito   3.75    2.50    1.00
  31 Mickey Mantle   21.00   14.00    6.00
  32 Glen Hobbie      2.50    1.70     .70     33.00   22.00    9.00
  33 Roy McMillan     2.50    1.70     .70
  34 Harvey Kuenn     2.50    1.70     .70
  35 Johnny Antonelli 2.50    1.70     .70     12.00    8.00    3.50
  36 Del Crandall     2.50    1.70     .70
```

1961 BAZOOKA (36)

1 13/16″ X 2 3/4″
2 3/4″ X 5 1/2″

CHUCK ESTRADA — BALTIMORE ORIOLES — pitcher — NO. 13 OF 36 CARDS
KEN BOYER — ST. LOUIS CARDINALS — 3rd base — NO. 14 OF 36 CARDS
HARVEY KUENN — SAN FRANCISCO GIANTS — outfield — NO. 15 OF 36 CARDS

The 1961 Bazooka set con-
tains 36 full color, blank
backed, numbered cards. The
set is almost identical in
format to the 1960 Bazooka
set except that the cards are
not in focus quite as clearly
as the 1960 set.

```
                         AS INDIVIDUALS          AS PANELS
                      MINT    VG-E    F-G       MINT    VG-E    F-G
COMPLETE SET        110.00   70.00   30.00    165.00  110.00   45.00
COMMON PLAYER         2.50    1.70     .70      XXXX    XXXX     XXX
COMMON PANEL          XXXX    XXXX     XXX      12.00    8.00    3.50

   1 Art Mahaffey      2.50    1.70     .70
   2 Mickey Mantle    21.00   14.00    6.00     33.00   22.00    9.00
   3 Ron Santo         3.00    2.00     .80
   4 Bud Daley         2.50    1.70     .70
   5 Roger Maris       7.50    5.00    2.00     12.00    8.00    3.50
   6 Eddie Yost        2.50    1.70     .70
   7 Minnie Minoso     3.00    2.50    1.00
   8 Dick Groat        3.00    2.00     .80     12.00    8.00    3.50
   9 Frank Malzone     2.50    1.70     .70
  10 Dick Donovan      2.50    1.70     .70
  11 Ed Mathews        6.00    4.00    1.60     12.00    8.00    3.50
  12 Jim Lemon         2.50    1.70     .70
  13 Chuck Estrada     2.50    1.70     .70
  14 Ken Boyer         3.75    2.50    1.00     12.00    8.00    3.50
  15 Harvey Kuenn      2.50    1.70     .70
  16 Ernie Broglio     2.50    1.70     .70
  17 Rocky Colavito    3.75    2.50    1.00     12.00    8.00    3.50
  18 Ted Kluszewski    3.75    2.50    1.00
  19 Ernie Banks       9.00    6.00    2.50
  20 Al Kaline         9.00    6.00    2.50     27.00   18.00    8.00
  21 Ed Bailey         2.50    1.70     .70
  22 Jim Perry         2.50    1.70     .70
  23 Willie Mays      16.50   11.00    4.50     27.00   18.00    8.00
  24 Bill Mazeroski    3.75    2.50    1.00
  25 Gus Triandos      2.50    1.70     .70
  26 Don Drysdale      4.50    3.00    1.20     12.00    8.00    3.50
  27 Frank Herrera     2.50    1.70     .70
  28 Earl Battey       2.50    1.70     .70
  29 Warren Spahn      6.00    4.00    1.60     15.00   10.00    4.00
  30 Gene Woodling     2.50    1.70     .70
  31 Frank Robinson    7.50    5.00    2.00     15.00   10.00    4.00
  32 Pete Runnels      2.50    1.70     .70
  33 Woodie Held       2.50    1.70     .70
  34 Norm Larker       2.50    1.70     .70
  35 Luis Aparicio     3.75    2.50    1.00     12.00    8.00    3.50
  36 Bill Tuttle       2.50    1.70     .70
```

1962 BAZOOKA (45)

1 13/16" X 2 3/4"
2 3/4" X 5 1/2"

JOHNNY ROMANO   ERNIE BANKS   NORM SIEBERN

The 1962 Bazooka set of 45 full color, blank backed, un-numbered cards was issued in panels of three on Bazooka bubble gum boxes. The cards below are numbered by panel alphabetically based on the last name of the player pictured on the far left card of the panel. The cards with an asterisk in the checklist below are more difficult to obtain than other cards in the set.

		AS INDIVIDUALS			AS PANELS		
		MINT	VG-E	F-G	MINT	VG-E	F-G
	COMPLETE SET	180.00	120.00	50.00	400.00	275.00	110.00
	COMMON PLAYER	2.25	1.50	.60	XXXX	XXXX	XXX
	COMMON PANEL	XXXX	XXXX	XXX	10.00	6.50	3.00
1	Bob Allison *	7.50	5.00	2.00			
2	Ed Mathews *	21.00	14.00	6.00	90.00	60.00	25.00
3	Vada Pinson *	7.50	5.00	2.00			
4	Earl Battey	2.25	1.50	.60			
5	Warren Spahn	6.00	4.00	1.60	12.00	8.00	3.50
6	Lee Thomas	2.25	1.50	.60			
7	Orlando Cepeda	3.25	2.25	.90			
8	Woodie Held	2.25	1.50	.60	10.00	6.50	3.00
9	Bob Aspromonte	2.25	1.50	.60			
10	Dick Howser	3.25	2.25	.90			
11	Bob Clemente	11.00	7.00	3.00	25.00	17.00	7.00
12	Al Kaline	9.00	6.00	2.50			
13	Joe Jay	2.25	1.50	.60			
14	Roger Maris	6.00·	4.00	1.60	15.00	10.00	4.00
15	Frank Howard	3.25	2.25	.90			
16	Sandy Koufax	9.00	6.00	2.50			
17	Jim Gentile	2.25	1.50	.60	15.00	10.00	4.00
18	Johnny Callison	2.25	1.50	.60			
19	Jim Landis	2.25	1.50	.60			
20	Ken Boyer	3.25	2.25	.90	10.00	6.50	3.00
21	Chuck Schilling	2.25	1.50	.60			
22	Art Mahaffey	2.25	1.50	.60			
23	Mickey Mantle	21.00	14.00	6.00	30.00	20.00	8.00
24	Dick Stuart	2.25	1.50	.60			
25	Ken McBride	2.25	1.50	.60			
26	Frank Robinson	7.50	5.00	2.00	18.00	12.00	5.00
27	Gil Hodges	6.00	4.00	1.60			
28	Milt Pappas	2.25	1.50·	.60			
29	Hank Aaron	15.00	10.00	4.00	25.00	17.00	7.00
30	Luis Aparicio	3.25	2.25	.90			
31	Johnny Romano *	7.50	5.00	2.00			
32	Ernie Banks *	30.00	20.00	8.00	90.00	60.00	25.00
33	Norm Siebern *	7.50	5.00	2.00			
34	Ron Santo	3.25	2.25	.90			
35	Norm Cash	3.25	2.25	.90	10.00	6.50	3.00
36	Jim Piersall	3.25	2.25	.90			
37	Don Schwall	2.25	1.50	.60			
38	Willie Mays	15.00	10.00	4.00	25.00	17.00	7.00
39	Norm Larker	2.25	1.50	.60			
40	Bill White	2.25	1.50	.60			
41	Whitey Ford	6.00	4.00	1.60	15.00	10.00	4.00
42	Rocky Colavito	3.25	2.25	.90			
43	Don Zimmer *	7.50	5.00	2.00			
44	Harmon Killebrew *	21.00	14.00	6.00	90.00	60.00	25.00
45	Gene Woodling *	7.50	5.00	2.00			

1963 BAZOOKA (36)

The 1963 Bazooka set of full color, blank backed, numbered cards was issued Bazooka bubble gum be This year marked a ch in format from prev Bazooka issues with a sm sized card being issued. card features a white with the player's name pr in red and the team pos printed in black on the The number appears in white border at the bo of the card. Three were issued per panel

	AS INDIVIDUALS			AS PANELS		
	MINT	VG-E	F-G	MINT	VG-E	F-G
COMPLETE SET	110.00	70.00	30.00	165.00	110.00	45.00
COMMON PLAYER	1.75	1.25	.50	XXXX	XXXX	XXX
COMMON PANEL	XXXX	XXXX	XXX	8.00	5.50	2.25
1 Mickey Mantle	21.00	14.00	6.00			
2 Bob Rodgers	1.75	1.25	.50	30.00	20.00	8.00
3 Ernie Banks	7.50	5.00	2.00			
4 Norm Siebern	1.75	1.25	.50			
5 Warren Spahn	4.50	3.00	1.20	12.00	8.00	3.50
6 Bill Mazeroski	1.75	1.25	.50			
7 Harmon Killebrew	4.50	3.00	1.20			
8 Dick Farrell	1.75	1.25	.50	25.00	17.00	7.00
9 Hank Aaron	13.50	9.00	4.00			
10 Dick Donovan	1.75	1.25	.50			
11 Jim Gentile	1.75	1.25	.50	21.00	14.00	6.00
12 Willie Mays	13.50	9.00	4.00			
13 Camilo Pascual	1.75	1.25	.50			
14 Bob Clemente	9.00	6.00	2.50	18.00	12.00	5.00
15 Johnny Callison	1.75	1.25	.50			
16 Carl Yastrzemski	11.00	7.00	3.00			
17 Don Drysdale	4.50	3.00	1.20	18.00	12.00	5.00
18 Johnny Romano	1.75	1.25	.50			
19 Al Jackson	1.75	1.25	.50			
20 Ralph Terry	1.75	1.25	.50	8.00	5.50	2.25
21 Bill Monbouquette	1.75	1.25	.50			
22 Orlando Cepeda	2.50	1.70	.70			
23 Stan Musial	11.00	7.00	3.00	21.00	14.00	6.00
24 Floyd Robinson	1.75	1.25	.50			
25 Chuck Hinton	1.75	1.25	.50			
26 Bob Purkey	1.75	1.25	.50	8.00	5.50	2.25
27 Ken Hubbs	2.50	1.70	.70			
28 Bill White	1.75	1.25	.50			
29 Ray Herbert	1.75	1.25	.50	15.00	10.00	4.00
30 Brooks Robinson	7.50	5.00	2.00			
31 Frank Robinson	7.50	5.00	2.00			
32 Lee Thomas	1.75	1.25	.50	15.00	10.00	4.00
33 Rocky Colavito	2.50	1.70	.70			
34 Al Kaline	7.50	5.00	2.00			
35 Art Mahaffey	1.75	1.25	.50	15.00	10.00	4.00
36 Tommy Davis	2.50	1.70	.70			

1963 BAZOOKA (41)
ALL—TIME GREATS

The 1963 Bazooka All-Time Greats set contains 41 black and white, numbered cards issued as inserts in boxes of Bazooka bubble gum. The cards feature bust shots with gold trim. The backs are yellow with black print containing vital information and a biography of the player. Many of the players are pictured not as they looked during their playing careers but as they looked many years after their playing days were through.

	MINT	VG-E	F-G
COMPLETE SET	75.00	50.00	20.00
COMMON PLAYER	1.50	1.00	.40
1 Joe Tinker	1.50	1.00	.40
2 Harry Heilmann	1.50	1.00	.40
3 Jack Chesbro	1.50	1.00	.40
4 Christy Mathewson	3.00	2.00	.80
5 Herb Pennock	1.50	1.00	.40
6 Cy Young	2.00	1.30	.55
7 Ed Walsh	1.50	1.00	.40
8 Nap Lajoie	2.00	1.30	.55

1963 BAZOOKA (CONTINUED)

	MINT	VG-E	F-G			MINT	VG-E	F-G
9 Eddie Plank	1.50	1.00	.40	25 Frank Chance	2.00	1.30	.55
10 Honus Wagner	3.00	2.00	.80	26 Fred Clarke	1.50	1.00	.40
11 Chief Bender	1.50	1.00	.40	27 Wilbert Robinson	1.50	1.00	.40
12 Walter Johnson	3.00	2.00	.80	28 Dazzy Vance	1.50	1.00	.40
13 Mordecai Brown	1.50	1.00	.40	29 Pete Alexander	2.00	1.30	.55
14 Rabbit Maranville	1.50	1.00	.40	30 Judge Landis	1.50	1.00	.40
15 Lou Gehrig	6.00	4.00	1.60	31 Willie Keeler	1.50	1.00	.40
16 Ban Johnson	1.50	1.00	.40	32 Rogers Hornsby	3.00	2.00	.80
17 Babe Ruth	9.00	6.00	2.50	33 Hugh Duffy	1.50	1.00	.40
18 Connie Mack	2.00	1.30	.55	34 Mickey Cochrane	2.00	1.30	.55
19 Hank Greenberg	1.50	1.00	.40	35 Ty Cobb	6.00	4.00	1.60
20 John McGraw	2.00	1.30	.55	36 Mel Ott	3.00	2.00	.80
21 Al Simmons	1.50	1.00	.40	37 Clark Griffith	1.50	1.00	.40
23 Jimmy Collins	1.50	1.00	.40	38 Ted Lyons	1.50	1.00	.40
24 Tris Speaker	2.00	1.30	.55	39 Cap Anson	2.00	1.30	.55
				40 Bill Dickey	2.00	1.30	.55
				41 Eddie Collins	1.50	1.00	.40

1964 BAZOOKA (36)

1 9/16" X 2 1/2"
2 1/2" X 4 11/16"

The 1964 Bazooka set of 36 full color, blank backed, numbered cards were issued in panels of three on the backs of Bazooka bubble gum boxes. Many players from the 1963 set have the same numbers; however, the pictures are different.

	AS INDIVIDUALS			AS PANELS		
	MINT	VG-E	F-G	MINT	VG-E	F-G
COMPLETE SET	110.00	70.00	30.00	165.00	110.00	45.00
COMMON PLAYER	1.75	1.25	.50	XXXX	XXXX	XXX
COMMON PANEL	XXXX	XXXX	XXX	7.50	5.00	2.00
1 Mickey Mantle	18.00	12.00	5.00			
2 Dick Groat	1.75	1.25	.50	30.00	20.00	8.00
3 Steve Barber	1.75	1.25	.50			
4 Ken McBride	1.75	1.25	.50			
5 Warren Spahn	4.50	3.00	1.20	10.00	6.50	3.00
6 Bob Friend	1.75	1.25	.50			
7 Harmon Killebrew	4.50	3.00	1.20			
8 Dick Farrell	1.75	1.25	.50	25.00	17.00	7.00
9 Hank Aaron	12.00	8.00	3.50			
10 Rich Rollins	1.75	1.25	.50			
11 Jim Gentile	1.75	1.25	.50	21.00	14.00	6.00
12 Willie Mays	12.00	8.00	3.50			
13 Camilo Pascual	1.75	1.25	.50			
14 Bob Clemente	9.00	6.00	2.50	15.00	10.00	4.00
15 Johnny Callison	1.75	1.25	.50			
16 Carl Yastrzemski	11.00	7.00	3.00			
17 Billy Williams	2.50	1.70	.70	18.00	12.00	5.00
18 Johnny Romano	1.75	1.25	.50			
19 Jim Maloney	1.75	1.25	.50			
20 Norm Cash	2.50	1.70	.70	10.00	6.50	3.00
21 Willie McCovey	4.50	3.00	1.20			
22 Jim Fregosi	1.75	1.25	.50			
23 George Altman	1.75	1.25	.50	7.50	5.00	2.00
24 Floyd Robinson	1.75	1.25	.50			
25 Chuck Hinton	1.75	1.25	.50			
26 Ron Hunt	1.75	1.25	.50	7.50	5.00	2.00
27 Gary Peters	1.75	1.25	.50			
28 Dick Ellsworth	1.75	1.25	.50			
29 Elston Howard	2.50	1.70	.70	15.00	10.00	4.00
30 Brooks Robinson	7.50	5.00	2.00			
31 Frank Robinson	7.50	5.00	2.00			
32 Sandy Koufax	9.00	6.00	2.50	21.00	14.00	6.00
33 Rocky Colavito	2.50	1.70	.70			
34 Al Kaline	7.50	5.00	2.00			
35 Ken Boyer	2.50	1.70	.70	15.00	10.00	4.00
36 Tommy Davis	2.50	1.70	.70			

1965 BAZOOKA (36)

The 1965 Bazooka set of 36 full color, blank backed, numbered cards was issued in panels of three on the backs of Bazooka bubble gum boxes. As in the previous two years, some of the players have the same numbers on their cards; however, all pictures are different from the previous two years.

	AS INDIVIDUALS			AS PANELS		
	MINT	VG-E	F-G	MINT	VG-E	F-G
COMPLETE SET	100.00	65.00	30.00	150.00	100.00	40.00
COMMON PLAYER	1.50	1.00	.40	XXXX	XXXX	XXX
COMMON PANEL	XXXX	XXXX	XXX	6.00	4.00	1.60
1 Mickey Mantle	15.00	10.00	4.00			
2 Larry Jackson	1.50	1.00	.40	25.00	17.00	7.00
3 Chuck Hinton	1.50	1.00	.40			
4 Tony Oliva	2.25	1.50	.60			
5 Dean Chance	1.50	1.00	.40	6.00	4.00	1.60
6 Jim O'Toole	1.50	1.00	.40			
7 Harmon Killebrew	4.50	3.00	1.20			
8 Pete Ward	1.50	1.00	.40	21.00	14.00	6.00
9 Hank Aaron	11.00	7.00	3.00			
10 Dick Radatz	1.50	1.00	.40			
11 Boog Powell	2.25	1.50	.60	21.00	14.00	6.00
12 Willie Mays	11.00	7.00	3.00			
13 Bob Veale	1.50	1.00	.40			
14 Bob Clemente	7.50	5.00	2.00	15.00	10.00	4.00
15 Johnny Callison	1.50	1.00	.40			
16 Joe Torre	2.25	1.50	.60			
17 Billy Williams	2.25	1.50	.60	7.50	5.00	2.00
18 Bob Chance	1.50	1.00	.40			
19 Bob Aspromonte	1.50	1.00	.40			
20 Joe Christopher	1.50	1.00	.40	6.00	4.00	1.60
21 Jim Bunning	2.25	1.50	.60			
22 Jim Fregosi	1.50	1.00	.40			
23 Bob Gibson	4.50	3.00	1.20	12.00	8.00	3.50
24 Juan Marichal	3.75	2.50	1.00			
25 Dave Wickersham	1.50	1.00	.40			
26 Ron Hunt	1.50	1.00	.40	6.00	4.00	1.60
27 Gary Peters	1.50	1.00	.40			
28 Ron Santo	2.25	1.50	.60			
29 Elston Howard	3.00	2.00	.80	15.00	10.00	4.00
30 Brooks Robinson	6.00	4.00	1.60			
31 Frank Robinson	6.00	4.00	1.60			
32 Sandy Koufax	7.50	5.00	2.00	21.00	14.00	6.00
33 Rocky Colavito	2.25	1.50	.60			
34 Al Kaline	6.00	4.00	1.60			
35 Ken Boyer	2.25	1.50	.60	15.00	10.00	4.00
36 Tommy Davis	2.25	1.50	.60			

1966 BAZOOKA (48)

The 1966 Bazooka set of 48 full color, blank backed, numbered cards was issued in panels of three on the backs of Bazooka bubble gum boxes. The set is distinguishable from the previous years by mention of a "48 card set" at the bottom of the card

	AS INDIVIDUALS			AS PANELS		
	MINT	VG-E	F-G	MINT	VG-E	F-G
COMPLETE SET	105.00	70.00	30.00	165.00	110.00	45.00
COMMON PLAYER	1.50	1.00	.40	XXXX	XXXX	XXX
COMMON PANEL	XXXX	XXXX	XXX	6.00	4.00	1.60
1 Sandy Koufax	7.50	5.00	2.00			
2 Willie Horton	1.50	1.00	.40	15.00	10.00	4.00
3 Frank Howard	2.25	1.50	.60			

1966 BAZOOKA (CONTINUED)

		MINT	VG-E	F-G		MINT	VG-E	F-G
4	Richie Allen	2.25	1.50	.60				
5	Mel Stottlemyre	1.50	1.00	.40		6.00	4.00	1.60
6	Tony Conigliaro	1.50	1.00	.40				
7	Mickey Mantle	15.00	10.00	4.00				
8	Leon Wagner	1.50	1.00	.40		21.00	14.00	6.00
9	Ed Kranepool	1.50	1.00	.40				
10	Juan Marichal	3.75	2.50	1.00				
11	Harmon Killebrew	4.50	3.00	1.20		12.00	8.00	3.50
12	Johnny Callison	1.50	1.00	.40				
13	Roy McMillan	1.50	1.00	.40				
14	Willie McCovey	4.50	3.00	1.20		10.00	6.50	3.00
15	Rocky Colavito	2.25	1.50	.60				
16	Willie Mays	11.00	7.00	3.00				
17	Sammy McDowell	1.50	1.00	.40		18.00	12.00	5.00
18	Vern Law	1.50	1.00	.40				
19	Jim Fregosi	1.50	1.00	.40				
20	Ron Fairly	1.50	1.00	.40		10.00	6.50	3.00
21	Bob Gibson	4.50	3.00	1.20				
22	Carl Yastrzemski	9.00	6.00	2.50				
23	Bill White	1.50	1.00	.40		15.00	10.00	4.00
24	Bob Aspromonte	1.50	1.00	.40				
25	Dean Chance	1.50	1.00	.40				
26	Bob Clemente	7.50	5.00	2.00		15.00	10.00	4.00
27	Tony Cloninger	1.50	1.00	.40				
28	Curt Blefary	1.50	1.00	.40				
29	Milt Pappas	1.50	1.00	.40		18.00	12.00	5.00
30	Hank Aaron	11.00	7.00	3.00				
31	Jim Bunning	2.25	1.50	.60				
32	Frank Robinson	6.00	4.00	1.60		12.00	8.00	3.50
33	Bill Skowron	2.25	1.50	.60				
34	Brooks Robinson	6.00	4.00	1.60				
35	Jim Wynn	1.50	1.00	.40		12.00	8.00	3.50
36	Joe Torre	2.25	1.50	.60				
37	Jim Grant	1.50	1.00	.40				
38	Pete Rose	13.50	9.00	4.00		21.00	14.00	6.00
39	Ron Santo	2.25	1.50	.60				
40	Tom Tresh	1.50	1.00	.40				
41	Tony Oliva	2.25	1.50	.60		10.00	6.50	3.00
42	Don Drysdale	3.75	2.50	1.00				
43	Pete Richert	1.50	1.00	.40				
44	Bert Campaneris	1.50	1.00	.40		6.00	4.00	1.60
45	Jim Maloney	1.50	1.00	.40				
46	Al Kaline	6.00	4.00	1.60				
47	Eddie Fisher	1.50	1.00	.40		15.00	10.00	4.00
48	Billy Williams	2.25	1.50	.60				

1967 BAZOOKA (48)

1 9/16" X 2 1/2"
2 1/2 X 4 11/16"

The 1967 Bazooka set of 48 full color, blank backed, numbered cards was issued in panels of three on the backs of Bazooka bubble gum boxes. This set is virtually identical to the 1966 set with the exception of 10 new cards as replacements for ten 1966 cards. The remaining 38 cards are identical in both pose and number. The replacement cards are listed in the checklist below with an asterisk.

TOMMY DAVIS
NEW YORK METS OF
NO. 37 OF 48 CARDS

PETE ROSE
CINCINNATI REDS 2B
NO. 38 OF 48 CARDS

RON SANTO
CHICAGO CUBS 3B
NO. 39 OF 48 CARDS

		AS INDIVIDUALS			AS PANELS		
		MINT	VG-E	F-G	MINT	VG-E	F-G
COMPLETE SET		90.00	60.00	25.00	135.00	90.00	40.00
COMMON PLAYER		1.50	1.00	.40	XXXX	XXXX	XXX
COMMON PANEL		XXXX	XXXX	XXX	6.00	4.00	1.60
1	Rick Reichardt *	1.50	1.00	.40			
2	Tommy Agee *	1.50	1.00	.40	6.00	4.00	1.60
3	Frank Howard *	2.25	1.50	.60			
4	Richie Allen	2.25	1.50	.60			
5	Mel Stottlemyre	1.50	1.00	.40	6.00	4.00	1.60
6	Tony Conigliaro	1.50	1.00	.40			
7	Mickey Mantle	15.00	10.00	4.00			
8	Leon Wagner	1.50	1.00	.40	21.00	14.00	6.00
9	Gary Peters *	1.50	1.00	.40			
10	Juan Marichal	3.75	2.50	1.00			
11	Harmon Killebrew	4.50	3.00	1.20	12.00	8.00	3.50
12	Johnny Callison	1.50	1.00	.40			
13	Denny McLain *	2.25	1.50	.60			
14	Willie McCovey	4.50	3.00	1.20	10.00	6.50	3.00
15	Rocky Colavito	2.25	1.50	.60			
16	Willie Mays	11.00	7.00	3.00			
17	Sammy McDowell	1.50	1.00	.40	18.00	12.00	5.00
18	Jim Kaat *	2.25	1.50	.60			
19	Jim Fregosi	1.50	1.00	.40			

29

	MINT	VG-E	F-G	MINT	VG-E	F-G
20 Ron Fairly	1.50	1.00	.40	10.00	6.50	3.00
21 Bob Gibson	4.50	3.00	1.20			
22 Carl Yastrzemski	9.00	6.00	2.50			
23 Bill White	1.50	1.00	.40	15.00	10.00	4.00
24 Bob Aspromonte	1.50	1.00	.40			
25 Dean Chance	1.50	1.00	.40			
26 Bob Clemente	7.50	5.00	2.00	15.00	10.00	4.00
27 Tony Cloninger	1.50	1.00	.40			
28 Curt Blefary	1.50	1.00	.40			
29 Phil Regan *	1.50	1.00	.40	18.00	12.00	5.00
30 Hank Aaron	11.00	7.00	3.00			
31 Jim Bunning	2.25	1.50	.60			
32 Frank Robinson	6.00	4.00	1.60	12.00	8.00	3.50
33 Ken Boyer *	2.25	1.50	.60			
34 Brooks Robinson	6.00	4.00	1.60			
35 Jim Wynn	1.50	1.00	.40	12.00	8.00	3.50
36 Joe Torre	2.25	1.50	.60			
37 Tommy Davis *	1.50	1.00	.40			
38 Pete Rose	11.00	7.00	3.00	21.00	14.00	6.00
39 Ron Santo	2.25	1.50	.60			
40 Tom Tresh	1.50	1.00	.40			
41 Tony Oliva	2.25	1.50	.60	10.00	6.50	3.00
42 Don Drysdale	3.75	2.50	1.00			
43 Pete Richert	1.50	1.00	.40			
44 Bert Campaneris	1.50	1.00	.40	6.00	4.00	1.60
45 Jim Maloney	1.50	1.00	.40			
46 Al Kaline	6.00	4.00	1.60			
47 Matty Alou *	1.50	1.00	.40	12.00	8.00	3.50
48 Billy Williams	2.25	1.50	.60			

1968 BAZOOKA (15)
TIPPS FROM THE TOPPS

3″ X 6 1/4″
1 1/4″ X 3 1/8″
5 1/2″ X 6 1/4″

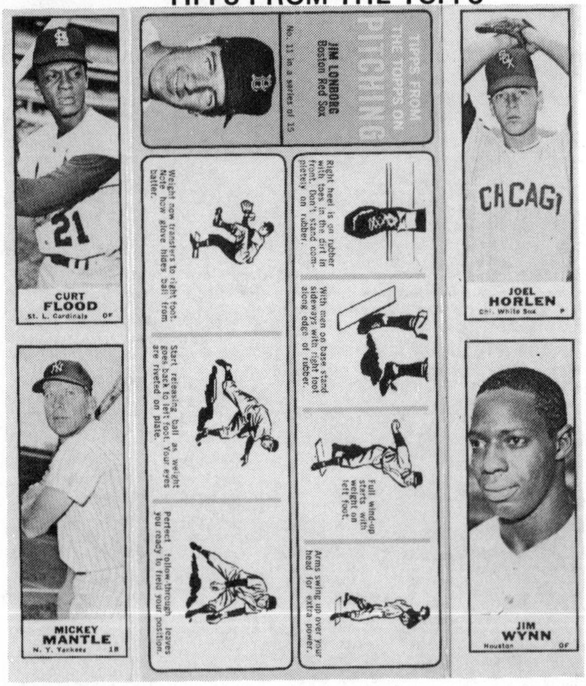

The 1968 Bazooka Tipps from the Topps is a set of 15 numbered boxes, each containing on the back panel a baseball playing tip from a star, and on the side panels four mini cards, two per side, in full color, measuring 1 1/4″ X 3″. Although the set contains a total of 60 of these small cards, 4 are repeated; therefore, there are but 56 different small cards.

	AS INDIVIDUALS			AS PANELS		
	MINT	VG-E	F-G	MINT	VG-E	F-G
COMPLETE SET	110.00	70.00	30.00	165.00	110.00	45.00
COMMON PANEL	XXXX	XXXX	XXX	6.00	4.00	1.60
COMMON PLAYER	1.00	.65	.30	XXXX	XXXX	XXX
1 Maury Wills,						
Bunting	3.00	2.00	.80			
Kaline	4.50	3.00	1.20			
Casanova	1.00	.65	.30	15.00	10.00	4.00
C. Boyer	1.00	.65	.30			
Seaver	4.50	3.00	1.20			
2 Carl Yastrzemski,						
Batting	7.50	5.00	2.00			
Hunter	1.50	1.00	.40			
Freehan	1.00	.65	.30	15.00	10.00	4.00
M. Alou	1.00	.65	.30			
Lefebvre	1.00	.65	.30			

```
 3 Bert Campaneris,
       Stealing Bases     1.50    1.00     .40
       McCarver           1.00     .65     .30
       Veale              1.00     .65     .30     9.00    6.00    2.50
       Fr. Robinson       3.75    2.50    1.00
       Knoop              1.00     .65     .30
 4 Maury Wills, Sliding   1.50    1.00     .40
       Holtzman           1.00     .65     .30
       Azcue              1.00     .65     .30     6.00    4.00    1.60
       T. Conigliaro      1.00     .65     .30
       White              1.00     .65     .30
 5 Julian Javier,
       The Double Play    1.50    1.00     .40
       Marichal           3.00    2.00     .80
       Petrocelli         1.00     .65     .30    15.00   10.00    4.00
       Pepitone           1.00     .65     .30
       Aaron              7.50    5.00    2.00
 6 Orlando Cepeda,
       Playing 1st Base   1.50    1.00     .40
       Santo              1.50    1.00     .40
       Drysdale           3.00    2.00     .80    15.00   10.00    4.00
       Rose               7.50    5.00    2.00
       Agee               1.00     .65     .30
 7 Bill Mazeroski,
       Playing 2nd Base   1.50    1.00     .40
       Roseboro           1.00     .65     .30
       Bunning            1.00     .65     .30     6.00    4.00    1.60
       F. Howard          1.50    1.00     .40
       Scott              1.00     .65     .30
 8 Brooks Robinson,
       Playing 3rd Base   6.00    4.00    1.60
       Gonzalez           1.00     .65     .30
       McGlothlin         1.00     .65     .30    15.00   10.00    4.00
       Horton             1.00     .65     .30
       Killebrew          3.00    2.00     .80
 9 Jim Fregosi,
       Playing Short      1.50    1.00     .40
       Alvis              1.00     .65     .30
       Gibson             3.00    2.00     .80     9.00    6.00    2.50
       Oliva              1.50    1.00     .40
       Pinson             1.50    1.00     .40
10 Joe Torre, Catching    1.50    1.00     .40
       Chance             1.00     .65     .30
       Jenkins            1.50    1.00     .40     7.50    5.00    2.00
       T. Davis           1.50    1.00     .40
       Monday             1.50    1.00     .40
11 Jim Lonborg,
       Pitching           1.50    1.00     .40
       Horlen             1.00     .65     .30
       Wynn               1.00     .65     .30    18.00   12.00    5.00
       Flood              1.50    1.00     .40
       Mantle            10.00    6.50    3.00
12 Mike McCormick,
       Fielding Pitcher   1.50    1.00     .40
       Mincher            1.00     .65     .30
       Perez              1.50    1.00     .40    12.00    8.00    3.50
       Clemente           6.00    4.00    1.60
       Downing            1.00     .65     .30
13 Frank Crosetti,
       Coaching           1.50    1.00     .40
       Carew              4.50    3.00    1.20
       Wilson             1.00     .65     .30    12.00    8.00    3.50
       Swoboda            1.00     .65     .30
       McCovey            3.75    2.50    1.00
14 Willie Mays,
       Playing the OF     7.50    5.00    2.00
       Allen              1.50    1.00     .40
       Peters             1.00     .65     .30    15.00   10.00    4.00
       B. Williams        1.50    1.00     .40
       Staub              1.50    1.00     .40
15 Lou Brock, Base
       Running            6.00    4.00    1.60
       Agee               1.00     .65     .30
       Rose               6.00    4.00    1.60    18.00   12.00    5.00
       Santo              1.50    1.00     .40
       Drysdale           3.00    2.00     .80
```

F213-9 COCA COLA

★ BASEBALL EXTRA ★

DOUBLE SHUTOUT BY ED REULBACH

Cub Pitcher Zips Dodgers Twice

ALL-TIME GREATS — ROGERS HORNSBY • ST. LOUIS CARDINALS Second Base

ALL-TIME GREATS — "RABBIT" MARANVILLE • BOSTON BRAVES Shortstop

ALL-TIME GREATS — CHRISTY MATHEWSON • NEW YORK GIANTS Pitcher

ALL-TIME GREATS — HONUS WAGNER • PITTSBURGH PIRATES Shortstop

Ed Reulbach, Chicago Cub hurler, made baseball history when he shut out the Brooklyn Dodgers in both games of a double-header, 5-0 and 3-0. It was the first time in Baseball this feat was accomplished. The victories, Reulbach's 21st and 22nd, helped his team keep pace with the Giants in their close pennant race. In the first game, he allowed five hits and one walk while striking out six. In the second game he was even more effective, doling out only three hits while fanning four. Reulbach extended his scoreless streak to thirty innings.

TOPPS BASEBALL TRADING CARDS ARE GREAT FUN
...EDUCATIONAL, TOO! COLLECT THE ENTIRE SET!

The 1969-1970 Bazooka Baseball Extra News cards contain 12 complete panels each comprising a large action shot of a significant event in baseball history and four small cards, comparable to those in the "Tipps from the Topps set of 1968", of Hall of Fame baseball players.

	AS INDIVIDUALS			AS PANELS		
	MINT	VG-E	F-G	MINT	VG-E	F-G
COMPLETE SET	90.00	60.00	25.00	125.00	80.00	30.00
COMMON PANEL	XXXX	XXXX	XXX	6.00	4.00	1.60
COMMON PLAYER	.50	.35	.15	XXXX	XXXX	XXX
1 No-Hit Duel by						
Toney & Vaughn	1.50	1.00	.40			
Cobb	3.75	2.50	1.00			
Keeler	.50	.35	.15	7.50	5.00	2.00
Brown	.50	.35	.15			
Plank	.75	.50	.20			
2 Alexander Conquers						
Yanks	3.00	2.00	.80			
Simmons	.50	.35	.15			
B. Johnson	.50	.35	.15	9.00	6.00	2.50
W. Johnson	2.50	1.70	.70			
Hornsby	2.50	1.70	.70			
3 Yanks' Lazzeri Sets						
AL Record	1.50	1.00	.40			
Mathewson	2.50	1.70	.70			
Bender	.50	.35	.15	6.00	4.00	1.60
Alexander	.75	.50	.20			
Young	.75	.50	.20			
4 HR Almost Hit Out						
of Stadium	4.50	3.00	1.20			
Gehrig	4.50	3.00	1.20			
Duffy	.50	.35	.15	12.00	8.00	3.50
Speaker	.75	.50	.20			
Tinker	.50	.35	.15			
5 Four Consecutive						
Homers by Lou	7.50	5.00	2.00			
McGraw	.75	.50	.20			
Chance	.75	.50	.20	18.00	12.00	5.00
Ruth	6.00	4.00	1.60			
Cochrane	.75	.50	.20			
6 No-Hit Game by						
Walter Johnson	4.50	3.00	1.20			
Young	.75	.50	.20			
W. Johnson	3.00	2.00	.80	10.50	7.00	3.00
Evers	.75	.50	.20			
McGraw	.75	.50	.20			
7 Twelve RBIs by						
Bottomley	1.50	1.00	.40			
Evers	.75	.50	.20			
Collins	.50	.35	.15	12.00	8.00	3.50
Gehrig	4.50	3.00	1.20			
Cobb	3.75	2.50	1.00			
8 Ty Ties Record	7.50	5.00	2.00			
Wagner	2.50	1.70	.70			
Cochrane	.50	.35	.15	15.00	10.00	4.00
Collins	.50	.35	.15			
Ott	1.50	1.00	.40			

```
 9 Babe Ruth Hits 3
     HR's in Game      9.00    6.00    2.50
     Anson             .75     .50     .20
     Speaker           .75     .50     .20    13.50    9.00    4.00
     Chesbro           .50     .35     .15
     Simmons           .50     .35     .15
10 Calls Shot in
     Series Game       9.00    6.00    2.50
     Maranville        .50     .35     .15
     Walsh             .50     .35     .15    15.00   10.00    4.00
     Lajoie           1.50    1.00     .40
     Mack              .75     .50     .20
11 Ruth's 60th HR Sets
     New Record        9.00    6.00    2.50
     Tinker            .50     .35     .15
     Lajoie           1.50    1.00     .40    15.00   10.00    4.00
     Ott              1.50    1.00     .40
     Chance            .75     .50     .20
12 Double Shutout by
     Ed Reulbach      1.00     .65     .30
     Hornsby          2.50    1.70     .70
     Maranville        .50     .35     .15     9.00    6.00    2.50
     Mathewson        2.50    1.70     .70
     Wagner           2.50    1.70     .70
```

1971 BAZOOKA (36)

2" X 2 5/8"
2 5/8" X 5 5/16"

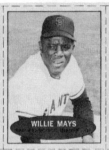

RANDY HUNDLEY   WILLIE MAYS   JIM HUNTER

The 1971 Bazooka set of 36 full color, unnumbered cards was issued in 12 panels of three cards each on the backs of boxes containing one cent Bazooka bubble gum. The panels are numbered in the checklist alphabetically by the player's last name on the left most card of the panel.

	AS INDIVIDUALS			AS PANELS		
	MINT	VG-E	F-G	MINT	VG-E	F-G
COMPLETE SET	50.00	35.00	14.00	75.00	50.00	20.00
COMMON PLAYER	.75	.50	.20	XXXX	XXXX	XXX
COMMON PANEL	XXX	XXX	XXX	3.00	2.00	.80
1 Tommie Agee	.75	.50	.20			
2 Harmon Killebrew	3.00	2.00	.80	10.00	6.50	3.00
3 Reggie Jackson	6.00	4.00	1.60			
4 Bert Campaneris	.75	.50	.20			
5 Pete Rose	6.00	4.00	1.60	9.00	6.00	2.50
6 Orlando Cepeda	.90	.60	.25			
7 Rico Carty	.90	.60	.25			
8 Johnny Bench	4.50	3.00	1.20	7.00	4.75	2.00
9 Tommy Harper	.75	.50	.20			
10 Bill Freehan	.75	.50	.20			
11 Roberto Clemente	4.50	3.00	1.20	6.00	4.00	1.60
12 Claude Osteen	.75	.50	.20			
13 Jim Fregosi	.75	.50	.20			
14 Billy Williams	.90	.60	.25	3.00	2.00	.80
15 Dave McNally	.75	.50	.20			
16 Randy Hundley	.75	.50	.20			
17 Willie Mays	6.00	4.00	1.60	9.00	6.00	2.50
18 Jim Hunter	1.50	1.00	.40			
19 Juan Marichal	1.50	1.00	.40			
20 Frank Howard	.90	.60	.25	3.75	2.50	1.00
21 Bill Melton	.75	.50	.20			
22 Willie McCovey	3.00	2.00	.80			
23 Carl Yastrzemski	6.00	4.00	1.60	11.00	7.00	3.00
24 Clyde Wright	.75	.50	.20			
25 Jim Merritt	.75	.50	.20			
26 Luis Aparicio	.90	.60	.25	3.00	2.00	.80
27 Bobby Murcer	.90	.60	.25			
28 Rico Petrocelli	.75	.50	.20			
29 Sam McDowell	.75	.50	.20	3.00	2.00	.80
30 Clarence Gaston	.75	.50	.20			
31 Brooks Robinson	4.50	3.00	1.20			
32 Hank Aaron	6.00	4.00	1.60	12.00	8.00	3.50
33 Larry Dierker	.75	.50	.20			
34 Rusty Staub	.90	.60	.25			
35 Bob Gibson	3.00	2.00	.80	5.00	3.50	1.40
36 Amos Otis	.90	.60	.25			

1958 BELL BRAND (10)   3" X 4"

ROY CAMPANELLA
Catcher LOS ANGELES DODGERS

Height: 5'10"   Weight: 218
Home: Glen Cove, New York
Throws: Right   Bats: Right
Born: November 19, 1921

Roy Campanella has been named The Most Valuable Player in the National League on 3 occasions! His finest season was in 1953 when he hit 41 home runs and piled up 142 runs batted in—an all-time high in Dodger history. In his ten campaigns with the Dodgers, Roy has hit 242 homers and only twice has dropped below 20.

MAJOR LEAGUE RECORD

YEAR	CLUB	GAMES	HITS	HR	RBI	AVG.
1948	Dodgers	83	72	9	45	.258
1949	"	130	125	22	82	.287
1950	"	126	123	31	89	.281
1951	"	143	164	33	108	.325
1952	"	128	126	22	97	.269
1953	"	144	162	41	142	.312
1954	"	111	82	19	51	.207
1955	"	123	142	32	107	.318
1956	"	124	85	20	73	.219
1957	"	103	80	13	62	.242

ROY CAMPANELLA

The 1958 Bell Brand Potato Chips set of 10 unnumbered cards features Los Angeles Dodgers only. The set is distinguished by a 1/4" dark green border. The Cimoli, Podres, and Snider cards are quite scarce. The ACC designation is F339-1.

	MINT	VG-E	F-G
COMPLETE SET	400.00	275.00	110.00
COMMON PLAYER(1-10)	21.00	14.00	6.00

	MINT	VG-E	F-G			MINT	VG-E	F-G
1 Campanella,Roy	21.00	14.00	6.00	6 Koufax,Sandy		50.00	35.00	15.00
2 Cimoli,Gino	70.00	45.00	20.00	7 Podres,Johnny		100.00	65.00	30.00
3 Drysdale,Don	35.00	24.00	10.00	8 Reese,Pee Wee		30.00	20.00	8.00
4 Gilliam,Jim	25.00	17.00	7.00	9 Snider,Duke		85.00	60.00	25.00
5 Hodges,Gil	35.00	24.00	10.00	10 Zimmer,Don		21.00	14.00	6.00

1960 BELL BRAND (20)   2 1/2" X 3 1/2"

SANDY KOUFAX
Left-Hand Pitcher   L.A. Dodgers

9 SANDY KOUFAX
Left-Hand Pitcher

Sandy tied the all-time record for strike-outs in a single game when he fanned eighteen Giants, matching the record held by Cleveland's Bob Feller. Sandy has the best strike-out average among currently active National League pitchers.

Start your collection of L. A. Dodger players! There's one in each package of 39c, 49c and 59c Bell Brand Potato Chips and the 29c, 49c Corn Chips.

The 1960 Bell Brand Potato Chips set of 20 full color numbered cards features Los Angeles Dodgers only. Because these cards were issued in packages of potato chips, many cards suffered from stains. Labine, Klippstein and Alston are somewhat more difficult to obtain than other cards in the set. ACC designation is F339...

	MINT	VG-E	F-G
COMPLETE SET	150.00	100.00	40.00
COMMON PLAYER(1-20)	6.00	4.00	1.50

	MINT	VG-E	F-G		MINT	VG-E	F-G
1 Larker,Norm	6.00	4.00	1.50	11 Essegian,Chuck	6.00	4.00	1.50
2 Snider,Duke	6.00	4.00	1.50	12 Klippstein,John	14.00	10.00	4.00
3 McDevitt,Danny	6.00	4.00	1.50	13 Roebuck,Ed	6.00	4.00	1.50
4 Gilliam,Jim	7.00	4.75	2.00	14 Demeter,Don	6.00	4.00	1.50
5 Repulski,Rip	6.00	4.00	1.50	15 Craig,Roger	6.00	4.00	1.50
6 Labine,Clem	11.00	7.00	3.00	16 Williams,Stan	6.00	4.00	1.50
7 Roseboro,John	6.00	4.00	1.50	17 Zimmer,Don	7.00	4.75	2.00
8 Furillo,Carl	7.00	4.75	2.00	18 Alston,Walt	11.00	7.00	3.00
9 Koufax,Sandy	18.00	12.00	5.00	19 Podres,Johnny	7.00	4.75	2.00
10 Pignatano,Joe	6.00	4.00	1.50	20 Wills,Maury	11.00	7.00	3.00

1961 BELL BRAND (20)   2 7/16'' X 3 1/2''

DUKE SNIDER
OUTFIELDER   L.A. DODGERS

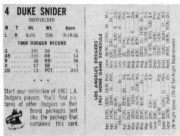

The 1961 Bell Brand Potato Chips set of 20 full color cards features Los Angeles Dodger players only and is numbered by the uniform numbers of the players. The cards are slightly smaller than the 1960 cards and are on thinner paper stock. The ACC designation is F339-3.

	MINT	VG-E	F-G
COMPLETE SET	120.00	80.00	30.00
COMMON PLAYER(1-51)	5.25	3.50	1.50

		MINT	VG-E	F-G
3	Davis,Willie	6.00	4.00	1.60
4	Snider,Duke	12.00	8.00	3.50
5	Larker,Norm	5.25	3.50	1.50
8	Roseboro,John	5.25	3.50	1.50
9	Moon,Wally	5.25	3.50	1.50
11	Lillis,Bob	5.25	3.50	1.50
12	Davis,Tom	6.00	4.00	1.60
14	Hodges,Gil	10.00	6.50	3.00
16	Demeter,Don	5.25	3.50	1.50
19	Gilliam,Jim	5.25	3.50	1.50

		MINT	VG-E	F-G
22	Podres,John	5.25	3.50	1.50
24	Alston,Walt	6.00	4.00	1.60
30	Wills,Maury	10.00	6.50	3.00
32	Koufax,Sandy	14.00	10.00	4.00
34	Sherry,Norm	5.25	3.50	1.50
37	Roebuck,Ed	5.25	3.50	1.50
38	Craig,Roger	5.25	3.50	1.50
40	Williams,Stan	5.25	3.50	1.50
43	Neal,Charlie	5.25	3.50	1.50
51	Sherry,Larry	5.25	3.50	1.50

1962 BELL BRAND (20)   2 7/16'' X 3 1/2''

DON DRYSDALE
PITCHER   L.A. DODGERS

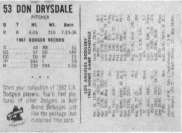

The 1962 Bell Brand set of 20 full color cards features Los Angeles Dodger players only and is numbered by the uniform numbers of the players. These cards were printed on a high quality glossy paper, much better than the previous two years, virtually eliminating the grease stains. This set is distinguished by a schedule on the backs of the cards. The ACC designation is F339-4.

	MINT	VG-E	F-G
COMPLETE SET	100.00	65.00	30.00
COMMON PLAYER(1-56)	4.50	3.00	1.25

		MINT	VG-E	F-G
3	Davis,Willie	5.25	3.50	1.50
4	Snider,Duke	12.50	8.50	3.50
6	Fairly,Ron	4.50	3.00	1.25
8	Roseboro,John	4.50	3.00	1.25
9	Moon,Wally	4.50	3.00	1.25
12	Davis,Tom	5.25	3.50	1.50
16	Perranoski,Ron	4.50	3.00	1.25
19	Gilliam,Jim	5.25	3.50	1.50
20	Spencer,Daryl	4.50	3.00	1.25
22	Podres,John	5.25	3.50	1.50

		MINT	VG-E	F-G
24	Alston,Walt	5.25	3.50	1.50
25	Howard,Frank	6.25	4.25	1.75
30	Wills,Maury	7.50	5.00	2.00
32	Koufax,Sandy	12.50	8.50	3.50
34	Sherry,Norm	4.50	3.00	1.25
37	Roebuck,Ed	4.50	3.00	1.25
40	Williams,Stan	4.50	3.00	1.25
51	Sherry,Larry	4.50	3.00	1.25
53	Drysdale,Don	10.00	6.50	3.00
56	Walls,Lee	4.50	3.00	1.25

1951 BERK ROSS (72)   2 1/16" X 2 1/2"

The 1951 Berk Ross set consists of 72 cards divided evenly into four series, designated in the checklist as A, B, C, and D. The cards were marketed in boxes containing two-card panels, without gum, and the set includes stars from other sports as well as baseball players. The ACC designation is W532.

	MINT	VG-E	F-G
COMPLETE SET	110.00	70.00	30.00
COMMON BASEBALL	1.10	.70	.30
COMMON NON-BB	.75	.50	.20

	MINT	VG-E	F-G			MINT	VG-E	F-G
A1 Al Rosen	3.00	2.00	.80	C1 Ralph Kiner		3.75	2.50	1.00
A2 Bob Lemon	3.75	2.50	1.00	C2 Bill Goodman		1.10	.70	.30
A3 Phil Rizzuto	3.75	2.50	1.00	C3 Allie Reynolds		2.00	1.30	.55
A4 Hank Bauer	2.00	1.30	.55	C4 Vic Raschi		2.00	1.30	.55
A5 Billy Johnson	1.10	.70	.30	C5 Joe Page		2.00	1.30	.55
A6 Jerry Coleman	1.50	1.00	.40	C6 Eddie Lopat		2.00	1.30	.55
A7 Johnny Mize	3.00	2.00	.80	C7 Andy Seminick		1.10	.70	.30
A8 Dom DiMaggio	2.00	1.30	.55	C8 Dick Sisler		1.10	.70	.30
A9 Richie Ashburn	2.00	1.30	.55	C9 Eddie Waitkus		1.10	.70	.30
A10 Del Ennis	1.10	.70	.30	C10 Ken Heintzelman		1.10	.70	.30
A11 Bob Cousy	2.00	1.30	.55	C11 Paul Unruh		.75	.50	.20
A12 Dick Schnittker	.75	.50	.20	C12 Jake LaMotta		2.00	1.30	.55
A13 Ezzard Charles	1.10	.70	.30	C13 Ike Williams		.75	.50	.20
A14 Leon Hart	1.10	.70	.30	C14 Wade Walker		.75	.50	.20
A15 James Martin	.75	.50	.20	C15 Rodney Franz		.75	.50	.20
A16 Ben Hogan	2.00	1.30	.55	C16 Sid Abel		1.10	.70	.30
A17 Bill Durnan	.75	.50	.20	C17 Claire Sherman		.75	.50	.20
A18 Bill Quackenbush	.75	.50	.20	C18 Jesse Owens		3.00	2.00	.80
B1 Stan Musial	9.00	6.00	2.50	D1 Gene Woodling		1.50	1.00	.40
B2 Warren Spahn	4.50	3.00	1.20	D2 Cliff Mapes		1.10	.70	.30
B3 Tom Henrich	2.00	1.30	.55	D3 Fred Sontort		1.10	.70	.30
B4 Yogi Berra	7.50	5.00	2.00	D4 Tommy Byrne		1.10	.70	.30
B5 Joe DiMaggio	18.00	12.00	5.00	D5 Whitey Ford		6.00	4.00	1.60
B6 Bobby Brown	1.10	.70	.30	D6 Jim Konstanty		1.50	1.00	.40
B7 Granny Hamner	1.10	.70	.30	D7 Russ Meyer		1.10	.70	.30
B8 Willie Jones	1.10	.70	.30	D8 Robin Roberts		3.75	2.50	1.00
B9 Stan Lopata	1.10	.70	.30	D9 Curt Simmons		1.10	.70	.30
B10 Mike Goliat	1.10	.70	.30	D10 Sam Jethroe		1.10	.70	.30
B11 Sherman White	.75	.50	.20	D11 Bill Sharman		1.50	1.00	.40
B12 Joe Maxim	.75	.50	.20	D12 Sandy Saddler		.75	.50	.20
B13 Ray Robinson	3.00	2.00	.80	D13 Margaret DuPont		.75	.50	.20
B14 Doak Walker	2.00	1.30	.55	D14 Arnold Galiffa		1.10	.70	.30
B15 Emil Sitko	.75	.50	.20	D15 Charlie Justice		1.50	1.00	.40
B16 Jack Stewart	.75	.50	.20	D16 Glen Cunningham		1.10	.70	.30
B17 Dick Button	1.10	.70	.30	D17 Gregory Rice		.75	.50	.20
B18 Melvin Patton	.75	.50	.20	D18 Harrison Dillard		.75	.50	.20

1956 TOPPS CHECKLISTS

1952 BERK ROSS (72)   2″ X 3″

HIT PARADE OF CHAMPIONS
Trade Mark Reg. U.S. Pat. Off.
MICKEY MANTLE
Outfielder, New York Yankees
Member of the N. Y. Yankees
World Champions

Born Commerce, Oklahoma
October 20, 1931
Height 5-10, Weight 175
Throws Right, Bats Left or Right
1951 Hit .267 in 96 Games

The 1952 Berk Ross set contains most of the top stars of the era. The backs of the Ewell Blackwell and Nelson Fox cards are transposed; this error was never corrected. Rizzuto appears twice in the set: swinging a bat and bunting.

	MINT	VG-E	F-G
COMPLETE SET	750.00	500.00	200.00
COMMON PLAYER(1-72)	4.50	3.00	1.25
1 Ashburn,Richie	6.00	4.00	1.50
2 Bauer,Hank	6.00	4.00	1.50
3 Berra,Yogi	20.00	13.00	5.50
4 Blackwell,Ewell	4.50	3.00	1.25
5 Brown,Bobby	4.50	3.00	1.25
6 Busby,Jim	4.50	3.00	1.25
7 Campanella,Roy	30.00	20.00	8.00
8 Carrasquel,Chico	4.50	3.00	1.25
9 Coleman,Jerry	4.50	3.00	1.25
10 Collins,Joe	4.50	3.00	1.25
11 Dark,Alvin	4.50	3.00	1.25
12 DiMaggio,Dom	7.50	5.00	2.00
13 DiMaggio,Joe	135.00	90.00	40.00
14 Doby,Larry	6.00	4.00	1.50
15 Doerr,Bobby	4.50	3.00	1.25
16 Elliott,Bob	4.50	3.00	1.25
17 Ennis,Del	4.50	3.00	1.25
18 Fain,Ferris	4.50	3.00	1.25
19 Feller,Bob	20.00	13.00	5.50
20 Fox,Nellie	6.00	4.00	1.50
21 Garver,Ned	4.50	3.00	1.25
22 Hartung,Clint	4.50	3.00	1.25
23 Hearn,Jim	4.50	3.00	1.25
24 Hodges,Gil	9.00	6.00	2.50
25 Irvin,Monte	7.50	5.00	2.00
26 Jansen,Larry	4.50	3.00	1.25
27 Jones,Sheldon	4.50	3.00	1.25
28 Kell,George	6.00	4.00	1.50
29 Kennedy,Monte	4.50	3.00	1.25
30 Kiner,Ralph	9.00	6.00	2.50
31 Koslo,Bob	4.50	3.00	1.25
32 Kuzava,Bob	4.50	3.00	1.25
33 Lemon,Bob	9.00	6.00	2.50
34 Lockman,Whitey	4.50	3.00	1.25

	MINT	VG-E	F-G
35 Lopat,Ed	6.00	4.00	1.50
36 Maglie,Sal	4.50	3.00	1.25
37 Mantle,Mickey	135.00	90.00	40.00
38 Martin,Billy	15.00	10.00	4.00
39 Mays,Willie	100.00	65.00	30.00
40 McDougald,Gil	6.00	4.00	1.50
41 Minoso,Minnie.	6.00	4.00	1.50
42 Mize,Johnny	9.00	6.00	2.50
43 Morgan,Tom	4.50	3.00	1.25
44 Mueller,Don.	4.50	3.00	1.25
45 Musial,Stan	60.00	40.00	15.00
46 Newcombe,Don	6.00	4.00	1.50
47 Noble,Ray	4.50	3.00	1.25
48 Ostrowski,Joe	4.50	3.00	1.25
49 Parnell,Mel	4.50	3.00	1.25
50 Raschi,Vic	6.00	4.00	1.50
51 Reese,Pee Wee	9.00	6.00	2.50
52 Reynolds,Allie	6.00	4.00	1.50
53 Rigney,Bill	4.50	3.00	1.25
54 Rizzuto,Phil (2)	9.00	6.00	2.50
55 Roberts,Robin	9.00	6.00	2.50
56 Robinson,Eddie	4.50	3.00	1.25
57 Robinson,Jackie	60.00	40.00	15.00
58 Roe,Preacher	6.00	4.00	1.50
59 Sain,Johnny	6.00	4.00	1.50
60 Schoendienst,Red	6.00	4.00	1.50
61 Snider,Duke	20.00	13.00	5.50
62 Spencer,George	4.50	3.00	1.25
63 Stanky,Eddie	6.00	4.00	1.50
64 Thompson,Hank	4.50	3.00	1.25
65 Thomson,Bobby	6.00	4.00	1.50
66 Wertz,Vic	4.50	3.00	1.25
67 Westlake,Wally	4.50	3.00	1.25
68 Westrum,Wes	4.50	3.00	1.25
69 Williams,Ted	80.00	55.00	25.00
70 Woodling,Gene	4.50	3.00	1.25
71 Zernial,Gus	4.50	3.00	1.25

1958 BOND BREAD (9)

2 1/2" X 3 1/2"

1958 Bond Bread set of nine unnumbered cards features players from the Buffalo Bisons of the International League. The ACC designation is D301.

	MINT	VG-E	F-G
COMPLETE SET	75.00	55.00	22.00
COMMON PLAYER(1-9)	6.50	4.25	1.75
1 Aber,Al	6.50	4.25	1.75
2 Caffie,Joe	6.50	4.25	1.75
3 Cavaretta,Phil	12.50	8.50	3.00

	MINT	VG-E	F-G
4 Coleman,Rip	6.50	4.25	1.75
5 Easter,Luke	35.00	25.00	10.00
6 Johnson,Ken	6.50	4.25	1.75
7 Ortiz,L.	6.50	4.25	1.75
8 Phillips,Jack	6.50	4.25	1.75
9 Small,Jim	6.50	4.25	1.75

1947 BOND BREAD (13)
JACKIE ROBINSON

2 1/4" X 3 1/2"

The 1947 Bond Bread Ja Robinson set features 13 c of Jackie in different ac or portrait poses. Card n ber 7 was issued in gre quantity than other card the set. The ACC designa is D302.

	MINT	VG-E	F-G
COMPLETE SET	2300.00	1600.00	650.00
COMMON PLAYER(1-13)	200.00	130.00	60.00
1 Sliding into base, cap ump in photo (horiz.)	200.00	130.00	60.00
2 Running down 3rd base line (verti.)	200.00	130.00	60.00
3 Batting, bat behind head, facing camera (verti.)	200.00	130.00	60.00
4 Moving towards second, throw almost to glove (horiz.)	200.00	130.00	60.00
5 Taking throw at first (horiz.)	200.00	130.00	60.00
6 Jumping high in air for ball (vert.)	200.00	130.00	60.00
7 Profile with glove in front of head, autographed (vert)	100.00	60.00	30.00

	MINT	VG-E	F-G
8 Leaping over 2nd base, ready to throw (vert)	200.00	130.00	60.00
9 Portrait-holding glove over head	200.00	130.00	60.00
10 Portrait-holding bat perpendicular to body	200.00	130.00	60.00
11 Reaching for throw,glove near ankle	200.00	130.00	60.00
12 Leaping for throw, no scoreboard in background	200.00	130.00	60.00
13 Portrait-holding bat parallel to body	200.00	130.00	60.00

1948 BOWMAN (48) B&W

2 1/8" X 2 1/2"

The 1948 Bowman set is considered to be the first set of the modern era. This black & white set contains twelve cards which are relatively more difficult to obtain than the other 36. These cards are marked with an (*) on the checklist below.

	MINT	VG-E	F-G
COMPLETE SET	300.00	200.00	80.00
COMMON PLAYER(1-36)	2.75	1.75	.75
COMMON PLAYER(37-48)	3.75	2.50	1.00

#	Player	MINT	VG-E	F-G
1	Elliot,Bob	6.00	3.00	1.00
2	Blackwell,Ewell	2.75	1.75	.75
3	Kiner,Ralph	10.00	6.50	3.00
4	Mize,Johnny	10.00	6.50	3.00
5	Feller,Bob	18.00	12.00	5.00
6	Berra,"Yogi"	18.00	12.00	5.00
7	Reiser,Peter*	10.00	6.50	3.00
8	Rizzuto,Phil*	30.00	20.00	8.00
9	Cooper,Walker	2.75	1.75	.75
10	Rosar,Buddy	2.75	1.75	.75
11	Lindell,Johnny	2.75	1.75	.75
12	Sain,Johnny	3.75	2.50	1.00
13	Marshall,Willard*	7.50	5.00	2.00
14	Reynolds,Allie	4.50	3.00	1.25
15	Joost,Eddie	2.75	1.75	.75
16	Lohrke,Jack*	7.50	5.00	2.00
17	Slaughter,Enos	7.50	5.00	2.00
18	Spahn,Warren	14.00	9.50	3.75
19	Henrich,Tommy	4.50	3.00	1.25
20	Kerr,Buddy*	7.50	5.00	2.00
21	Fain,Ferris	2.75	1.75	.75
22	Bevins,Floyd*	7.50	5.00	2.00
23	Jansen,Larry	2.75	1.75	.75
24	Leonard,"Dutch"*	7.50	5.00	2.00

#	Player	MINT	VG-E	F-G
25	McCoskey,Barney	2.75	1.75	.75
26	Shea,Frank*	7.50	5.00	2.00
27	Gordon,Sid	2.75	1.75	.75
28	Verbam,Emil*	7.50	5.00	2.00
29	Page,Joe*	10.00	6.50	3.00
30	Lockman,Whitey*	7.50	5.00	2.00
31	McCahan,Bill	2.75	1.75	.75
32	Rigney,Bill	2.75	1.75	.75
33	Johnson,Bill	2.75	1.75	.75
34	Jones,Sheldon*	7.50	5.00	2.00
35	Sternweiss,"Snuffy	2.75	1.75	.75
36	Musial,Stan	50.00	35.00	15.00
37	Hartung,Clint	3.75	2.50	1.00
38	Schoendienst,"Red"	4.50	3.00	1.25
39	Galan,Augie	3.75	2.50	1.00
40	Marion,Marty	4.50	3.00	1.25
41	Barney,Rex	3.75	2.50	1.00
42	Pope,Ray	3.75	2.50	1.00
43	Edwards,Bruce	3.75	2.50	1.00
44	Wyrostek,Johnny	3.75	2.50	1.00
45	Sauer,Hank	4.50	3.00	1.25
46	Wehmeier,Herman	3.75	2.50	1.00
47	Thomson,Bobby	6.00	4.00	1.50
48	Koslo,"Dave"	3.75	2.50	1.00

1949 BOWMAN PCL (36)

2 1/8" X 2 1/2"

1949 Bowman Pacific Coast League set is one of the scarcest sets of modern times. It is not a Bowman regular issue, and there is still considerable doubt as to whether or not this set was officially released for sale. Pacific League players only are portrayed.

	MINT	VG-E	F-G
COMPLETE SET	6750.00	4500.00	1800.00
COMMON PLAYER(1-36)	200.00	130.00	50.00

#	Player	MINT	VG-E	F-G
1	Anthony,Lee	200.00	130.00	50.00
2	Metkovich,George	200.00	130.00	50.00
3	Hodgin,Ralph	200.00	130.00	50.00
4	Woods,George	200.00	130.00	50.00
5	Rescigno,Xavier	200.00	130.00	50.00
6	Grasso,Mickey	200.00	130.00	50.00
7	Rucker,Johnny	200.00	130.00	50.00
8	Brewer,Jack	200.00	130.00	50.00
9	D'Allessandro,Dom	200.00	130.00	50.00
10	Gassaway,Charlie	200.00	130.00	50.00
11	Freitas,Tony	200.00	130.00	50.00
12	Maltzberger,Gordon	200.00	130.00	50.00
13	Jensen,John	200.00	130.00	50.00
14	White,Joyner	200.00	130.00	50.00
15	Storey,Harvey	200.00	130.00	50.00
16	Lajeski,Dick	200.00	130.00	50.00

#	Player	MINT	VG-E	F-G
17	Glosson,Albie	200.00	130.00	50.00
18	Raimondi,Bill	200.00	130.00	50.00
19	Holcombe,Ken	200.00	130.00	50.00
20	Ross,Don	200.00	130.00	50.00
21	Coscarart,Pete	200.00	130.00	50.00
22	York,Tony	200.00	130.00	50.00
23	Mooty,Jake	200.00	130.00	50.00
24	Adams,Charles	200.00	130.00	50.00
25	Scarsella,Les	200.00	130.00	50.00
26	Marty,Joe	200.00	130.00	50.00
27	Kelleher,Frank	200.00	130.00	50.00
28	Handley,Lee	200.00	130.00	50.00
29	Besse,Herman	200.00	130.00	50.00
30	Lazor,John	200.00	130.00	50.00
31	Malone,Eddie	200.00	130.00	50.00
32	Robays,Maurice Van	200.00	130.00	50.00
33	Tabor,Jim	200.00	130.00	50.00
34	Handiley,Gene	200.00	130.00	50.00
35	Seats,Tom	200.00	130.00	50.00
36	Burnett,Ora	200.00	130.00	50.00

Hall's Nostalgia

If you're looking for those missing baseball cards in your collectio
why not try buying them from Hall's Nostalgia? We have seve
hundred thousand cards from 1880 to date. If you can visit o
store, you are welcome to browse around. However, we also ser
over 10,000 mail order customers and would be happy to add yo
name to the growing list. Just send a stamped - self addressec
envelope, and 50¢ for handling, along with your want list, and w
will promptly send out a price quote for your specific needs. V
also carry thousands of sport publications so send $1.00 for c
current publication list.

BASEBALL CARDS WANTED

Paying 35% up to 100% of this guide.
Always check with us before you sell.

Call or Write

Hall's
Nostalgi

21-25 Mystic Street
Dept. P G 4, Box 408
Arlington, MA 02174

1- (617) 646-7757

NOW OPEN —
HALL'S NOSTALGIA #2
389 Chatham Street
Lynn, MA 01904
(617) 595-7757

CERTIFIED APPRAISERS
MID-AM ANTIQUE
APPRAISERS ASSOCIATION
REGISTERED MEMBER

40

No: 50 of a Series of 240
JACKIE ROBINSON
Second Base—Brooklyn Dodgers
Born: Cairo, Georgia, January 31, 1919
Bats: Right   Throws: Right   Ht.: 6.0   Wt.: 190
When Brooklyn signed him to Montreal Royal contract, he became first Negro to enter rank: of pro ball. As Royals' regular second baseman for 1946 he led International League in batting with .349. When he joined Dodgers in 1947 he was switched to first base. Led National League in stolen bases with 29, hit .296 and was named Rookie of Year. Last year he finished with same average, .296 and batted in 85 runs.

#202—OFFICIAL BASEBALL RING
Made of durable metal. Adjustable—fits any size finger. Beautiful silverplate oxidized finish brings out detail of official Baseball Emblem. Baseball of white plastic. Sides of ring show Baseball and Crossed Bats design. Send only 15c and 3 Baseball wrappers to BASEBALL, P.O. BOX 491 NEW YORK 46, N. Y.

(Not valid where contrary to State laws.)
Offer expires 12/31/49 ©Bowman Gum, Inc. 1949

The 1949 Set is Bowman's first color set and the most difficult Bowman regular issue to complete. The high numbers 145-240 are somewhat scarce. Card nos. 4, 78, 83, 85, 86, 88, and 98 exist with or without the player's name printed on the front of the card, i.e., no name on front (NNOF). Card nos. 109, 124, 126, 127, 132, and 143 exist with printed (PR) or script (SCR) name on the back of the card. Cards up to no. 144 were issued in series of 36 cards except that no. 4 was included with the third series.

	MINT	VG-E	F-G
COMPLETE SET	2250.00	1500.00	650.00
COMMON (1-37,74-108)	3.00	2.00	.80
COMMON PLAYER(38-73)	3.75	2.50	1.00
COMMON PLAYER(109-144)	2.00	1.30	.55
COMMON PLAYER(145-240)	13.50	9.00	4.00

	MINT	VG-E	F-G
1 Bickford,Vern	8.00	4.00	1.50
2 Lockman,Whitey	2.75	1.75	.75
3 Porterfield,Bob	2.75	1.75	.75
4A Priddy,Jerry(NNOF	3.50	2.40	1.00
4B Priddy,Jerry(NOF)	8.50	5.75	2.25
5 Sauer,Hank	3.50	2.40	1.00
6 Cavaretta,Phil	3.50	2.40	1.00
7 Dobson,Joe	2.75	1.75	.75
8 Dickson,Murray	2.75	1.75	.75
9 Fain,Ferris	3.50	2.40	1.00
10 Gray,Ted	2.75	1.75	.75
11 Boudreau,Lou	8.50	5.75	2.25
12 Michaels,Cass	2.75	1.75	.75
13 Chesnes,Bob	2.75	1.75	.75
14 Simmons,Curt	3.50	2.40	1.00
15 Garver,Ned	2.75	1.75	.75
16 Kozar,Al	2.75	1.75	.75
17 Torgeson,Earl	2.75	1.75	.75
18 Thomson,Bobby	4.25	3.00	1.25
19 Brown,Bobby	2.75	1.75	.75
20 Hermanski,Gene	2.75	1.75	.75
21 Baumholtz,Frank	2.75	1.75	.75
22 Lowrey,"Peanuts"	2.75	1.75	.75
23 Doerr,Bobby	3.50	2.40	1.00
24 Musial,Stan	50.00	35.00	15.00
25 Scheib,Carl	2.75	1.75	.75
26 Kell,George	3.50	2.40	1.00
27 Feller,Bob	18.00	12.00	5.00
28 Kolloway,Don	2.75	1.75	.75
29 Kiner,Ralph	8.50	5.75	2.25
30 Seminick,Andy	2.75	1.75	.75
31 Kokos,Dick	2.75	1.75	.75
32 Yost,Eddie	2.75	1.75	.75
33 Spahn,Warren	11.00	7.00	3.00
34 Koslo,Dave	2.75	1.75	.75
35 Raschi,Vic	3.50	2.40	1.00
36 Reese,"Peewee"	8.50	5.75	2.25
37 Wyrostek,John	2.75	1.75	.75
38 Verban,Emil	3.50	2.40	1.00
39 Goodman,Billy	3.50	2.40	1.00
40 Munger"Red"	3.50	2.40	1.00
41 Brissie,Lou	3.50	2.40	1.00
42 Evers,"Hoot"	3.50	2.40	1.00
43 Mitchell,Dale	3.50	2.40	1.00
44 Philley,Dave	3.50	2.40	1.00
45 Westlake,Wally	3.50	2.40	1.00
46 Roberts,Robin	8.50	5.75	2.25
47 Sain,Johnny	4.25	3.00	1.25
48 Marshall,Willard	3.50	2.40	1.00
49 Shea,Frank	3.50	2.40	1.00
50 Robinson,Jackie	50.00	35.00	15.00
51 Wehmeier,Herman	3.50	2.40	1.00
52 Schmitz,Johnny	3.50	2.40	1.00
53 Kramer,Jack	3.50	2.40	1.00
54 Marion,Marty	4.25	3.00	1.25
55 Joost,Eddie	3.50	2.40	1.00
56 Mullin,Pat	3.50	2.40	1.00
57 Bearden,Gene	3.50	2.40	1.00
58 Elliott,Bob	3.50	2.40	1.00
59 Lohrke,Jack	3.50	2.40	1.00
60 Berra,"Yogi"	24.00	16.00	7.00
61 Barney,Rex	3.50	2.40	1.00
62 Hatton,Grady	3.50	2.40	1.00
63 Pafko,Andy	3.50	2.40	1.00
64 DiMaggio,Dom	5.50	3.75	1.75
65 Slaughter,Enos	5.50	3.75	1.75
66 Valo,Elmer	3.50	2.40	1.00

	MINT	VG-E	F-G
67 Dark,Alvin	4.25	3.00	1.25
68 Jones,Sheldon	3.50	2.40	1.00
69 Henrich,Tommy	5.50	3.75	1.75
70 Furillo,Carl	5.50	3.75	1.75
71 Stephens,Vern	3.50	2.40	1.00
72 Holmes,Tommy	4.25	3.00	1.25
73 Cox,Billy	3.50	2.40	1.00
74 McBride,Tom	2.75	1.75	.75
75 Mayo,Eddie	2.75	1.75	.75
76 Nicholson,Bill	2.75	1.75	.75
77 Donham,Ernie	2.75	1.75	.75
78A Zoldak,Sam(NNOF)	3.50	2.40	1.00
78B Zoldak,Sam(NOF)	8.50	5.75	2.25
79 Northey,Ron	2.75	1.75	.75
80 McCahan,Bill	2.75	1.75	.75
81 Stallcup,Virgil	2.75	1.75	.75
82 Page,Joe	2.75	1.75	.75
83A Scheffing,Bob (NNOF)	3.50	2.40	1.00
83B Scheffing,Bob(NOF	8.50	5.75	2.25
84 Campanella,Roy	36.00	24.00	10.00
85A Mize,Johnny(NNOF)	8.50	5.75	2.25
85B Mize,Johnny(NOF)	18.00	12.00	5.00
86A Pesky,Johnny(NNOF	3.50	2.40	1.00
86B Pesky,Johnny(NOF)	8.50	5.75	2.25
87 Gumpert,Randy	2.75	1.75	.75
88A Salkeld,Bill(NNOF)	3.50	2.40	1.00
88B Salkeld,Bill(NNOF	8.50	5.75	2.25
89 Platt,Mizell	2.75	1.75	.75
90 Coan,Gil	2.75	1.75	.75
91 Wakefield,Dick	2.75	1.75	.75
92 Jones,Willie	2.75	1.75	.75
93 Stevens,Ed	2.75	1.75	.75
94 Vernon,"Mickey"	3.50	2.40	1.00
95 Pollet,Howie	2.75	1.75	.75
96 Wright,Taft	2.75	1.75	.75
97 Litwhiler,Danny	2.75	1.75	.75
98A Rizzuto,Phil(NNOF	8.50	5.75	2.25
98B Rizzuto,Phil(NOF)	24.00	16.00	7.00
99 Gustine,Frank	2.75	1.75	.75
100 Hodges,Gil	8.50	5.75	2.25
101 Gordon,Sid	2.75	1.75	.75
102 Spence,Stan	2.75	1.75	.75
103 Tipton,Joe	2.75	1.75	.75
104 Stanky,Ed	3.50	2.40	1.00
105 Kennedy,Bill	2.75	1.75	.75
106 Early,Jake	2.75	1.75	.75
107 Lake,Eddie	2.75	1.75	.75
108 Heintzelman,Ken	2.75	1.75	.75
109A Fitzgerald,Ed(PR)	2.75	1.75	.75
109B Fitzgerald,Ed(SCR	5.50	3.75	1.75
110 Wynn,Early	5.50	3.75	1.75
111 Schoendienst,"Red"	3.50	2.40	1.00
112 Chapman,Sam	1.75	1.15	.50
113 LaManno,Ray	1.75	1.15	.50
114 Reynolds,Allie	3.50	2.40	1.00
115 Leonard,"Dutch"	1.75	1.15	.50
116 Hatton,Joe	1.75	1.15	.50
117 Cooper,Walker	1.75	1.15	.50
118 Mele,Sam	1.75	1.15	.50
119 Baker,Floyd	1.75	1.15	.50
120 Fannin,Cliff	1.75	1.15	.50
121 Christman,Mark	1.75	1.15	.50
122 Vico,George	1.75	1.15	.50
123 Blatnick,Johnny	1.75	1.15	.50
124A Murtaugh,Danny(PR	2.75	1.75	.75
124B Murtaugh,Danny (SCR)	5.50	3.75	1.75
125 Keltner,Ken	1.75	1.15	.50
126A Brazle,Al(PRINT)	2.75	1.75	.75
126B Brazle,Al(SCRIPT)	5.50	3.75	1.75

1949 BOWMAN (CONTINUED)

	MINT	VG-E	F-G			MINT	VG-E	F-G
127A Majeski,"Hank"(PR	2.75	1.75	.75	181 Niarhos,Gus		13.50	9.00	4.00
127B Majeski,"Hank"	5.50	3.75	1.75	182 Peck,Hall		13.50	9.00	4.00
(SCR)				183 Stringer,Lou		13.50	9.00	4.00
128 Vander Meer,Johnny	3.50	2.40	1.00	184 Chipman,Bob		13.50	9.00	4.00
129 Johnson,Bill	1.75	1.15	.50	185 Reiser,Pete		16.50	11.00	4.50
130 Walker,Harry	1.75	1.15	.50	186 Kerr,"Buddy"		13.50	9.00	4.00
131 Lehner,Paul	1.75	1.15	.50	187 Marchildon,Phil		13.50	9.00	4.00
132A Evans,Al(PRINT)	2.75	1.75	.75	188 Drews,Karl		13.50	9.00	4.00
132B Evans,Al(SCRIPT)	5.50	3.75	1.75	189 Wooten,Earl		13.50	9.00	4.00
133 Robinson,Aaron	1.75	1.15	.50	190 Hearn,Jim		13.50	9.00	4.00
134 Borowy,Hank	1.75	1.15	.50	191 Haynes,Joe		13.50	9.00	4.00
135 Rojek,Stan	1.75	1.15	.50	192 Gumbert,Harry		13.50	9.00	4.00
136 Edwards,"Hank"	1.75	1.15	.50	193 Trinkle,Ken		13.50	9.00	4.00
137 Wilks,Ted	1.75	1.15	.50	194 Branca,Ralph		14.00	9.50	3.75
138 Rosar,"Buddy"	1.75	1.15	.50	195 Bockman,Eddie		13.50	9.00	4.00
139 Arft,Hank	1.75	1.15	.50	196 Hutchinson,Fred		16.50	11.00	4.50
140 Scarborough,Rae	1.75	1.15	.50	197 Lindell,Johnny		13.50	9.00	4.00
141 Lupien,Ulysses	1.75	1.15	.50	198 Gromek,John		13.50	9.00	4.00
142 Waitkus,Eddie	1.75	1.15	.50	199 Hughson,"Tex"		13.50	9.00	4.00
143A Dillinger,Bob(PRI	2.75	1.75	.75	200 Dobernic,Jess		13.50	9.00	4.00
143B Dillinger,Bob	5.50	3.75	1.75	201 Sisti,Sibby		13.50	9.00	4.00
(SCRIPT)				202 Jansen,Larry		13.50	9.00	4.00
144 Haefner,"Mickey"	1.75	1.15	.50	203 McCosky,Barney		13.50	9.00	4.00
145 Donnelly,Sylvester	13.50	9.00	4.00	204 Savage,Bob		13.50	9.00	4.00
146 McCormick,"Mike"	13.50	9.00	4.00	205 Sisler,Dick		13.50	9.00	4.00
147 Singleton,"Bert"	13.50	9.00	4.00	206 Edwards,Bruce		13.50	9.00	4.00
148 Swift,Bob	13.50	9.00	4.00	207 Hopp,Johnny		13.50	9.00	4.00
149 Partee,Roy	13.50	9.00	4.00	208 Trout,"Dizzy"		13.50	9.00	4.00
150 Clark,Allie	13.50	9.00	4.00	209 Keller,Charlie		16.50	11.00	4.50
151 Harris,Mickey	13.50	9.00	4.00	210 Gordon,Joe		14.00	9.50	3.75
152 Maddern,Clarence	13.50	9.00	4.00	211 Ferriss,"Boo"		13.50	9.00	4.00
153 Masi,Phil	13.50	9.00	4.00	212 Hamner,Ralph		13.50	9.00	4.00
154 Hartung,Clint	13.50	9.00	4.00	213 Barrett,"Red"		13.50	9.00	4.00
155 Guerra,"Mickey"	13.50	9.00	4.00	214 Ashburn,Richie		22.50	15.00	6.50
156 Zarilla,Al	13.50	9.00	4.00	215 Higbe,Kirby		13.50	9.00	4.00
157 Masterson,Walt	13.50	9.00	4.00	216 Rowe,"Schoolboy"		16.50	11.00	4.50
158 Brecheen,Harry	14.00	9.50	3.75	217 Pieretti,Marion		13.50	9.00	4.00
159 Moulder,Glen	13.50	9.00	4.00	218 Kryhoski,Dick		13.50	9.00	4.00
160 Blackburn,Jim	13.50	9.00	4.00	219 Trucks,"Fire"		13.50	9.00	4.00
161 Thompson,"Jocko"	13.50	9.00	4.00	220 McCarthy,Johnny		13.50	9.00	4.00
162 Roe,"Preacher"	21.00	14.00	6.00	221 Muncrief,Bob		13.50	9.00	4.00
163 McCullough,Clyde	13.50	9.00	4.00	222 Kellner,Alex		13.50	9.00	4.00
164 Wertz,Vic	14.00	9.50	3.75	223 Hofmann,Bobby		13.50	9.00	4.00
165 Stirnweiss,"Snuffy"	13.50	9.00	4.00	224 Paige,"Satchell"		300.00	200.00	80.00
166 Tresh,Mike	13.50	9.00	4.00	225 Coleman,Gerry		14.00	9.50	3.75
167 Martin,"Babe"	13.50	9.00	4.00	226 Snider,"Duke"		165.00	110.00	45.00
168 Lake,Doyle	13.50	9.00	4.00	227 Ostermueller,Fritz		13.50	9.00	4.00
169 Heath,Jeff	13.50	9.00	4.00	228 Mayo,Jackie		13.50	9.00	4.00
170 Rigney,Bill	13.50	9.00	4.00	229 Lopat,Ed		18.00	12.00	5.00
171 Fowler,Dick	13.50	9.00	4.00	230 Galan,Augie		13.50	9.00	4.00
172 Pellagrini,Eddie	13.50	9.00	4.00	231 Johnson,Earl		13.50	9.00	4.00
173 Stewart,Eddie	13.50	9.00	4.00	232 McQuinn,George		13.50	9.00	4.00
174 Moore,Terry	14.00	9.50	3.75	233 Doby,Larry		21.00	14.00	6.00
175 Appling,Luke	22.50	15.00	6.50	234 Sewell,"Rip"		13.50	9.00	4.00
176 Raffensberger,Ken	13.50	9.00	4.00	235 Russell,Jim		13.50	9.00	4.00
177 Lopata,Stan	13.50	9.00	4.00	236 Sanford,Fred		13.50	9.00	4.00
178 Brown,Tom	13.50	9.00	4.00	237 Kennedy,Monte		13.50	9.00	4.00
179 Casey,Hugh	13.50	9.00	4.00	238 Lemon,Bob		55.00	37.50	17.00
180 Berry,Connie	13.50	9.00	4.00	239 McCormick,Frank		13.50	9.00	4.00
				240 Young,"Babe"		14.00	9.50	3.75

1950 BOWMAN (252)   2 1/8'' X 2 1/2''

ROY CAMPANELLA
Catcher—Brooklyn Dodgers
Born: Philadelphia, Nov. 19, 1921
Height: 5-9½   Weight: 180
Bats: Right   Throws: Right
In his second big-league year (1949)
Roy led National League catchers
appearing in 100 or more games with a
fielding percentage of .985. Hit .287
in 130 games, banged 22 homers, drove
in 82 runs. Was the NL all-star catcher.
Dodgers first noted Roy when he played
against them on an all-star Negro team
in an exhibition game.
No. 75 in the 1950 SERIES of BASEBALL Picture Cards
© 1950 Bowman Gum, Inc., Phila., Pa., U. S. A.

The Bowman set of 252 color cards showed a marked improvement in the quality and color over the 1949 issue. The "low numbers", 1-72, are more difficult to obtain than the higher numbers.

	MINT	VG-E	F-G			MINT	VG-E	F-G
COMPLETE SET	825.00	550.00	225.00	7 Hegan,Jim		5.25	3.50	1.50
COMMON PLAYER(1-72)	5.25	3.50	1.50	8 Kell,George		6.00	4.00	1.60
COMMON PLAYER(73-252)	1.80	1.20	.50	9 Wertz,Vic		5.25	3.50	1.50
				10 Henrich,Tommy		7.50	5.00	2.00
1 Parnell,Mel	15.00	5.00	2.00	11 Rizzuto,Phil		13.00	9.00	4.00
2 Stephens,Vern	5.25	3.50	1.50	12 Page,Joe		6.00	4.00	1.60
3 DiMaggio,Dom	7.50	5.00	2.00	13 Fain,Ferris		6.00	4.00	1.60
4 Zernial,Gus	5.25	3.50	1.50	14 Kellner,Alex		5.25	3.50	1.50
5 Kuzava,Bob	5.25	3.50	1.50	15 Kozar,Al		5.25	3.50	1.50
6 Feller,Bob	22.50	15.00	6.50	16 Sievers,Roy		5.25	3.50	1.50

#	Name	MINT	VG-E	F-G
17	Hudson,Sid	5.25	3.50	1.50
18	Robinson,Eddie	5.25	3.50	1.50
19	Spahn,Warren	13.00	9.00	4.00
20	Elliott,Bob	5.25	3.50	1.50
21	Reese,"Peewee"	10.00	6.50	3.00
22	Robinson,Jackie	45.00	30.00	12.00
23	Newcombe,Don	7.50	5.00	2.00
24	Schmitz,Johnny	5.25	3.50	1.50
25	Sauer,Hank	6.00	4.00	1.60
26	Hatton,Grady	5.25	3.50	1.50
27	Wehmeier,Herman	5.25	3.50	1.50
28	Thomson,Bobby	7.50	5.00	2.00
29	Stanky,Eddie	6.00	4.00	1.60
30	Waitkus,Eddie	5.25	3.50	1.50
31	Ennis,Del	6.00	4.00	1.60
32	Roberts,Robin	10.00	6.50	3.00
33	Kiner,Ralph	10.00	6.50	3.00
34	Dickson,Murry	5.25	3.50	1.50
35	Slaughter,Enos	7.50	5.00	2.00
36	Kazak,Eddie	5.25	3.50	1.50
37	Appling,Luke	7.50	5.00	2.00
38	Wight,Bill	5.25	3.50	1.50
39	Doby,Larry	6.00	4.00	1.60
40	Lemon,Bob	10.00	6.50	3.00
41	Evers,"Hoot"	5.25	3.50	1.50
42	Houtteman,Art	5.25	3.50	1.50
43	Doerr,Bobby	6.00	4.00	1.60
44	Dobson,Joe	5.25	3.50	1.50
45	Zarilla,Al	5.25	3.50	1.50
46	Berra,"Yogi"	24.00	16.00	7.00
47	Coleman,Jerry	6.00	4.00	1.60
48	Brissie,Lou	5.25	3.50	1.50
49	Valo,Elmer	5.25	3.50	1.50
50	Kokos,Dick	5.25	3.50	1.50
51	Garver,Ned	5.25	3.50	1.50
52	Mele,Sam	5.25	3.50	1.50
53	Vollmer,Clyde	5.25	3.50	1.50
54	Coan,Gil	5.25	3.50	1.50
55	Kerr,"Buddy"	5.25	3.50	1.50
56	Crandell,Del	6.00	4.00	1.60
57	Bickford,Vern	5.25	3.50	1.50
58	Furillo,Carl	7.50	5.00	2.00
59	Branca,Ralph	6.00	4.00	1.60
60	Pafko,Andy	5.25	3.50	1.50
61	Rush,Bob	5.25	3.50	1.50
62	Kluszewski,Ted	7.50	5.00	2.00
63	Blackwell,Ewell	6.00	4.00	1.60
64	Dark,Al	6.00	4.00	1.60
65	Koslo,Dave	5.25	3.50	1.50
66	Jansen,Larry	5.25	3.50	1.50
67	Jones,Willie	5.25	3.50	1.50
68	Simmons,Curt	6.00	4.00	1.60
69	Westlake,Wally	5.25	3.50	1.50
70	Chesnes,Bob	5.25	3.50	1.50
71	Schoendienst,"Red"	6.00	4.00	1.60
72	Pollet,Howie	5.25	3.50	1.50
73	Marshall,Willard	1.80	1.20	.50
74	Antonelli,Johnny	2.50	1.70	.70
75	Campanella,Roy	30.00	20.00	8.00
76	Barney,Rex	1.80	1.20	.50
77	Snider,Duke	16.50	11.00	4.50
78	Owen,Mickey	1.80	1.20	.50
79	Vandermeer,Johnny	2.50	1.70	.70
80	Fox,Howard	1.80	1.20	.50
81	Northey,Ron	1.80	1.20	.50
82	Lockman,Whitey	1.80	1.20	.50
83	Jones,Sheldon	1.80	1.20	.50
84	Ashburn,Richie	5.00	3.50	1.50
85	Heintzleman,Ken	1.80	1.20	.50
86	Rojek,Stan	1.80	1.20	.50
87	Werle,Bill	1.80	1.20	.50
88	Marion,Marty	2.50	1.70	.70
89	Munger,"Red"	1.80	1.20	.50
90	Brecheen,Harry	1.80	1.20	.50
91	Michaels,Cass	1.80	1.20	.50
92	Majeski,Hank	1.80	1.20	.50
93	Bearden,Gene	1.80	1.20	.50
94	Boudreau,Lou	7.50	5.00	2.00
95	Robinson,Aaron	1.80	1.20	.50
96	Trucks,Virgil	1.80	1.20	.50
97	McDermott,Maurice	1.80	1.20	.50
98	Williams,Ted	50.00	35.00	15.00
99	Goodman,Billy	1.80	1.20	.50
100	Raschi,Vic	2.50	1.70	.70
101	Brown,Bobby	1.80	1.20	.50
102	Johnson,Billy	1.80	1.20	.50
103	Joost,Eddie	1.80	1.20	.50
104	Chapman,Sam	1.80	1.20	.50
105	Dillinger,Bob	1.80	1.20	.50
106	Fannin,Cliff	1.80	1.20	.50
107	Dente,Sam	1.80	1.20	.50
108	Scarborough,Ray	1.80	1.20	.50
109	Gordon,Sid	1.80	1.20	.50
110	Holmes,Tommy	2.50	1.70	.70
111	Cooper,Walker	1.80	1.20	.50
112	Hodges,Gil	10.00	6.50	3.00
113	Hermanski,Gene	1.80	1.20	.50
114	Terwilliger,Wayne	1.80	1.20	.50
115	Smalley,Roy	1.80	1.20	.50
116	Stallcup,Virgil	1.80	1.20	.50
117	Rigney,Bill	1.80	1.20	.50
118	Hartung,Clint	1.80	1.20	.50
119	Sisler,Dick	1.80	1.20	.50
120	Thompson,John	1.80	1.20	.50
121	Seminick,Andy	1.80	1.20	.50
122	Hopp,Johnny	1.80	1.20	.50
123	Restelli,Dino	1.80	1.20	.50
124	McCullough,Clyde	1.80	1.20	.50
125	Rice,Del	1.80	1.20	.50
126	Brazle,Al	1.80	1.20	.50
127	Philley,Dave	1.80	1.20	.50
128	Masi,Phil	1.80	1.20	.50
129	Gordon,Joe	2.50	1.70	.70
130	Mitchell,Dale	1.80	1.20	.50
131	Gromek,Steve	1.80	1.20	.50
132	Vernon,James	2.50	1.70	.70
133	Kolloway,Don	1.80	1.20	.50
134	Trout,Paul	1.80	1.20	.50
135	Mullin,Pat	1.80	1.20	.50
136	Rosar,Warren	1.80	1.20	.50
137	Pesky,Johnny	2.50	1.70	.70
138	Reynolds,Allie	3.75	2.50	1.00
139	Mize,Johnny	7.50	5.00	2.00
140	Suder,Pete	1.80	1.20	.50
141	Coleman,Joe	1.80	1.20	.50
142	Lollar,Sherman	1.80	1.20	.50
143	Stewart,Eddie	1.80	1.20	.50
144	Evans,Al	1.80	1.20	.50
145	Graham,Jack	1.80	1.20	.50
146	Baker,Floyd	1.80	1.20	.50
147	Garcia,Mike	2.50	1.70	.70
148	Wynn,Early	7.50	5.00	2.00
149	Swift,Bob	1.80	1.20	.50
150	Vico,George	1.80	1.20	.50
151	Hutchinson,Fred	2.50	1.70	.70
152	Kinder,Ellis	1.80	1.20	.50
153	Masterson,Walt	1.80	1.20	.50
154	Niarhos,Gus	1.80	1.20	.50
155	Shea,Frank	1.80	1.20	.50
156	Sanford,Fred	1.80	1.20	.50
157	Guerra,Mike	1.80	1.20	.50
158	Lehner,Paul	1.80	1.20	.50
159	Tipton,Joe	1.80	1.20	.50
160	Harris,Mickey	1.80	1.20	.50
161	Robertson,Sherry	1.80	1.20	.50
162	Yost,Eddie	1.80	1.20	.50
163	Torgeson,Earl	1.80	1.20	.50
164	Sisti,Sibby	1.80	1.20	.50
165	Edwards,Bruce	1.80	1.20	.50
166	Hatton,Joe	1.80	1.20	.50
167	Roe,"Preacher"	3.75	2.50	1.00
168	Scheffing,Bob	1.80	1.20	.50
169	Edwards,Hank	1.80	1.20	.50
170	Leonard,"Dutch"	1.80	1.20	.50
171	Gumbert,Harry	1.80	1.20	.50
172	Lowery,"Peanuts"	1.80	1.20	.50
173	Merriman,Lloyd	1.80	1.20	.50
174	Thompson,Hank	1.80	1.20	.50
175	Kennedy,Monte	1.80	1.20	.50
176	Donnelly,Sylvester	1.80	1.20	.50
177	Borowy,Hank	1.80	1.20	.50
178	Fitzgerald,Eddie	1.80	1.20	.50
179	Diering,Chuck	1.80	1.20	.50
180	Walker,Harry	1.80	1.20	.50
181	Pieretti,Marino	1.80	1.20	.50
182	Zoldak,Sam	1.80	1.20	.50
183	Haefner,Mickey	1.80	1.20	.50
184	Gumpert,Randy	1.80	1.20	.50
185	Judson,Howie	1.80	1.20	.50
186	Keltner,Ken	1.80	1.20	.50
187	Stringer,Lou	1.80	1.20	.50
188	Johnson,Earl	1.80	1.20	.50
189	Friend,Owen	1.80	1.20	.50
190	Wood,Ken	1.80	1.20	.50
191	Starr,Dick	1.80	1.20	.50
192	Chipman,Bob	1.80	1.20	.50
193	Reiser,"Pete"	2.50	1.70	.70
194	Cox,Billy	1.80	1.20	.50
195	Cavaretta,Phil	2.50	1.70	.70
196	Lade,Doyle	1.80	1.20	.50
197	Wyrostek,Johnny	1.80	1.20	.50
198	Litwiler,Danny	1.80	1.20	.50
199	Kramer,Jack	1.80	1.20	.50
200	Higby,Kirby	1.80	1.20	.50
201	Castiglione,Pete	1.80	1.20	.50
202	Chambers,Cliff	1.80	1.20	.50
203	Murtaugh,Danny	1.80	1.20	.50

1950 BOWMAN (CONTINUED)

		MINT	VG-E	F-G
204	Hamner,Granny	1.80	1.20	.50
205	Goliat,Mike	1.80	1.20	.50
206	Lopata,Stan	1.80	1.20	.50
207	Lanier,Max	1.80	1.20	.50
208	Hearn,Jim	1.80	1.20	.50
209	Lindell,Johnny	1.80	1.20	.50
210	Gray,Ted	1.80	1.20	.50
211	Keller,Charley	2.50	1.70	.70
212	Priddy,Gerry	1.80	1.20	.50
213	Scheib,Carl	1.80	1.20	.50
214	Fowler,Dick	1.80	1.20	.50
215	Lopat,Ed	3.75	2.50	1.00
216	Porterfield,Bob	1.80	1.20	.50
217	Stengel,Casey	16.50	11.00	4.50
218	Mapes,Cliff	1.80	1.20	.50
219	Bauer,Hank	3.75	2.50	1.00
220	Mueller,Don	6.00	4.00	1.60
221	Mueller,Don	1.80	1.20	.50
222	Morgan,Bobby	1.80	1.20	.50
223	Russell,Jim	1.80	1.20	.50
224	Banta,Jack	1.80	1.20	.50
225	Sawyer,Eddie	2.50	1.70	.70
226	Konstanty,Jim	3.75	2.50	1.00
227	Miller,Bob	1.80	1.20	.50

		MINT	VG-E	F-G
228	Nicholson,Bill	1.80	1.20	.50
229	Frisch,Frank	7.50	5.00	2.00
230	Serena,Bill	1.80	1.20	.50
231	Ward,Preston	1.80	1.20	.50
232	Rosen,Al	6.00	4.00	1.60
233	Clark,Allie	1.80	1.20	.50
234	Shantz,Bobby	2.50	1.70	.70
235	Gilbert,Harold	1.80	1.20	.50
236	Cain,Bob	1.80	1.20	.50
237	Salkeld,Bill	1.80	1.20	.50
238	Jones,Vernal	1.80	1.20	.50
239	Howerton,Bill	1.80	1.20	.50
240	Lake,Eddie	1.80	1.20	.50
241	Berry,Neil	1.80	1.20	.50
242	Kryhoski,Dick	1.80	1.20	.50
243	Groth,Johnny	1.80	1.20	.50
244	Coogan,Dale	1.80	1.20	.50
245	Papai,Al	1.80	1.20	.50
246	Dropo,Walt	1.80	1.20	.50
247	Noren,Irv	1.80	1.20	.50
248	Jethroe,Sam	2.50	1.70	.70
249	Stirnweiss,"Snuffy"	1.80	1.20	.50
250	Coleman,Ray	1.80	1.20	.50
251	Moss,John	1.80	1.20	.50
252	Demars,Billy	6.00	2.00	.80

1951 BOWMAN (324)　　　　2 1/8″ X 3 1/8″

ROBIN ROBERTS

Pitcher—Philadelphia Phillies
Born: Springfield, Ill., Sept. 30, 1926
Height 6 ft.　　　　Weight: 190
Bats: Left　　　　Throws: Right

Robin soared high in 1950, his second full major-league season. In winning his 20th game, on the last day of the campaign, he copped the National League pennant for Philadelphia, in a do-or-die stand against the rampaging Dodgers. Final record was 20-11. Tied for lead in shut-outs with five. Pitched 3 shut-outs in row. Won 7 straight. Had a 15-16 record in 1949. Signed for big bonus.

No. 3 in the 1951 SERIES

BASEBALL
PICTURE CARDS
©1951 Bowman Gum, Inc., Phila., Pa., U.S.A.

The 1951 Bowman set, many of the cards of which are exact poses taken from the 1950 set, is Bowman's largest single issue. Its high nos., 253-324 are much more difficult to obtain than the low numbers, and the high numbers contain the "true" rookie cards of Mickey Mantle and Willie Mays. Card no. 195 portrays a caricature sketch of Paul Richards rather than the normal line drawing likeness as players on the other cards in the set are portrayed. The full name of the player appears on the face of the card.

		MINT	VG-E	F-G
	COMPLETE SET	1500.00	1000.00	400.00
	COMMON PLAYER(1-252)	1.80	1.20	.50
	COMMON PLAYER(253-324)	7.00	4.50	2.00
1	Ford,Whitey	50.00	20.00	8.00
2	Berra,"Yogi"	24.00	16.00	7.00
3	Roberts,Robin	7.50	5.00	2.00
4	Ennis,Del	2.50	1.70	.70
5	Mitchell,Dale	2.50	1.70	.70
6	Newcombe,Don	5.00	3.50	1.50
7	Hodges,Gil	7.50	5.00	2.00
8	Lehner,Paul	1.80	1.20	.50
9	Chapman,Sam	1.80	1.20	.50
10	Schoendienst,"Red"	3.75	2.50	1.00
11	Munger,"Red"	1.80	1.20	.50
12	Majeski,Hank	1.80	1.20	.50
13	Stanky,Eddie	2.50	1.70	.70
14	Dark,Al	2.50	1.70	.70
15	Pesky,Johnny	2.50	1.70	.70
16	McDermott,Maurice	1.80	1.20	.50
17	Castiglione,Pete	1.80	1.20	.50
18	Coan,Gil	1.80	1.20	.50
19	Gordon,Sid	1.80	1.20	.50
20	Crandall,Del	2.50	1.70	.70
21	Stirnweiss,"Snuffy"	1.80	1.20	.50
22	Sauer,Hank	2.50	1.70	.70
23	Evers,"Hoot"	1.80	1.20	.50
24	Blackwell,Ewell	2.50	1.70	.70
25	Raschi,Vic	2.50	1.70	.70
26	Rizzuto,Phil	10.00	6.50	3.00
27	Konstanty,Jim	2.50	1.70	.70
28	Waitkus,Eddie	1.80	1.20	.50
29	Clark,Allie	1.80	1.20	.50
30	Feller,Bob	16.50	11.00	4.50
31	Campanella,Roy	24.00	16.00	7.00
32	Snider,Duke	15.00	10.00	4.00
33	Hooper,Bob	1.80	1.20	.50
34	Marion,Marty	2.50	1.70	.70

		MINT	VG-E	F-G
35	Zarilla,Al	1.80	1.20	.50
36	Dobson,Joe	1.80	1.20	.50
37	Lockman,Whitey	1.80	1.20	.50
38	Evans,Al	1.80	1.20	.50
39	Scarborough,Ray	1.80	1.20	.50
40	Bell,Gus	1.80	1.20	.50
41	Yost,Eddie	1.80	1.20	.50
42	Bickford,Vern	1.80	1.20	.50
43	DeMars,Billy	1.80	1.20	.50
44	Smalley,Roy	1.80	1.20	.50
45	Houtteman,Art	1.80	1.20	.50
46	Kell,George (1941)	6.00	4.00	1.60
47	Hatton,Grady	1.80	1.20	.50
48	Raffensberger,Ken	1.80	1.20	.50
49	Coleman,Jerry	2.50	1.70	.70
50	Mize,Johnny	7.50	5.00	2.00
51	Seminick,Andy	1.80	1.20	.50
52	Sisler,Dick	1.80	1.20	.50
53	Lemon,Bob	7.50	5.00	2.00
54	Boone,Ray	1.80	1.20	.50
55	Hermanski,Gene	1.80	1.20	.50
56	Branca,Ralph	2.50	1.70	.70
57	Kellner,Alex	1.80	1.20	.50
58	Slaughter,Enos	6.00	4.00	1.60
59	Gumpert,Randy	1.80	1.20	.50
60	Carrasquel,"Chico"	1.80	1.20	.50
61	Hearn,Jim	1.80	1.20	.50
62	Boudreau,Lou	7.50	5.00	2.00
63	Dillinger,Bob	1.80	1.20	.50
64	Werle,Bill	1.80	1.20	.50
65	Vernon,"Mickey"	2.50	1.70	.70
66	Elliott,Bob	1.80	1.20	.50
67	Sievers,Roy	1.80	1.20	.50
68	Kokos,Dick	1.80	1.20	.50
69	Schmitz,Johnny	1.80	1.20	.50
70	Northey,Ron	1.80	1.20	.50
71	Priddy,Jerry	1.80	1.20	.50
72	Merriman,Lloyd	1.80	1.20	.50

	MINT	VG-E	F-G
73 Byrne,Tommy	1.80	1.20	.50
74 Johnson,Billy	1.80	1.20	.50
75 Meyer,Russ	1.80	1.20	.50
76 Lopata,Stan	1.80	1.20	.50
77 Goliat,Mike	1.80	1.20	.50
78 Wynn,Early	6.00	4.00	1.60
79 Hegan,Jim	1.80	1.20	.50
80 Reese,"Peewee"	7.50	5.00	2.00
81 Furillo,Carl	3.75	2.50	1.00
82 Tipton,Joe	1.80	1.20	.50
83 Scheib,Carl	1.80	1.20	.50
84 McCoskey,Barney	1.80	1.20	.50
85 Kazak,Eddie	1.80	1.20	.50
86 Brecheen,Harry	1.80	1.20	.50
87 Baker,Floyd	1.80	1.20	.50
88 Robinson,Eddie	1.80	1.20	.50
89 Thompson,"Hank"	1.80	1.20	.50
90 Koslo,Dave	1.80	1.20	.50
91 Vollmer,Clyde	1.80	1.20	.50
92 Stephens,Vern	1.80	1.20	.50
93 O'Connell,Danny	1.80	1.20	.50
94 McCullough,Clyde	1.80	1.20	.50
95 Robertson,Sherry	1.80	1.20	.50
96 Consuegra,Sandy	1.80	1.20	.50
97 Kuzava,Bob	1.80	1.20	.50
98 Marshall,Willard	1.80	1.20	.50
99 Torgeson,Earl	1.80	1.20	.50
100 Lollar,Sherm	1.80	1.20	.50
101 Friend,Owen	1.80	1.20	.50
102 Leonard,"Dutch"	1.80	1.20	.50
103 Pafko,Andy	1.80	1.20	.50
104 Trucks,Virgil	1.80	1.20	.50
105 Kolloway,Don	1.80	1.20	.50
106 Mullin,Pat	1.80	1.20	.50
107 Wyrostek,Johnny	1.80	1.20	.50
108 Stallcup,Virgil	1.80	1.20	.50
109 Reynolds,Allie	3.75	2.50	1.00
110 Brown,Bobby	1.80	1.20	.50
111 Simmons,Curt	1.80	1.20	.50
112 Jones,Willie	1.80	1.20	.50
113 Nicholson,Bill	1.80	1.20	.50
114 Zoldak,Sam	1.80	1.20	.50
115 Gromek,Steve	1.80	1.20	.50
116 Edwards,Bruce	1.80	1.20	.50
117 Miksis,Eddie	1.80	1.20	.50
118 Roe,Preacher	3.75	2.50	1.00
119 Joost,Eddie	1.80	1.20	.50
120 Coleman,Joe	1.80	1.20	.50
121 Staley,Gerry	1.80	1.20	.50
122 Garagiola,Joe	7.50	5.00	2.00
123 Judson,Howie	1.80	1.20	.50
124 Niarhos,Gus	1.80	1.20	.50
125 Rigney,Bill	1.80	1.20	.50
126 Thomson,Bobby	3.75	2.50	1.00
127 Maglie,Sal	2.50	1.70	.70
128 Kinder,Ellis	1.80	1.20	.50
129 Batts,Matt	1.80	1.20	.50
130 Saffell,Tom	1.80	1.20	.50
131 Chambers,Cliff	1.80	1.20	.50
132 Michaels,Cass	1.80	1.20	.50
133 Dente,Sam	1.80	1.20	.50
134 Spahn,Warren	10.00	6.50	3.00
135 Cooper,Walker	1.80	1.20	.50
136 Coleman,Ray	1.80	1.20	.50
137 Starr,Dick	1.80	1.20	.50
138 Cavaretta,Phil	2.50	1.70	.70
139 Lade,Doyle	1.80	1.20	.50
140 Lake,Eddie	1.80	1.20	.50
141 Hutchinson,Fred	2.50	1.70	.70
142 Robinson,Aaron	1.80	1.20	.50
143 Kluszewski,Ted	3.75	2.50	1.00
144 Wehmeier,Herman	1.80	1.20	.50
145 Sanford,Fred	1.80	1.20	.50
146 Hopp,Johnny	2.50	1.70	.70
147 Heintzelman,Ken	1.80	1.20	.50
148 Hamner,Granny	1.80	1.20	.50
149 Church,"Bubba"	1.80	1.20	.50
150 Garcia,Mike	2.50	1.70	.70
151 Doby,Larry	3.75	2.50	1.00
152 Abrams,Cal	1.80	1.20	.50
153 Barney,Rex	1.80	1.20	.50
154 Suder,Pete	1.80	1.20	.50
155 Brissie,Lou	1.80	1.20	.50
156 Rice,Del	1.80	1.20	.50
157 Brazle,Al	1.80	1.20	.50
158 Diering,Chuck	1.80	1.20	.50
159 Stewart,Eddie	1.80	1.20	.50
160 Masi,Phil	1.80	1.20	.50
161 Westrum,Wes	1.80	1.20	.50
162 Jansen,Larry	1.80	1.20	.50
163 Kennedy,Monte	1.80	1.20	.50
164 Wight,Bill	1.80	1.20	.50

	MINT	VG-E	F-G
165 Williams,Ted	50.00	35.00	15.00
166 Rojek,Stan	1.80	1.20	.50
167 Dickson,Murry	1.80	1.20	.50
168 Mele,Sam	1.80	1.20	.50
169 Hudson,Sid	1.80	1.20	.50
170 Sisti,Sibby	1.80	1.20	.50
171 Kerr,Buddy	1.80	1.20	.50
172 Garver,Ned	1.80	1.20	.50
173 Arft,Hank	1.80	1.20	.50
174 Owen,Mickey	1.80	1.20	.50
175 Terwilliger,Wayne	1.80	1.20	.50
176 Wertz,Vic	1.80	1.20	.50
177 Keller,Charlie	2.50	1.70	.70
178 Gray,Ted	1.80	1.20	.50
179 Litwiler,Danny	1.80	1.20	.50
180 Fox,Howie	1.80	1.20	.50
181 Stengel,Casey	13.00	9.00	4.00
182 Ferrick,Tom	1.80	1.20	.50
183 Bauer,Hank	2.50	1.70	.70
184 Sawyer,Eddie	1.80	1.20	.50
185 Bloodworth,Jimmy	1.80	1.20	.50
186 Ashburn,Richie	3.75	2.50	1.00
187 Rosen,Al	5.00	3.50	1.50
188 Avila,Bobby	1.80	1.20	.50
189 Palica,Erv	1.80	1.20	.50
190 Hatton,Joe	1.80	1.20	.50
191 Hitchcock,Billy	1.80	1.20	.50
192 Wyse,Hank	1.80	1.20	.50
193 Wilks,Ted	1.80	1.20	.50
194 Lowery,"Peanuts"	1.80	1.20	.50
195 Richards,Paul	5.00	3.50	1.50
196 Pierce,Billy	2.50	1.70	.70
197 Cain,Bob	1.80	1.20	.50
198 Irvin,Monte	6.00	4.00	1.60
199 Jones,Sheldon	1.80	1.20	.50
200 Kramer,Jack	1.80	1.20	.50
201 O'Neill,Steve	1.80	1.20	.50
202 Guerra,Mike	1.80	1.20	.50
203 Law,Vernon	1.80	1.20	.50
204 Lombardi,Vic	1.80	1.20	.50
205 Grasso,Mickey	1.80	1.20	.50
206 Marrero,Conrado	1.80	1.20	.50
207 Southworth,Billy	1.80	1.20	.50
208 Donnelly,Blix	1.80	1.20	.50
209 Wood,Ken	1.80	1.20	.50
210 Moss,Les	1.80	1.20	.50
211 Jeffcoat,Hal	1.80	1.20	.50
212 Rush,Bob	1.80	1.20	.50
213 Berry,Neil	1.80	1.20	.50
214 Swift,Bob	1.80	1.20	.50
215 Peterson,Ken	1.80	1.20	.50
216 Ryan,Connie	1.80	1.20	.50
217 Page,Joe	2.50	1.70	.70
218 Lopat,Ed	3.75	2.50	1.00
219 Woodling,Gene	2.50	1.70	.70
220 Miller,Bob	1.80	1.20	.50
221 Whitman,Dick	1.80	1.20	.50
222 Tucker,Thurman	1.80	1.20	.50
223 Vandermeer,Johnny	3.75	2.50	1.00
224 Cox,Billy	1.80	1.20	.50
225 Bankhead,Dan	1.80	1.20	.50
226 Dykes,Jimmy	2.50	1.70	.70
227 Shantz,Bobby	2.50	1.70	.70
228 Boyer,Cloyd	1.80	1.20	.50
229 Howerton,Bill	1.80	1.20	.50
230 Lanier,Max	1.80	1.20	.50
231 Aloma,Luis	1.80	1.20	.50
232 Fox,Nelson	5.00	3.50	1.50
233 Durocher,Leo	5.00	3.50	1.50
234 Hartung,Clint	1.80	1.20	.50
235 Lohrke,Jack	1.80	1.20	.50
236 Rosar,Warren	1.80	1.20	.50
237 Goodman,Billy	1.80	1.20	.50
238 Reiser,Peter	2.50	1.70	.70
239 MacDonald,Bill	1.80	1.20	.50
240 Haynes,Joe	1.80	1.20	.50
241 Noren,Irv	1.80	1.20	.50
242 Jethroe,Sam	1.80	1.20	.50
243 Antonelli,Johnny	2.50	1.70	.70
244 Fannin,Cliff	1.80	1.20	.50
245 Berardino,John	2.50	1.70	.70
246 Serena,Bill	1.80	1.20	.50
247 Ramazotti,Bob	1.80	1.20	.50
248 Klippstein,Johnny	1.80	1.20	.50
249 Groth,Johnny	1.80	1.20	.50
250 Borowy,Hank	1.80	1.20	.50
251 Ramsdell,Billy	1.80	1.20	.50
252 Howell,Dixie	1.80	1.20	.50
253 Mantle,Mickey	325.00	200.00	80.00
254 Jensen,Jackie	10.00	6.50	3.00
255 Candini,Milo	7.00	4.50	2.00
256 Sylvestri,Ken	7.00	4.50	2.00
257 Tebbetts,Birdie	7.50	5.00	2.00

		MINT	VG-E	F-G
258	Easter,Luke	7.50	5.00	2.00
259	Dressen,Chuck	7.50	5.00	2.00
260	Erskine,Carl	10.00	6.50	3.00
261	Moses,Wally	7.50	5.00	2.00
262	Zernial,Gus	7.50	5.00	2.00
263	Pollet,Howie	7.00	4.50	2.00
264	Richmond,Don	7.00	4.50	2.00
265	Bilko,Steve	7.00	4.50	2.00
266	Dorish,Harry	7.00	4.50	2.00
267	Holcomb,Ken	7.00	4.50	2.00
268	Mueller,Don	7.00	4.50	2.00
269	Noble,Ray	7.00	4.50	2.00
270	Nixon,Willard	7.00	4.50	2.00
271	Wright,Tommy	7.00	4.50	2.00
272	Meyer,Billy	7.00	4.50	2.00
273	Murtaugh,Danny	7.50	5.00	2.00
274	Metkovich,George	7.00	4.50	2.00
275	Harris,Bucky	10.00	6.50	3.00
276	Quinn,Frank	7.00	4.50	2.00
277	Hartsfield,Roy	7.00	4.50	2.00
278	Roy,Norman	7.00	4.50	2.00
279	Delsing,Jim	7.00	4.50	2.00
280	Overmire,Frank	7.00	4.50	2.00
281	Widmar,Al	7.00	4.50	2.00
282	Frisch,Frank	13.00	9.00	4.00
283	Dubiel,Walt	7.00	4.50	2.00
284	Bearden,Gene	7.00	4.50	2.00
285	Lipon,Johnny	7.00	4.50	2.00
286	Usher,Bob	7.00	4.50	2.00
287	Blackburn,Jim	7.00	4.50	2.00
288	Adams,Bobby	7.00	4.50	2.00
289	Mapes,Cliff	7.00	4.50	2.00
290	Dickey,Bill	22.50	15.00	6.50

		MINT	VG-E	F-G
291	Henrich,Tommy	10.00	6.50	3.00
292	Pellegrini,Eddie	7.00	4.50	2.00
293	Johnson,Ken	7.00	4.50	2.00
294	Thompson,Jocko	7.00	4.50	2.00
295	Lopez,Al	13.00	9.00	4.00
296	Kennedy,Bob	7.50	5.00	2.00
297	Philley,Dave	7.00	4.50	2.00
298	Astroth,Joe	7.00	4.50	2.00
299	King,Clyde	7.00	4.50	2.00
300	Rice,Hal	7.00	4.50	2.00
301	Glaviano,Tommy	7.00	4.50	2.00
302	Busby,Jim	7.00	4.50	2.00
303	Rotblatt,Marv	7.00	4.50	2.00
304	Gettell,Al	7.00	4.50	2.00
305	Mays,Willie	300.00	200.00	80.00
306	Piersall,Jim	10.00	6.50	3.00
307	Masterson,Walt	7.00	4.50	2.00
308	Beard,Ted	7.00	4.50	2.00
309	Queen,Mel	7.00	4.50	2.00
310	Dusak,Erv	7.00	4.50	2.00
311	Harris,Mickey	7.00	4.50	2.00
312	Mauch,Gene	10.00	6.50	3.00
313	Mueller,Ray	7.00	4.50	2.00
314	Sain,Johnny	10.00	6.50	3.00
315	Taylor,Zack	7.00	4.50	2.00
316	Pillette,Duane	7.00	4.50	2.00
317	Burgess,"Smoky"	7.50	5.00	2.00
318	Hacker,Warren	7.00	4.50	2.00
319	Rolfe,"Red"	7.50	5.00	2.00
320	White,Hal	7.00	4.50	2.00
321	Johnson,Earl	7.00	4.50	2.00
322	Sewell,Luke	7.50	5.00	2.00
323	Adcock,Joe	7.50	5.00	2.00
324	Pramesa,Johnny	10.00	6.50	3.00

1952 BOWMAN (252)

2 1/8'' X 3 1/8''

BOB FELLER

Pitcher—Cleveland Indians
Born: Van Meter, Iowa, Nov. 5, 1918
Height: 6 ft.   Weight: 185
Bats: Right   Throws: Right

Pitched the third no-hitter of career in 1951. Won 22 games and lost 8. Once Bob struck out 18 batters in one 9-inning game, a modern major-league record. Holds big-time record of 348 strikeouts in a season. Up to 1952 had 230 wins in majors against only 131 losses.

No. 43 in the 1952 SERIES

BASEBALL
PICTURE CARDS

The 1952 Bowman issue of 252 cards contains a series of high numbers (Nos. 217—252) which are more difficult to obtain than the other cards in the set. A facsimile autograph of the player is printed on the face of the card.

	MINT	VG-E	F-G
COMPLETE SET	825.00	550.00	225.00
COMMON PLAYER(1-180)	1.80	1.20	.50
COMMON PLAYER(181-216)	1.50	1.00	.40
COMMON PLAYER(217-252)	3.50	2.25	.90

		MINT	VG-E	F-G
1	Berra,"Yogi"	40.00	20.00	8.00
2	Thomson,Bobby	3.75	2.50	1.00
3	Hutchinson,Fred	2.50	1.70	.70
4	Roberts,Robin	7.50	5.00	2.00
5	Minoso,"Minnie"	3.75	2.50	1.00
6	Stallcup,Virgil	1.80	1.20	.50
7	Garcia,Mike	2.50	1.70	.70
8	Reese,"Peewee"	7.50	5.00	2.00
9	Stephens,Vern	1.80	1.20	.50
10	Hooper,Bob	1.80	1.20	.50
11	Kiner,Ralph	7.50	5.00	2.00
12	Surkont,Max	1.80	1.20	.50
13	Mapes,Cliff	1.80	1.20	.50
14	Chambers,Cliff	1.80	1.20	.50
15	Mele,Sam	1.80	1.20	.50
16	Lown,"Turk"	1.80	1.20	.50
17	Lopat,Ed	3.75	2.50	1.00
18	Mueller,Don	1.80	1.20	.50
19	Cain,Bob	1.80	1.20	.50
20	Jones,Willie	1.80	1.20	.50
21	Fox,Nelson	3.75	2.50	1.00
22	Ramsdell,Willard	1.80	1.20	.50
23	Lemon,Bob	7.50	5.00	2.00
24	Furillo,Carl	3.75	2.50	1.00
25	McDermott,"Mickey"	1.80	1.20	.50

		MINT	VG-E	F-G
26	Joost,Eddie	1.80	1.20	.50
27	Garagiola,Joe	7.50	5.00	2.00
28	Hartsfield,Ray	1.80	1.20	.50
29	Garver,Ned	1.80	1.20	.50
30	Schoendienst,"Red"	2.50	1.70	.70
31	Yost,Eddie	1.80	1.20	.50
32	Miksis,Eddie	1.80	1.20	.50
33	McDougald,Gil	2.50	1.70	.70
34	Dark,Alvin	2.50	1.70	.70
35	Hamner,Granny	1.80	1.20	.50
36	Michaels,Cass	1.80	1.20	.50
37	Raschi,Vic	2.50	1.70	.70
38	Lockman,Whitey	1.80	1.20	.50
39	Wertz,Vic	1.80	1.20	.50
40	Church,"Bubba"	1.80	1.20	.50
41	Carrasquel,Chico	1.80	1.20	.50
42	Wyrostek,Johnny	1.80	1.20	.50
43	Feller,Bob	15.00	10.00	4.00
44	Campanella,Roy	24.00	16.00	7.00
45	Pesky,Johny	1.80	1.20	.50
46	Scheib,Carl	1.80	1.20	.50
47	Castiglione,Pete	1.80	1.20	.50
48	Bickford,Vern	1.80	1.20	.50
49	Hearn,Jim	1.80	1.20	.50
50	Staley,Gerry	1.80	1.20	.50
51	Coan,Gil	1.80	1.20	.50
52	Rizzuto,Phil	10.00	6.50	3.00
53	Ashburn,Richie	3.75	2.50	1.00
54	Pierce,Billy	2.50	1.70	.70

	MINT	VG-E	F-G			MINT	VG-E	F-G
55 Raffensberger,Ken	1.80	1.20	.50	148 Heintzelman,Ken	1.80	1.20	.50
56 King,Clyde	1.80	1.20	.50	149 Judson,Howie	1.80	1.20	.50
57 Vollmer,Clyde	1.80	1.20	.50	150 Wehmeier,Herman	1.80	1.20	.50
58 Majeski,Hank	1.80	1.20	.50	151 Rosen,Al	5.00	3.50	1.50
59 Dickson,Murry	1.80	1.20	.50	152 Cox,Billy	1.80	1.20	.50
60 Gordon,Sid	1.80	1.20	.50	153 Hatfield,Fred	1.80	1.20	.50
61 Byrne,Tommy	1.80	1.20	.50	154 Fain,Ferris	2.50	1.70	.70
62 Presko,Joe	1.80	1.20	.50	155 Meyer,Billy	1.80	1.20	.50
63 Noren,Irv	1.80	1.20	.50	156 Spahn,Warren	10.00	6.50	3.00
64 Smalley,Roy	1.80	1.20	.50	157 Delsing,Jim	1.80	1.20	.50
65 Bauer,Hank	2.50	1.70	.70	158 Harris,Bucky	6.00	4.00	1.60
66 Maglie,Sal	1.80	1.20	.50	159 Leonard,"Dutch"	1.80	1.20	.50
67 Groth,Johnny	1.80	1.20	.50	160 Stanky,Eddie	2.50	1.70	.70
68 Busby,Jim	1.80	1.20	.50	161 Jensen,Jackie	2.50	1.70	.70
69 Adcock,Joe	2.50	1.70	.70	162 Irvin,Monte	6.00	4.00	1.60
70 Erskine,Carl	2.50	1.70	.70	163 Lipon,Johnny	1.80	1.20	.50
71 Law,Vernon	1.80	1.20	.50	164 Ryan,Connie	1.80	1.20	.50
72 Torgeson,Earl	1.80	1.20	.50	165 Rogovin,Saul	1.80	1.20	.50
73 Coleman,Gerry	1.80	1.20	.50	166 Adams,Bobby	1.80	1.20	.50
74 Westrum,Wes	1.80	1.20	.50	167 Avila,Bobby	1.80	1.20	.50
75 Kell,George	2.50	1.70	.70	168 Roe,"Preacher"	3.75	2.50	1.00
76 Ennis,Del	1.80	1.20	.50	169 Dropo,Walt	1.80	1.20	.50
77 Robinson,Eddie	1.80	1.20	.50	170 Astroth,Joe	1.80	1.20	.50
78 Merriman,Lloyd	1.80	1.20	.50	171 Queen,Mel	1.80	1.20	.50
79 Brissie,Lou	1.80	1.20	.50	172 St. Claire,Ebba	1.80	1.20	.50
80 Hodges,Gil	7.50	5.00	2.00	173 Bearden,Gene	1.80	1.20	.50
81 Goodman,Billy	1.80	1.20	.50	174 Grasso,Mickey	1.80	1.20	.50
82 Zernial,Gus	1.80	1.20	.50	175 Jackson,Ransom	1.80	1.20	.50
83 Pollet,Howie	1.80	1.20	.50	176 Brecheen,Harry	1.80	1.20	.50
84 Jethroe,Sam	1.80	1.20	.50	177 Woodling,Gene	2.50	1.70	.70
85 Marion,Marty	2.50	1.70	.70	178 Williams,Dave	1.80	1.20	.50
86 Abrams,Cal	1.80	1.20	.50	179 Suder,Pete	1.80	1.20	.50
87 Vernon,Mickey	2.50	1.70	.70	180 Fitzgerald,Eddie	1.80	1.20	.50
88 Edwards,Bruce	1.80	1.20	.50	181 Collins,Joe	1.50	1.00	.40
89 Hitchcock,Billy	1.80	1.20	.50	182 Koslo,Dave	1.50	1.00	.40
90 Jansen,Larry	1.80	1.20	.50	183 Mullin,Pat	1.50	1.00	.40
91 Kolloway,Don	1.80	1.20	.50	184 Simmons,Curt	1.50	1.00	.40
92 Waitkus,Eddie	1.80	1.20	.50	185 Stewart,Eddie	1.50	1.00	.40
93 Richards,Paul	1.80	1.20	.50	186 Smith,Frank	1.50	1.00	.40
94 Sewell,Luke	1.80	1.20	.50	187 Hegan,Jim	1.50	1.00	.40
95 Easter,Luke	1.80	1.20	.50	188 Dressen,Charlie	1.50	1.00	.40
96 Branca,Ralph	2.50	1.70	.70	189 Piersall,Jim	2.50	1.70	.70
97 Marshall,Willard	1.80	1.20	.50	190 Fowler,Dick	1.50	1.00	.40
98 Dykes,Jimmy	1.80	1.20	.50	191 Friend,Bob	1.50	1.00	.40
99 McCullough,Clyde	1.80	1.20	.50	192 Cusick,John	1.50	1.00	.40
100 Sisti,Sibby	1.80	1.20	.50	193 Young,Bobby	1.50	1.00	.40
101 Mantle,Mickey	165.00	110.00	45.00	194 Porterfield,Bob	1.50	1.00	.40
102 Lowery,"Peanuts"	1.80	1.20	.50	195 Baumholtz,Frank	1.50	1.00	.40
103 Haynes,Joe	1.80	1.20	.50	196 Musial,Stan	50.00	35.00	15.00
104 Jeffcoat,Hal	1.80	1.20	.50	197 Silvera,Charlie	1.50	1.00	.40
105 Brown,Bobby	1.80	1.20	.50	198 Diering,Chuck	1.50	1.00	.40
106 Gumpert,Randy	1.80	1.20	.50	199 Gray,Ted	1.50	1.00	.40
107 Rice,Del	1.80	1.20	.50	200 Silvestri,Ken	1.50	1.00	.40
108 Metkovich,George	1.80	1.20	.50	201 Coleman,Ray	1.50	1.00	.40
109 Morgan,Tom	1.80	1.20	.50	202 Perkowski,Harry	1.50	1.00	.40
110 Lanier,Max	1.80	1.20	.50	203 Gromek,Steve	1.50	1.00	.40
111 Evers,"Hoot"	1.80	1.20	.50	204 Pafko,Andy	1.50	1.00	.40
112 Burgess,"Smokey"	1.80	1.20	.50	205 Masterson,Walt	1.50	1.00	.40
113 Zarilla,Al	1.80	1.20	.50	206 Valo,Elmer	1.50	1.00	.40
114 Hiller,Frank	1.80	1.20	.50	207 Strickland,George	1.50	1.00	.40
115 Doby,Larry	3.75	2.50	1.00	208 Cooper,Walker	1.50	1.00	.40
116 Snider,Duke	15.00	10.00	4.00	209 Littlefield,Dick	1.50	1.00	.40
117 Wight,Bill	1.80	1.20	.50	210 Wilson,Archie	1.50	1.00	.40
118 Murray,Ray	1.80	1.20	.50	211 Minner,Paul	1.50	1.00	.40
119 Howerton,Bill	1.80	1.20	.50	212 Hemus,Solly	1.50	1.00	.40
120 Nichols,Chet	1.80	1.20	.50	213 Kennedy,Monte	1.50	1.00	.40
121 Corwin,Al	1.80	1.20	.50	214 Boone,Ray	1.50	1.00	.40
122 Johnson,Billy	1.80	1.20	.50	215 Jones,Sheldon	1.50	1.00	.40
123 Hudson,Sid	1.80	1.20	.50	216 Batts,Matt	1.50	1.00	.40
124 Tebbetts,"Birdie"	1.80	1.20	.50	217 Stengel,Casey	21.00	14.00	6.00
125 Fox,Howie	1.80	1.20	.50	218 Mays,Willie	180.00	120.00	50.00
126 Cavaretta,Phil	2.50	1.70	.70	219 Berry,Neil	3.50	2.25	.90
127 Sisler,Dick	1.80	1.20	.50	220 Meyer,Russ	3.50	2.25	.90
128 Newcombe,Don	5.00	3.50	1.50	221 Kretlow,Lou	3.50	2.25	.90
129 Niarhos,Gus	1.80	1.20	.50	222 Howell,"Dixie"	3.50	2.25	.90
130 Clark,Allie	1.80	1.20	.50	223 Simpson,Harry	3.50	2.25	.90
131 Swift,Bob	1.80	1.20	.50	224 Schmitz,Johnny	3.50	2.25	.90
132 Cole,Dave	1.80	1.20	.50	225 Wilber,Del	3.50	2.25	.90
133 Kryhoski,Dick	1.80	1.20	.50	226 Kellner,Alex	3.50	2.25	.90
134 Brazle,Al	1.80	1.20	.50	227 Sukeforth,Clyde	3.50	2.25	.90
135 Harris,Mickey	1.80	1.20	.50	228 Chipman,Bob	3.50	2.25	.90
136 Hermanski,Gene	1.80	1.20	.50	229 Arft,Hank	3.50	2.25	.90
137 Rojek,Stan	1.80	1.20	.50	230 Shea,Frank	3.50	2.25	.90
138 Wilks,Ted	1.80	1.20	.50	231 Fondy,Dee	3.50	2.25	.90
139 Priddy,Jerry	1.80	1.20	.50	232 Slaughter,Enos	10.00	6.50	3.00
140 Scarborough,Ray	1.80	1.20	.50	233 Kuzava,Bob	3.50	2.25	.90
141 Edwards,Hank	1.80	1.20	.50	234 Fitzsimmons,Fred	3.50	2.25	.90
142 Wynn,Early	6.00	4.00	1.60	235 Souchock,Steve	3.50	2.25	.90
143 Consuegra,Sandy	1.80	1.20	.50	236 Brown,Tommy	3.50	2.25	.90
144 Hatton,Joe	1.80	1.20	.50	237 Lollar,Sherman	3.50	2.25	.90
145 Mize,Johnny	7.50	5.00	2.00	238 McMillan,Roy	3.50	2.25	.90
146 Durocher,Leo	5.00	3.50	1.50	239 Mitchell,Dale	3.50	2.25	.90
147 Stuart,Marlin	1.80	1.20	.50	240 Loes,Billy	3.50	2.25	.90

	MINT	VG-E	F-G			MINT	VG-E	F-G
241 Parnell,Mel	3.50	2.25	.90		247 Pramesa,John	3.50	2.25	.90
242 Kell,Everett	3.50	2.25	.90		248 Werle,Bill	3.50	2.25	.90
243 Munger,"Red"	3.50	2.25	.90		249 Thompson,"Hank"	3.50	2.25	.90
244 Burdette,Lew	7.50	5.00	2.00		250 Delock,Ivan	3.50	2.25	.90
245 Schmees,George	3.50	2.25	.90		251 Lohrke,Jack	3.50	2.25	.90
246 Snyder,Jerry	3.50	2.25	.90		252 Crosetti,Frank	16.00	6.00	2.00

1953 BOWMAN COLOR (160)   2 1/2" X 3 3/4"

The 1953 Bowman Color set, considered by many to be the best looking set of the modern era, contains Kodachrome photographs with no names or facsimile autographs on the face. Numbers 113-160 are somewhat more difficult to obtain. Card no. 159 is actually a picture of Floyd Baker.

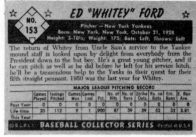

	MINT	VG-E	F-G			MINT	VG-E	F-G
COMPLETE SET	1400.00	900.00	400.00		56 Cain,Bob	3.75	2.50	1.00
COMMON PLAYER(1-112)	3.75	2.50	1.00		57 Boudreau,Lou	7.50	5.00	2.00
COMMON PLAYER(113-128)	11.00	7.00	3.00		58 Marshall,Willard	3.75	2.50	1.00
COMMON PLAYER(129-160)	7.00	4.50	2.00		59 Mantle,Mickey	175.00	115.00	50.00
					60 Hamner,Granny	3.75	2.50	1.00
1 Williams,Dave	9.00	3.00	1.00		61 Kell,George	4.50	3.00	1.25
2 Wertz,Vic	3.75	2.50	1.00		62 Kluszewski,Ted	6.00	4.00	1.50
3 Jethroe,Sam	3.75	2.50	1.00		63 McDougald,Gil	4.50	3.00	1.25
4 Houtteman,Art	3.75	2.50	1.00		64 Simmons,Curt	3.75	2.50	1.00
5 Gordon,Sid	3.75	2.50	1.00		65 Roberts,Robin	9.00	6.00	2.50
6 Ginsberg,Joe	3.75	2.50	1.00		66 Parnell,Mel	3.75	2.50	1.00
7 Chiti,Harry	3.75	2.50	1.00		67 Clark,Mel	3.75	2.50	1.00
8 Rosen,Al	6.00	4.00	1.50		68 Reynolds,Allie	6.00	4.00	1.50
9 Rizzuto,Phil	13.00	9.00	4.00		69 Grimm,Charley	3.75	2.50	1.00
10 Ashburn,Richie	6.00	4.00	1.50		70 Courtney,Clint	3.75	2.50	1.00
11 Shantz,Bobby	4.50	3.00	1.25		71 Minner,Paul	3.75	2.50	1.00
12 Erskine,Carl	4.50	3.00	1.25		72 Gray,Ted	3.75	2.50	1.00
13 Zerniel,Gus	3.75	2.50	1.00		73 Pierce,Billy	4.50	3.00	1.25
14 Loes,Billy	3.75	2.50	1.00		74 Mueller,Don	3.75	2.50	1.00
15 Busby,Jim	3.75	2.50	1.00		75 Rogovin,Saul	3.75	2.50	1.00
16 Friend,Bob	4.50	3.00	1.25		76 Hearn,Jim	3.75	2.50	1.00
17 Staley,Jerry	3.75	2.50	1.00		77 Grasso,Mickey	3.75	2.50	1.00
18 Fox,Nelson	6.00	4.00	1.50		78 Furillo,Carl	6.00	4.00	1.50
19 Dark,Alvin	4.50	3.00	1.25		79 Boone,Ray	3.75	2.50	1.00
20 Lenhardt,Don	3.75	2.50	1.00		80 Kiner,Ralph	7.50	5.00	2.00
21 Garagiola,Joe	9.00	6.00	2.50		81 Slaughter,Enos	7.50	5.00	2.00
22 Porterfield,Bob	3.75	2.50	1.00		82 Astroth,Joe	3.75	2.50	1.00
23 Wehmeier,Herman	3.75	2.50	1.00		83 Daniels,Jack	3.75	2.50	1.00
24 Jensen,Jackie	4.50	3.00	1.25		84 Bauer,Hank	6.00	4.00	1.50
25 Evers,"Hoot"	3.75	2.50	1.00		85 Hemus,Solly	3.75	2.50	1.00
26 McMillan,Roy	3.75	2.50	1.00		86 Simpson,Harry	3.75	2.50	1.00
27 Raschi,Vic	4.50	3.00	1.25		87 Perkowski,Harry	3.75	2.50	1.00
28 Burgess,"Smokey"	3.75	2.50	1.00		88 Dobson,Joe	3.75	2.50	1.00
29 Avila,Bobby	3.75	2.50	1.00		89 Consuegra,Sandy	3.75	2.50	1.00
30 Cavaretta,Phil	4.50	3.00	1.25		90 Nuxhall,Joe	4.50	3.00	1.25
31 Dykes,Jimmy	4.50	3.00	1.25		91 Souchock,Steve	3.75	2.50	1.00
32 Musial,Stan	65.00	45.00	20.00		92 Hodges,Gil	13.00	9.00	4.00
33 Reese,"Peewee"	13.00	9.00	4.00		93 Rizzuto & Martin	24.00	16.00	7.00
34 Coan,Gil	3.75	2.50	1.00		94 Addis,Bob	3.75	2.50	1.00
35 McDermott,Maurice	3.75	2.50	1.00		95 Moses,Wally	3.75	2.50	1.00
36 Minoso,"Minnie"	6.00	4.00	1.50		96 Maglie,Sal	4.50	3.00	1.25
37 Wilson,Jim	3.75	2.50	1.00		97 Mathews,Ed	13.00	9.00	4.00
38 Byrd,Harry	3.75	2.50	1.00		98 Rodriguez,Hector	3.75	2.50	1.00
39 Richards,Paul	4.50	3.00	1.25		99 Spahn,Warren	13.00	9.00	4.00
40 Doby,Larry	4.50	3.00	1.25		100 Wight,Bill	3.75	2.50	1.00
41 White,Sammy	3.75	2.50	1.00		101 Schoendienst,Red	6.00	4.00	1.50
42 Brown,Tommy	3.75	2.50	1.00		102 Hegan,Jim	3.75	2.50	1.00
43 Garcia,Mike	4.50	3.00	1.25		103 Ennis,Del	3.75	2.50	1.00
44 Bauer,Berra,Mantle	36.00	24.00	10.00		104 Easter,Luke	3.75	2.50	1.00
45 Dropo,Walt	3.75	2.50	1.00		105 Joost,Eddie	3.75	2.50	1.00
46 Campanella,Roy	30.00	20.00	8.00		106 Raffensberger,Ken	3.75	2.50	1.00
47 Garver,Ned	3.75	2.50	1.00		107 Kellner,Alex	3.75	2.50	1.00
48 Sauer,Hank	4.50	3.00	1.25		108 Adams,Bobby	3.75	2.50	1.00
49 Stanky,Eddie	4.50	3.00	1.25		109 Wood,Ken	3.75	2.50	1.00
50 Kretlow,Lou	3.75	2.50	1.00		110 Rush,Bob	3.75	2.50	1.00
51 Irvin,Monte	7.50	5.00	2.00		111 Dyck,Jim	3.75	2.50	1.00
52 Marion,Marty	4.50	3.00	1.25		112 Atwell,Toby	3.75	2.50	1.00
53 Rice,Del	3.75	2.50	1.00		113 Drews,Karl	11.00	7.00	3.00
54 Carrasquel,Chico	3.75	2.50	1.00		114 Feller,Bob	60.00	40.00	15.00
55 Durocher,Leo	6.00	4.00	1.50					

	MINT	VG-E	F-G
115 Boyer,Cloyd	11.00	7.00	3.00
116 Yost,Eddie	11.00	7.00	3.00
117 Snider,Duke	150.00	90.00	40.00
118 Martin,Billy	36.00	24.00	10.00
119 Mitchell,Dale	11.00	7.00	3.00
120 Stuart,Marlin	11.00	7.00	3.00
121 Berra,Yogi	120.00	75.00	30.00
122 Serena,Bill	11.00	7.00	3.00
123 Lipon,Johnny	11.00	7.00	3.00
124 Dressen,Charlie	11.00	7.00	3.00
125 Hatfield,Ray	11.00	7.00	3.00
126 Corwin,Al	11.00	7.00	3.00
127 Kryhoski,Dick	11.00	7.00	3.00
128 Lockman,Whitey	11.00	7.00	3.00
129 Meyer,Russ	7.00	4.50	2.00
130 Michaels,Cass	7.00	4.50	2.00
131 Ryan,Connie	7.00	4.50	2.00
132 Hutchinson,Fred	9.00	6.00	2.50
133 Jones,Willie	7.00	4.50	2.00
134 Pesky,Johnny	7.50	5.00	2.00
135 Morgan,Bobby	7.00	4.50	2.00
136 Brideweiser,Jim	7.00	4.50	2.00
137 Dente,Sam	7.00	4.50	2.00

	MINT	VG-E	F-G
138 Church,Bubba	7.00	4.50	2.00
139 Runnels,Pete	7.00	4.50	2.00
140 Brazle,Al	7.00	4.50	2.00
141 Shea,Frank	7.00	4.50	2.00
142 Miggins,Larry	7.00	4.50	2.00
143 Lopez,Al	13.00	9.00	4.00
144 Hacker,Warren	7.00	4.50	2.00
145 Shuba,George	7.00	4.50	2.00
146 Wynn,Early	22.50	15.00	6.50
147 Koshorek,Clem	7.00	4.50	2.00
148 Goodman,Billy	7.00	4.50	2.00
149 Corwin,Al	7.00	4.50	2.00
150 Scheib,Carl	7.00	4.50	2.00
151 Adcock,Joe	11.00	7.00	3.00
152 Vollmer,Clyde	7.00	4.50	2.00
153 Ford,Whitey	55.00	35.00	15.00
154 Lown,Turk	7.00	4.50	2.00
155 Clark,Allie	7.00	4.50	2.00
156 Surkont,Max	7.00	4.50	2.00
157 Lollar,Sherman	7.00	4.50	2.00
158 Fox,Howard	7.00	4.50	2.00
159 Vernon,Mickey	11.00	7.00	3.00
160 Abrams,Cal	10.00	5.00	2.00

1953 BOWMAN B&W (64)   2 1/2'' X 3 3/4''

The 1953 Bowman Black and White set contains photograph fronts exactly like the color set of 1953. Although they suffer aesthetically from the lack of color, the '53 Black and Whites are popular among collectors because of the difficulty in completing the set.

☆ ☆ **IRV NOREN** ☆
NO. 45
Outfield — New York Yankees
Born: Jamestown, New York, November 29, 1924
Height: 6 ft.; Weight: 190; Bats: Left; Throws: Left

Last year was only the third in the majors for Irv; his first with the Yanks. He began the season with Washington, and after appearing in 12 games for the Senators, was traded to the Yanks. Hit .323 with Fort Worth in '48 and .330 for Hollywood the next season. Batted .295 as a rookie for the Senators. Tied an American League record for putouts by an outfielder in a game with 11.

	MAJOR LEAGUE BATTING RECORD							FIELDING RECORD			
	Games Played	Times at Bat	Runs Scored	No. of Hits	Home Runs	Runs Bat. In	Bat. Ave.	Put Outs	No. of Assists	No. of Errors	Field. Ave.
Past Year	105	321	40	76	5	23	.237	137	5	0	1.000
Life time	372	1372	204	378	27	207	.270	1057	54	23	.985
This Year											

B G H L I **BASEBALL COLLECTOR SERIES** Printed in U.S.A

	MINT	VG-E	F-G
COMPLETE SET	700.00	450.00	200.00
COMMON PLAYER(1-64)	9.00	6.00	2.50
1 Bell,Gus	20.00	8.00	3.00
2 Nixon,Willard	9.00	6.00	2.50
3 Rigney,Bill	9.00	6.00	2.50
4 Mullin,Pat	9.00	6.00	2.50
5 Fondy,Dee	9.00	6.00	2.50
6 Murray,Ray	9.00	6.00	2.50
7 Seminick,Andy	9.00	6.00	2.50
8 Suder,Pete	9.00	6.00	2.50
9 Masterson,Walt	9.00	6.00	2.50
10 Sisler,Dick	9.00	6.00	2.50
11 Gernert,Dick	9.00	6.00	2.50
12 Jackson,Randy	9.00	6.00	2.50
13 Tipton,Joe	9.00	6.00	2.50
14 Nicholson,Bill	9.00	6.00	2.50
15 Mize,Johnny	27.00	18.00	8.00
16 Miller,Stu	9.00	6.00	2.50
17 Trucks,Virgil	9.00	6.00	2.50
18 Hoeft,Billy	9.00	6.00	2.50
19 Lapalme,Paul	9.00	6.00	2.50
20 Robinson,Eddie	9.00	6.00	2.50
21 Podbielan,Clarence	9.00	6.00	2.50
22 Batts,Matt	9.00	6.00	2.50
23 Mizell,Wilmer	9.00	6.00	2.50
24 Wilber,Del	9.00	6.00	2.50
25 Sain,Johnny	18.00	12.00	5.50
26 Roe,"Preacher"	18.00	12.00	5.50
27 Lemon,Bob	27.00	18.00	8.00
28 Wilhelm,Hoyt	18.00	12.00	5.50
29 Hudson,Sid	9.00	6.00	2.50
30 Cooper,Walker	9.00	6.00	2.50
31 Woodling,Gene	10.00	6.50	3.00

	MINT	VG-E	F-G
32 Bridges,Rocky	9.00	6.00	2.50
33 Kuzava,Bob	9.00	6.00	2.50
34 St. Claire,Ebba	9.00	6.00	2.50
35 Wyrostek,Johnny	9.00	6.00	2.50
36 Piersall,Jim	18.00	12.00	5.50
37 Jeffcoat,Hal	9.00	6.00	2.50
38 Cole,Dave	9.00	6.00	2.50
39 Stengel,Casey	110.00	70.00	30.00
40 Jansen,Larry	9.00	6.00	2.50
41 Ramazotti,Bob	9.00	6.00	2.50
42 Judson,Howie	9.00	6.00	2.50
43 Bevan,Hal	9.00	6.00	2.50
44 Delsing,Jim	9.00	6.00	2.50
45 Noren,Irv	9.00	6.00	2.50
46 Harris,Bucky	16.00	11.00	5.00
47 Lohrke,Jack	9.00	6.00	2.50
48 Ridzek,Steve	9.00	6.00	2.50
49 Baker,Floyd	9.00	6.00	2.50
50 Leonard,Dutch	9.00	6.00	2.50
51 Burdette,Lou	12.00	8.00	3.50
52 Branca,Ralph	10.00	6.50	3.00
53 Martin,Morris	9.00	6.00	2.50
54 Miller,Billy	9.00	6.00	2.50
55 Johnson,Don	9.00	6.00	2.50
56 Smalley,Roy	9.00	6.00	2.50
57 Pafko,Andy	9.00	6.00	2.50
58 Konstanty,Jim	10.00	6.50	3.00
59 Pillette,Duane	9.00	6.00	2.50
60 Cox,Billy	9.00	6.00	2.50
61 Gorman,Tom	9.00	6.00	2.50
62 Thomas,Keith	9.00	6.00	2.50
63 Gromek,Steve	9.00	6.00	2.50
64 Hansen,Andy	12.00	6.00	2.50

The 1954 Bowman set contains the modern era's most publicized variation card. Number 66 exists as both Ted Williams and Jim Piersall (who is also number 210 in the set). The Williams card is considered by some to be scarcest post-war regular issue card. The set price below does not include number 6 Williams.

EDDIE MATHEWS NO. 64

The youngster is touted as a junior Babe Ruth. In his second season in the majors Eddie swatted 47 home runs to win the League's title. He hit 30 homers which set a National League record for most homers on the road in a season. In addition, the shy youngster knocked in 135 runs, had 31 doubles, 8 triples and an average of .302. He lost the slugging title by two-tenths of a point, with a percentage of .6269 to Duke Snider's .6271.

Who made 8 doubles in 3 consecutive games establishing a major league record?

	MINT	VG-E	F-G
COMPLETE SET	420.00	280.00	120.00
COMMON PLAYER(1-128)	.70	.50	.20
COMMON PLAYER(129-224)	.90	.60	.25

#	Player	MINT	VG-E	F-G
1	Rizzuto,Phil	18.00	8.00	3.00
2	Jensen,Jackie	1.75	1.15	.50
3	Fricano,Marion	.70	.50	.20
4	Hooper,Bob	.70	.50	.20
5	Hunter,Bill	.70	.50	.20
6	Fox,Nelson	2.50	1.70	.70
7	Dropo,Walt	.70	.50	.20
8	Busby,Jim	.70	.50	.20
9	Williams,Davey	.70	.50	.20
10	Erskine,Carl	.70	.50	.20
11	Gordon,Sid	.70	.50	.20
12	McMillan,Roy	.70	.50	.20
13	Minner,Paul	.70	.50	.20
14	Staley,Gerry	.70	.50	.20
15	Ashburn,Richie	2.50	1.70	.70
16	Wilson,Jim	.70	.50	.20
17	Gorman,Tom	.70	.50	.20
18	Evers,"Hoot"	.70	.50	.20
19	Shantz,Bobby	1.00	.65	.30
20	Houtteman,Art	.70	.50	.20
21	Wertz,Vic	.70	.50	.20
22	Mele,Sam	.70	.50	.20
23	Kuenn,Harvey	1.35	.90	.40
24	Porterfield,Bob	.70	.50	.20
25	Westrum,Wes	.70	.50	.20
26	Cox,Billy	.70	.50	.20
27	Cole,Dick	.70	.50	.20
28	Greengrass,Jim	.70	.50	.20
29	Klippstein,Johnny	.70	.50	.20
30	Rice,Del	.70	.50	.20
31	Burgess,"Smokey"	1.00	.65	.30
32	Crandall,Del	1.00	.65	.30
33	Raschi,Vic	1.75	1.15	.50
34	White,Sammy	.70	.50	.20
35	Joost,Eddie	.70	.50	.20
36	Strickland,George	.70	.50	.20
37	Kokos,Dick	.70	.50	.20
38	Minoso,"Minnie"	2.50	1.70	.70
39	Garver,Ned	.70	.50	.20
40	Coan,Gil	.70	.50	.20
41	Dark,Alvin	1.00	.65	.30
42	Loes,Billy	.70	.50	.20
43	Friend,Bob	1.00	.65	.30
44	Perkowski,Harry	.70	.50	.20
45	Kiner,Ralph	6.50	4.50	2.00
46	Repulski,Rip	.70	.50	.20
47	Hamner,Granny	.70	.50	.20
48	Dittmer,Jack	.70	.50	.20
49	Byrd,Harry	.70	.50	.20
50	Kell,George	1.35	.90	.40
51	Kellner,Alex	.70	.50	.20
52	Ginsberg,Joe	.70	.50	.20
53	Lenhardt,Don	.70	.50	.20
54	Carrasquel,Chico	.70	.50	.20
55	Delsing,Jim	.70	.50	.20
56	McDermott,Maurice	.70	.50	.20
57	Wilhelm,Hoyt	2.50	1.70	.70
58	Reese,"Peewee"	6.50	4.50	2.00
59	Schultz,Bob	.70	.50	.20
60	Baczewski,Fred	.70	.50	.20

#	Player	MINT	VG-E	F-G
61	Miksis,Eddie	.70	.50	.20
62	Slaughter,Enos	3.75	2.50	1.00
63	Torgeson,Earl	.70	.50	.20
64	Mathews,Eddie	6.50	4.50	2.00
65	Mantle,Mickey	75.00	50.00	20.00
66A	Piersall,Jim	45.00	30.00	12.00
66B	Williams,Ted	650.00	400.00	150.00
67	Scheib,Carl	.70	.50	.20
68	Avila,Bobby	.70	.50	.20
69	Courtney,Clint	.70	.50	.20
70	Marshall,Willard	.70	.50	.20
71	Gray,Ted	.70	.50	.20
72	Yost,Eddie	.70	.50	.20
73	Mueller,Don	.70	.50	.20
74	Gilliam,Jim	2.50	1.70	.70
75	Surkont,Max	.70	.50	.20
76	Nuxhall,Joe	1.00	.65	.30
77	Roth,Bob	.70	.50	.20
78	Yvars,Sal	.70	.50	.20
79	Simmons,Curt	1.00	.65	.30
80	Logan,Johnny	.70	.50	.20
81	Coleman,Jerry	1.00	.65	.30
82	Goodman,Billy	.70	.50	.20
83	Murray,Ray	.70	.50	.20
84	Doby,Larry	1.75	1.15	.50
85	Dyck,Jim	.70	.50	.20
86	Dorish,Harry	.70	.50	.20
87	Lund,Don	.70	.50	.20
88	Umphlett,Tom	.70	.50	.20
89	Mays,Willie	60.00	40.00	15.00
90	Campanella,Roy	18.00	12.00	5.00
91	Abrams,Cal	.70	.50	.20
92	Raffensberger,Ken	.70	.50	.20
93	Serena,Bill	.70	.50	.20
94	Hemus,Solly	.70	.50	.20
95	Roberts,Robin	6.50	4.50	2.00
96	Adcock,Joe	1.00	.65	.30
97	McDougald,Gil	1.00	.65	.30
98	Kinder,Ellis	.70	.50	.20
99	Suder,Pete	.70	.50	.20
100	Garcia,Mike	1.00	.65	.30
101	Larsen,Don	1.75	1.15	.50
102	Pierce,Billy	1.35	.90	.40
103	Souchock,Steve	.70	.50	.20
104	Shea,Frank	.70	.50	.20
105	Maglie,Sal	1.00	.65	.30
106	Labine,Clem	.70	.50	.20
107	LaPalme,Paul	.70	.50	.20
108	Adams,Bobby	.70	.50	.20
109	Smalley,Roy	.70	.50	.20
110	Schoendienst,"Red"	1.75	1.15	.50
111	Dickson,Murry	.70	.50	.20
112	Pafko,Andy	.70	.50	.20
113	Reynolds,Allie	2.50	1.70	.70
114	Nixon,Willard	.70	.50	.20
115	Bollweg,Don	.70	.50	.20
116	Easter,Luke	1.00	.65	.30
117	Kryhoski,Dick	.70	.50	.20
118	Boyd,Bob	.70	.50	.20
119	Hatfield,Fred	.70	.50	.20
120	Hoderlein,Mel	.70	.50	.20
121	Katt,Ray	.70	.50	.20

	MINT	VG-E	F-G
122 Furillo,Carl	2.50	1.70	.70
123 Atwell,Toby	.70	.50	.20
124 Bell,Gus	.70	.50	.20
125 Hacker,Warren	.70	.50	.20
126 Chambers,Cliff	.70	.50	.20
127 Ennis,Del	1.00	.65	.30
128 St. Claire,Ebba	.70	.50	.20
129 Bauer,Hank	1.75	1.15	.50
130 Bolling,Milt	.90	.60	.25
131 Astroth,Joe	.90	.60	.25
132 Feller,Bob	12.50	8.50	3.50
133 Pillette,Duane	.90	.60	.25
134 Aloma,Luis	.90	.60	.25
135 Pesky,Johnny	.90	.60	.25
136 Vollmer,Clyde	.90	.60	.25
137 Corwin,Al	.90	.60	.25
138 Hodges,Gil	9.00	6.00	2.50
139 Ward,Preston	.90	.60	.25
140 Rogovin,Saul	.90	.60	.25
141 Garagiola,Joe	6.50	4.50	2.00
142 Brazle,Al	.90	.60	.25
143 Jones,Willie	.90	.60	.25
144 Johnson,Ernie	.90	.60	.25
145 Martin,Billy	6.50	4.50	2.00
146 Gernert,Dick	.90	.60	.25
147 DeMaestri,Joe	.90	.60	.25
148 Mitchell,Dale	.90	.60	.25
149 Young,Bob	.90	.60	.25
150 Michaels,Cass	.90	.60	.25
151 Mullin,Pat	.90	.60	.25
152 Vernon,Mickey	.90	.60	.25
153 Lockman,Whitey	.90	.60	.25
154 Newcombe,Don	2.50	1.70	.70
155 Thomas,Frank	.90	.60	.25
156 Bridges,Rocky	.90	.60	.25
157 Lown,"Turk"	.90	.60	.25
158 Miller,Stu	.90	.60	.25
159 Lindell,Johnny	.90	.60	.25
160 O'Connell,Danny	.90	.60	.25
161 Berra,"Yogi"	15.00	10.00	4.00
162 Lepcio,Ted	.90	.60	.25
163 Philley,Dave	.90	.60	.25
164 Wynn,Early	6.50	4.50	2.00
165 Groth,Johnny	.90	.60	.25
166 Consuegra,Sandy	.90	.60	.25
167 Hoeft,Billy	.90	.60	.25
168 Fitzgerald,Ed	.90	.60	.25
169 Jansen,Larry	.90	.60	.25
170 Snider,Duke	13.00	9.00	4.00
171 Bernier,Carlos	.90	.60	.25
172 Seminick,Andy	.90	.60	.25

	MINT	VG-E	F-G
173 Fondy,Dee	.90	.60	.25
174 Castiglione,Pete	.90	.60	.25
175 Clark,Mel	.90	.60	.25
176 Bickford,Vern	.90	.60	.25
177 Ford,"Whitey"	9.00	6.00	2.50
178 Wilber,Del	.90	.60	.25
179 Martin,Morris	.90	.60	.25
180 Tipton,Joe	.90	.60	.25
181 Moss,Les	.90	.60	.25
182 Lollar,Sherman	.90	.60	.25
183 Batts,Matt	.90	.60	.25
184 Grasso,Mickey	.90	.60	.25
185 Spencer,Daryl	.90	.60	.25
186 Meyer,Russ	.90	.60	.25
187 Law,Vernon	.90	.60	.25
188 Smith,Frank	.90	.60	.25
189 Jackson,Randy	.90	.60	.25
190 Presko,Joe	.90	.60	.25
191 Drews,Karl	.90	.60	.25
192 Burdette,Lou	1.35	.90	.40
193 Robinson,Eddie	.90	.60	.25
194 Hudson,Sid	.90	.60	.25
195 Cain,Bob	.90	.60	.25
196 Lemon,Bob	6.50	4.50	2.00
197 Kretlow,Lou	.90	.60	.25
198 Trucks,Virgil	.90	.60	.25
199 Gromek,Steve	.90	.60	.25
200 Marrero,Conrado	.90	.60	.25
201 Thomson,Bobby	2.50	1.70	.70
202 Shuba,George	.90	.60	.25
203 Janowicz,Vic	.90	.60	.25
204 Collum,Jackie	.90	.60	.25
205 Jeffcoat,Hal	.90	.60	.25
206 Bilko,Steve	.90	.60	.25
207 Lopata,Stan	.90	.60	.25
208 Antonelli,Johnny	.90	.60	.25
209 Woodling,Gene	1.35	.90	.40
210 Piersall,Jim	3.75	2.50	1.00
211 Robertson,Al	.90	.60	.25
212 Friend,Owen	.90	.60	.25
213 Littlefield,Dick	.90	.60	.25
214 Fain,Ferris	.90	.60	.25
215 Bucha,Johnny	.90	.60	.25
216 Snyder,Jerry	.90	.60	.25
217 Thompson,Henry	.90	.60	.25
218 Roe,"Preacher"	2.50	1.70	.70
219 Rice,Hal	.90	.60	.25
220 Landrith,Hobie	.90	.60	.25
221 Baumholtz,Frank	.90	.60	.25
222 Luna,Memo	.90	.60	.25
223 Ridzik,Steve	.90	.60	.25
224 Bruton,Bill	1.75	1.15	.50

1955 BOWMAN (320) 2 1/2" X 3 3/4"

The 1955 Bowman set, also known as "the Television set" because all the players are portrayed within a T.V. border, includes the first cards of umpires in a major set. High numbers 225—320 are more difficult to obtain than the lower numbers. Card nos. 48 Milt Bolling and 204 Frank Bolling exist with each others backs, as do card nos. 101 Don Johnson and 157 Ernie Johnson. Card no. 132 Harvey Kuenn exsists with the name spelled correctly and also incorrectly spelled "Kueen".

	MINT	VG-E	F-G
°LETE SET	400.00	275.00	100.00
¹ON PLAYER(1-96)	.50	.35	.12
¹ON PLAYER(97-224)	.40	.26	.10
¹ON PLAYER(225-320)	1.65	1.10	.45
Wilhelm,Hoyt	7.00	2.00	.80
Dark,Alvin	.60	.40	.15
Coleman,Joe	.50	.35	.12
Waitkus,Eddie	.50	.35	.12
Robertson,Jim	.50	.35	.12
Suder,Pete	.50	.35	.12

	MINT	VG-E	F-G
7 Baker,Gene	.50	.35	.12
8 Hacker,Warren	.50	.35	.12
9 McDougald,Gil	.50	.35	.12
10 Rizzuto,Phil	.50	.35	.12
11 Bruton,Billy	.50	.35	.12
12 Pafko,Andy	.50	.35	.12
13 Vollmer,Clyde	.50	.35	.12
14 Keriazakos,Gus	.50	.35	.12
15 Sullivan,Frank	.50	.35	.12
16 Piersall,Jim	.90	.60	.25

	MINT	VG-E	F-G
17 Ennis,Del	.50	.35	.12
18 Lopata,Stan	.50	.35	.12
19 Avila,Bobby	.50	.35	.12
20 Smith,Al	.50	.35	.12
21 Hoak,Don	.50	.35	.12
22 Campanella,Roy	11.00	7.00	3.00
23 Kaline,Al	9.00	6.00	2.50
24 Aber,Al	.50	.35	.12
25 Minoso,Minnie	1.75	1.15	.50
26 Trucks,Virgil	.50	.35	.12
27 Ward,Preston	.50	.35	.12
28 Cole,Dick	.50	.35	.12
29 Schoendienst,Red	.90	.60	.25
30 Sarni,Bill	.50	.35	.12
31 Temple,Johnny	.50	.35	.12
32 Post,Wally	.50	.35	.12
33 Fox,Nelson	1.75	1.15	.50
34 Courtney,Clint	.50	.35	.12
35 Tuttle,Bill	.50	.35	.12
36 Belardi,Wayne	.50	.35	.12
37 Reese,Peewee	6.50	4.50	2.00
38 Wynn,Early	5.00	3.50	1.40
39 Darnell,Bob	.50	.35	.12
40 Wertz,Vic	.50	.35	.12
41 Clark,Mel	.50	.35	.12
42 Greenwood,Bob	.50	.35	.12
43 Buhl,Bob	.50	.35	.12
44 O'Connell,Danny	.50	.35	.12
45 Umphlett,Tom	.50	.35	.12
46 Vernon,Mickey	.60	.40	.15
47 White,Sammy	.50	.35	.12
48A Bolling,Milt (corr)	2.75	1.75	.75
48B Bolling,Milt (error)	.90	.60	.25
49 Greengrass,Jim	.50	.35	.12
50 Landrith,Hobie	.50	.35	.12
51 Tappe,Elvin	.50	.35	.12
52 Rice,Hal	.50	.35	.12
53 Kellner,Alex	.50	.35	.12
54 Bollweg,Don	.50	.35	.12
55 Abrams,Cal	.50	.35	.12
56 Cox,Billy	.50	.35	.12
57 Friend,Bob	.60	.40	.15
58 Thomas,Frank	.50	.35	.12
59 Ford,Whitey	6.50	4.50	2.00
60 Slaughter,Enos	2.75	1.75	.75
61 LaPalme,Paul	.50	.35	.12
62 Lint,Royce	.50	.35	.12
63 Noren,Irv	.50	.35	.12
64 Simmons,Curt	.60	.40	.15
65 Zimmer,Don	.90	.60	.25
66 Shuba,George	.50	.35	.12
67 Larsen,Don	1.75	1.15	.50
68 Howard,Elston	1.75	1.15	.50
69 Hunter,Bill	.50	.35	.12
70 Burdette,Lou	.90	.60	.25
71 Jolly,Dave	.50	.35	.12
72 Nichols,Chet	.50	.35	.12
73 Yost,Eddie	.50	.35	.12
74 Snyder,Jerry	.50	.35	.12
75 Lawrence,Brooks	.50	.35	.12
76 Poholsky,Tom	.50	.35	.12
77 McDonald,Jim	.50	.35	.12
78 Coan,Gil	.50	.35	.12
79 Miranda,Willie	.50	.35	.12
80 Limmer,Lou	.50	.35	.12
81 Morgan,Bob	.50	.35	.12
82 Walls,Lee	.50	.35	.12
83 Surkont,Max	.50	.35	.12
84 Freese,George	.50	.35	.12
85 Michaels,Cass	.50	.35	.12
86 Gray,Ted	.50	.35	.12
87 Jackson,Randy	.50	.35	.12
88 Bilko,Steve	.50	.35	.12
89 Boudreau,Lou	5.00	3.50	1.40
90 Dittmar,Art	.50	.35	.12
91 Marlowe,Dick	.50	.35	.12
92 Zuverink,George	.50	.35	.12
93 Seminick,Andy	.50	.35	.12
94 Thompson,Hank	.60	.40	.15
95 Maglie,Sal	.60	.40	.15
96 Narleski,Ray	.50	.35	.12
97 Podres,Johnny	.90	.60	.25
98 Gilliam,Jim	1.75	1.15	.50
99 Coleman,Jerry	.60	.40	.15
100 Morgan,Tom	.40	.26	.10
101A Johnson,Don (corr)	2.75	1.75	.75
101B Johnson,Don (error)	.90	.60	.25
102 Thomson,Bobby	1.75	1.15	.50
103 Mathews,Eddie	5.00	3.50	1.40
104 Porterfield,Bob	.40	.26	.10
105 Schmitz,Johnny	.40	.26	.10

	MINT	VG-E	F-G
106 Rice,Del	.40	.26	.10
107 Hemus,Solly	.40	.26	.10
108 Kretlow,Lou	.40	.26	.10
109 Stephens,Vern	.40	.26	.10
110 Miller,Bob	.40	.26	.10
111 Ridzik,Steve	.40	.26	.10
112 Hamner,Granny	.40	.26	.10
113 Hall,Bob	.40	.26	.10
114 Janowicz,Vic	.40	.26	.10
115 Bowman,Roger	.40	.26	.10
116 Consuegra,Sandy	.40	.26	.10
117 Groth,Johnny	.40	.26	.10
118 Adams,Bobby	.40	.26	.10
119 Astroth,Joe	.40	.26	.10
120 Burtschy,Ed	.40	.26	.10
121 Crawford,Rufus	.40	.26	.10
122 Corwin,Al	.40	.26	.10
123 Grissom,Marv	.40	.26	.10
124 Antonelli,Johnny	.60	.40	.15
125 Giel,Paul	.40	.26	.10
126 Goodman,Billy	.40	.26	.10
127 Majeski,Hank	.40	.26	.10
128 Garcia,Mike	.60	.40	.15
129 Naragon,Hal	.40	.26	.10
130 Ashburn,Richie	1.75	1.15	.50
131 Marshall,Willard	.40	.26	.10
132A Kuenn,Harvey (corr)	2.75	1.75	.75
132B Kuenn,Harvey (error)	.90	.60	.25
133 King,Charles	.40	.26	.10
134 Feller,Bob	9.00	6.00	2.50
135 Merriman,Lloyd	.40	.26	.10
136 Bridges,Rocky	.40	.26	.10
137 Talbot,Bob	.40	.26	.10
138 Williams,Davey	.40	.26	.10
139 Shantz Brothers	.90	.60	.25
140 Shantz,Bobby	.60	.40	.15
141 Westrum,Wes	.40	.26	.10
142 Regalado,Rudy	.40	.26	.10
143 Newcombe,Don	1.75	1.15	.50
144 Houtteman,Art	.40	.26	.10
145 Nieman,Bob	.40	.26	.10
146 Liddle,Don	.40	.26	.10
147 Mele,Sam	.40	.26	.10
148 Chakales,Bob	.40	.26	.10
149 Boyer,Cloyd	.40	.26	.10
150 Klaus,Bill	.40	.26	.10
151 Bridewser,Jim	.40	.26	.10
152 Klippstein,Johnny	.40	.26	.10
153 Robinson,Eddie	.40	.26	.10
154 Lary,Frank	.40	.26	.10
155 Staley,Gerry	.40	.26	.10
156 Hughes,Jim	.40	.26	.10
157A Johnson,Ernie (corr)	2.75	1.75	.75
157B Johnson,Ernie (error)	.90	.60	.25
158 Hodges,Gil	5.00	3.50	1.40
159 Byrd,Harry	.40	.26	.10
160 Skowron,Bill	.90	.60	.25
161 Batts,Matt	.40	.26	.10
162 Maxwell,Charlie	.40	.26	.10
163 Gordon,Sid	.40	.26	.10
164 Atwell,Toby	.40	.26	.10
165 McDermott,Maurice	.40	.26	.10
166 Busby,Jim	.40	.26	.10
167 Grim,Bob	.40	.26	.10
168 Berra,Yogi	9.00	6.00	2.50
169 Furillo,Carl	1.75	1.15	.50
170 Erskine,Carl	.90	.60	.25
171 Roberts,Robin	5.00	3.50	1.40
172 Jones,Willie	.40	.26	.10
173 Carrasquel,Chico	.40	.26	.10
174 Lollar,Sherman	.40	.26	.10
175 Shantz,Wilmer	.40	.26	.10
176 DeMaestri,Joe	.40	.26	.10
177 Nixon,Willard	.40	.26	.10
178 Brewer,Tom	.40	.26	.10
179 Aaron,Hank	24.00	16.00	7.00
180 Logan,Johnny	.40	.26	.10
181 Miksis,Eddie	.40	.26	.10
182 Rush,Bob	.40	.26	.10
183 Katt,Ray	.40	.26	.10
184 Mays,Willie	24.00	16.00	7.00
185 Raschi,Vic	.90	.60	.25
186 Grammas,Alex	.40	.26	.10
187 Hatfield,Fred	.40	.26	.10
188 Garver,Ned	.40	.26	.10
189 Collum,Jack	.40	.26	.10
190 Baczewski,Fred	.40	.26	.10
191 Lemon,Bob	5.00	3.50	1.40
192 Strickland,George	.40	.26	.10
193 Judson,Howie	.40	.26	.10

	MINT	VG-E	F-G
94 Nuxhall,Joe	.60	.40	.15
95A Palica,Erv (w/tr)	2.75	1.75	.75
95B Palica,Erv (w/o tr)	.60	.40	.15
96 Meyer,Russ	.40	.26	.10
97 Kiner,Ralph	5.00	3.50	1.40
98 Pope,Dave	.40	.26	.10
99 Law,Vernon	.60	.40	.15
00 Littlefield,Dick	.40	.26	.10
01 Reynolds,Allie	1.75	1.15	.50
02 Mantle,Mickey	30.00	20.00	8.00
03 Gromek,Steve	.40	.26	.10
04A Bolling,Frank (corr)	2.75	1.75	.75
04B Bolling,Frank (error)	.90	.60	.25
05 Repulski,Rip	.40	.26	.10
06 Beard,Ralph	.40	.26	.10
07 Shea,Frank	.40	.26	.10
08 Fitzgerald,Eddy	.40	.26	.10
09 Burgess,Smokey	.40	.26	.10
10 Torgeson,Earl	.40	.26	.10
11 Dixon,Sonny	.40	.26	.10
12 Dittmer,Jack	.40	.26	.10
13 Kell,George	.90	.60	.25
14 Pierce,Billy	.90	.60	.25
15 Kuzava,Bob	.40	.26	.10
16 Roe,Preacher	.90	.60	.25
17 Crandall,Del	.60	.40	.15
18 Adcock,Joe	.60	.40	.15
19 Lockman,Whitey	.40	.26	.10
20 Hearn,Jim	.40	.26	.10
21 Brown,Hector	.40	.26	.10
22 Kemmerer,Russ	.40	.26	.10
23 Jeffcoat,Hal	.40	.26	.10
24 Fondy,Dee	.40	.26	.10
25 Richards,Paul	2.75	1.75	.75
26 McKinley,W. (UMP)	2.75	1.75	.75
27 Baumholtz,Frank	1.65	1.10	.45
28 Phillips,John	1.65	1.10	.45
29 Brosnan,Jim	2.75	1.75	.75
30 Brazle,Al	1.65	1.10	.45
31 Konstanty,Jim	2.75	1.75	.75
32 Tebbetts,Birdie	1.75	1.15	.50
33 Serena,Bill	1.65	1.10	.45
34 Bartell,Dick	1.65	1.10	.45
35 Paparella,J.(UMP)	2.75	1.75	.75
36 Dickson,Murry	1.65	1.10	.45
37 Wyrostek,Johnny	1.65	1.10	.45
38 Stanky,Eddie	2.75	1.75	.75
39 Rommel,Edwin(UMP)	2.75	1.75	.75
40 Loes,Billy	1.75	1.15	.50
41 Pesky,Johnny	2.75	1.75	.75
42 Banks,Ernie	45.00	30.00	12.00
43 Bell,Gus	1.75	1.15	.50
44 Pillette,Duane	1.65	1.10	.45
45 Miller,Bill	1.65	1.10	.45
46 Bauer,Hank	5.00	3.50	1.40
47 Leonard,Dutch	1.65	1.10	.45
48 Dorish,Harry	1.65	1.10	.45
49 Gardner,Billy	1.65	1.10	.45
50 Napp,Larry(UMP)	2.75	1.75	.75
51 Jok,Stan	1.65	1.10	.45
52 Smalley,Roy	1.65	1.10	.45
53 Wilson,Jim	1.65	1.10	.45
54 Flowers,Bennett	1.65	1.10	.45
55 Runnels,Pete	1.65	1.10	.45
56 Friend,Owen	1.65	1.10	.45
57 Alston,Tom	1.65	1.10	.45
58 Stevens,John(UMP)	2.75	1.75	.75
59 Mossi,Don	1.65	1.10	.45

	MINT	VG-E	F-G
260 Hurley,Edwin(UMP)	2.75	1.75	.75
261 Moryn,Walt	1.65	1.10	.45
262 Lemon,Jim	1.65	1.10	.45
263 Joost,Eddie	1.65	1.10	.45
264 Henry,Bill	1.65	1.10	.45
265 Barlick,Albert (UMP)	2.75	1.75	.75
266 Fornieles,Mike	1.65	1.10	.45
267 Honochick,George (UMP)	2.75	1.75	.75
268 Hawes,Roy Lee	1.65	1.10	.45
269 Amalfitano,Joe	1.65	1.10	.45
270 Fernandez,Chico	1.65	1.10	.45
271 Hooper,Bob	1.65	1.10	.45
272 Flaherty,John(UMP)	2.75	1.75	.75
273 Church,Bubba	1.65	1.10	.45
274 Delsing,Jim	1.65	1.10	.45
275 Grieve,William (UMP)	2.75	1.75	.75
276 Delock,Ike	1.65	1.10	.45
277 Runge,Ed(UMP)	2.75	1.75	.75
278 Neal,Charles	1.75	1.15	.50
279 Soar,Hank(UMP)	2.75	1.75	.75
280 McCullough,Clyde	1.65	1.10	.45
281 Berry,Charles(UMP)	2.75	1.75	.75
282 Cavaretta,Phil	2.75	1.75	.75
283 Chylak,Nestor(UMP)	2.75	1.75	.75
284 Jackowski,Bill(UMP	2.75	1.75	.75
285 Dropo,Walt	1.75	1.15	.50
286 Secory,Frank(UMP)	2.75	1.75	.75
287 Mrozinski,Ron	1.65	1.10	.45
288 Smith,Dick	1.65	1.10	.45
289 Gore,Arthur(UMP)	2.75	1.75	.75
290 Freeman,Hershell	1.65	1.10	.45
291 Dascoli,Frank(UMP)	2.75	1.75	.75
292 Blaylock,Marv	1.65	1.10	.45
293 Gorman,Thomas(UMP)	2.75	1.75	.75
294 Moses,Wally	1.75	1.15	.50
295 Ballanfort,Lee (UMP)	2.75	1.75	.75
296 Virdon,Bill	6.50	4.50	2.00
297 Boggess,Dusty(UMP)	2.75	1.75	.75
298 Grimm,Charlie	1.75	1.15	.50
299 Warneke,Lon(UMP)	2.75	1.75	.75
300 Byrne,Tommy	1.65	1.10	.45
301 Engeln,William (UMP)	2.75	1.75	.75
302 Malzone,Frank	1.75	1.15	.50
303 Conlan,Jocko(UMP)	6.50	4.50	2.00
304 Chiti,Harry	1.65	1.10	.45
305 Umont,Frank(UMP)	2.75	1.75	.75
306 Cerv,Bob	1.75	1.15	.50
307 Pinelli,Babe(UMP)	2.75	1.75	.75
308 Lopez,Al	6.50	4.50	2.00
309 Dixon,Hal(UMP)	2.75	1.75	.75
310 Lehman,Ken	1.65	1.10	.45
311 Goetz,Lawrence (UMP)	2.75	1.75	.75
312 Wight,Bill	1.65	1.10	.45
313 Donatelli,A.(UMP)	5.00	3.50	1.40
314 Mitchell,Dale	1.65	1.10	.45
315 Hubbard,Cal(UMP)	6.50	4.50	2.00
316 Fricano,Marion	1.65	1.10	.45
317 Summers,William (UMP)	2.75	1.75	.75
318 Hudson,Sid	1.65	1.10	.45
319 Schroll,Albert	1.65	1.10	.45
320 Susce,George Jr.	1.75	1.15	.50

1953-54 BRIGGS (37)

ERWIN PORTERFIELD, Pitcher
Born August 10, 1924, at Newport, Va.
THROWS RIGHT — BATS RIGHT

HANK BAUER

2 1/4" X 3 1/2"

The 1953-54 Briggs hot dog set of 37 full color, blank backed, unnumbered cards was issued in the Washington, D.C., area only. Twenty-five of the cards contain Washington Senator players while the other 12 cards portray players from the three New York teams. The poses are similar to those used in the Dan Dee Potato Chips issue. The ACC designation is F154.

	MINT	VG-E	F-G
COMPLETE SET	3300.00	2200.00	900.00
COMMON PLAYERS (W)	65.00	45.00	20.00
COMMON PLAYERS (NY)	75.00	50.00	20.00
W 1 Jim Busby	65.00	45.00	20.00
W 2 Tommy Bryne	65.00	45.00	20.00
W 3 Sonny Dixon	65.00	45.00	20.00
W 4 Ed Fitzgerald	65.00	45.00	20.00
W 5 Mickey Grasso	65.00	45.00	20.00
W 6 Mel Hoderlein	65.00	45.00	20.00
W 7 Jackie Jensen	90.00	60.00	25.00
W 8 Connie Marrero	65.00	45.00	20.00
W 9 Carmen Mauro	75.00	50.00	20.00
W10 Walt Masterson	65.00	45.00	20.00
W11 Mickey McDermott	65.00	45.00	20.00
W12 Bob Oldis	65.00	45.00	20.00
W13 Bob Porterfield	65.00	45.00	20.00
W14 Pete Runnels	75.00	50.00	20.00
W15 Johnny Schmitz	65.00	45.00	20.00
W16 Angel Scull	65.00	45.00	20.00
W17 Spec Shea	65.00	45.00	20.00

	MINT	VG-E	F-G
W18 Chuck Stobbs	65.00	45.00	20.00
W19 Wayne Terwilliger	65.00	45.00	20.00
W20 Joe Tipton	65.00	45.00	20.00
W21 Tom Umphlett	65.00	45.00	20.00
W22 Mickey Vernon	90.00	60.00	25.00
W23 Clyde Vollmer	65.00	45.00	20.00
W24 Gene Werbil	90.00	60.00	25.00
W25 Eddie Yost	75.00	50.00	20.00
NY 1 Hank Bauer	90.00	60.00	25.00
NY 2 Carl Erskine	90.00	60.00	25.00
NY 3 Gil Hodges	135.00	90.00	40.00
NY 4 Monte Irvin	120.00	80.00	35.00
NY 5 Whitey Lockman	75.00	50.00	20.00
NY 6 Mickey Mantle	650.00	450.00	200.00
NY 7 Willie Mays	500.00	350.00	140.00
NY 8 Gil McDougald	90.00	60.00	25.00
NY 9 Don Mueller	75.00	50.00	20.00
NY10 Don Newcombe	100.00	65.00	30.00
NY11 Phil Rizzuto	135.00	90.00	40.00
NY12 Duke Snider	200.00	130.00	55.00

1977 BURGER KING YANKEES (24)   2 1/2" X 3 1/2"

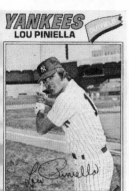

The cards in this set marked with an asterisk have different poses than those cards in the regular Topps set. The checklist card is unnumbered and the Piniella card was issued subsequent to the original printing.

	MINT	VG-E	F-G
COMPLETE SET	19.00	13.00	5.00
COMMON PLAYER(1-24)	.25	.17	.07

	MINT	VG-E	F-G
1 Team - Martin	.50	.35	.15
2 Munson,Thurman*	1.50	1.00	.40
3 Healy,Fran	.25	.17	.07
4 Hunter,Jim	.50	.35	.15
5 Figueroa,Ed	.25	.17	.07
6 Gullett,Don*	.35	.24	.10
7 Torrez,Mike*	.50	.35	.15
8 Holtzman,Ken	.35	.24	.10
9 Tidrow,Dick	.25	.17	.07
10 Lyle,Sparky	.35	.24	.10
11 Guidry,Ron	.75	.50	.20
12 Chambliss,Chris	.35	.24	.10

	MINT	VG-E	F-G
13 Randolph,Willie*	.50	.35	.15
14 Dent,Bucky*	.50	.35	.15
15 Nettles,Graig*	.50	.35	.15
16 Stanley,Fred	.25	.17	.07
17 Jackson,Reggie	1.50	1.00	.40
18 Rivers,Mickey	.35	.24	.10
19 White,Roy	.35	.24	.10
20 Wynn,Jim*	.35	.24	.10
21 Blair,Paul*	.35	.24	.10
22 May,Carlos	.25	.17	.07
23 Piniella,Lou	12.00	8.00	3.00
Checklist	.05	.03	.01

1978 BURGER KING ASTROS (23)   2 1/2" X 3 1/2"

J. R. RICHARD

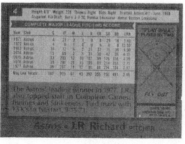

Released in local Burger King outlets during the 1978 season, this Astros series contains the standard 22 numbered player cards and one un-numbered checklist. The player poses found to differ from the regular Topps issue are marked with astericks.

	MINT	VG-E	F-G
COMPLETE SET	6.50	4.50	2.00
COMMON PLAYER(1-23)	.25	.17	.07

	MINT	VG-E	F-G
1 Virdon,Bill	.35	.24	.10
2 Ferguson,Joe	.25	.17	.07
3 Herrman,Ed	.25	.17	.07
4 Richard,J. R.	.60	.40	.15
5 Niekro,Joe	.35	.24	.10
6 Bannister,Floyd	.25	.17	.07
7 Andujar,Joaquin	.25	.17	.07
8 Forsch,Ken	.25	.17	.07
9 Lemongello,Mark	.25	.17	.07
10 Sambito,Joe	.35	.24	.10
11 Pentz,Gene	.25	.17	.07

	MINT	VG-E	F-G
12 Watson,Bob	.35	.24	.10
13 Gonzales,Julio	.25	.17	.07
14 Cabell,Enos	.25	.17	.07
15 Metzger,Roger	.25	.17	.07
16 Howe,Art	.25	.17	.07
17 Cruz,Jose	.35	.24	.10
18 Cedeno,Cesar	.60	.40	.15
19 Puhl,Terry	.35	.24	.10
20 Howard,Wilbur	.25	.17	.07
21 Bergman,Dave*	.35	.24	.10
22 Alou,Jesus*	.35	.24	.10
Checklist	.03	.02	.01

1978 BURGER KING RANGERS (23)   2 1/2" X 3 1/2"

BUMP WILLS

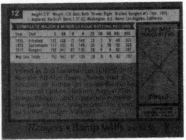

This set of 22 numb
player cards and one
numbered checklist was
sued regionally by B
King in 1978. Astericks
note poses different
those found in the re
Topps cards of this

	MINT	VG-E	F-G
COMPLETE SET	7.00	4.75	2.00
COMMON PLAYER(1-23)	.25	.17	.07
1 Hunter,Billy	.35	.24	.10
2 Sundberg,Jim	.50	.35	.15
3 Ellis,John	.25	.17	.07
4 Alexander,Doyle	.25	.17	.07
5 Matlack,Jon	.35	.24	.10
6 Ellis,Doc	.25	.17	.07
7 Medich,Doc	.35	.24	.10
8 Jenkins,Ferguson	.50	.35	.15
9 Barker,Len	.35	.24	.10
10 Cleveland,Reggie	.25	.17	.07
11 Hargrove,Mike	.35	.24	.10

	MINT	VG-E	F-G
12 Wills,Bump	.35	.24	.10
13 Harrah,Toby	.35	.24	.10
14 Campaneris,Bert	.35	.24	.10
15 Alomar,Sandy	.25	.17	.07
16 Bevacqua,Kurt	.25	.17	.07
17 Oliver,Al	.50	.35	.15
18 Beniquez,Juan	.25	.17	.07
19 Washington,Claudel	.25	.17	.07
20 Zisk,Richie	.50	.35	.15
21 Lowenstein,John	.25	.17	.07
22 Thompson,Bobby	.25	.17	.07
Checklist	.03	.02	.01

1978 BURGER KING TIGERS (23)   2 1/2" X 3 1/2"

RUSTY STAUB

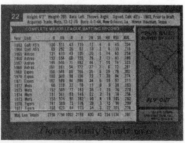

Twenty-three color car
players and one num
checklist—comprise the
Burger King Tigers set
in the Detroit area. The
marked with an asterisk
tain photos different
those appearing on the
regular issue cards of
year.

	MINT	VG-E	F-G
COMPLETE SET	7.00	4.75	2.00
COMMON PLAYER(1-23)	.25	.17	.07
1 Houk,Ralph	.35	.24	.10
2 May,Milt	.25	.17	.07
3 Wockenfuss,John	.25	.17	.07
4 Fidrych,Mark	.50	.35	.15
5 Rozema,Dave	.25	.17	.07
6 Billingham,Jack*	.35	.24	.10
7 Slaton,Jim*	.35	.24	.10
8 Morris,Jack	.35	.24	.10
9 Hiller,John	.35	.24	.10
10 Foucault,Steve	.25	.17	.07
11 Wilcox,Milt	.25	.17	.07

	MINT	VG-E	F-G
12 Thompson,Jason	.35	.24	.10
13 Whitaker,Lou	.35	.24	.10
14 Rodriquez,Aurelio	.25	.17	.07
15 Trammel,Alan*	.50	.35	.15
16 Dillard,Steve	.25	.17	.07
17 Mankowski,Phil	.25	.17	.07
18 Kemp,Steve	.50	.35	.15
19 LeFlore,Ron	.50	.35	.15
20 Corcoran,Tim	.25	.17	.07
21 Stanley,Mickey	.35	.24	.10
22 Staub,Rusty	.35	.24	.10
Checklist	.03	.02	.01

1978 BURGER KING YANKEES (23)   2 1/2" X 3 1/2"

CLIFF JOHNSON

These cards were distributed in packs of three players plus a checklist at Burger King's New York area outlets. Cards with an asterisk have different poses than those in the Topps regular issue.

	MINT	VG-E	F-G
COMPLETE SET	5.25	3.50	1.50
COMMON PLAYER(1-23)	.21	.14	.06
1 Martin,Billy	.40	.26	.10
2 Munson,Thurman	.80	.55	.20
3 Johnson,Cliff	.21	.14	.06
4 Guidry,Ron	.40	.26	.10
5 Figueroa,Ed	.21	.14	.06
6 Tidrow,Dick	.21	.14	.06
7 Hunter,Jim	.40	.26	.10
8 Gullett,Don	.21	.14	.06
9 Lyle,Sparky	.30	.20	.08
10 Gossage,Rich*	.40	.26	.10
11 Eastwick,Rawly*	.30	.20	.08

	MINT	VG-E	F-G
12 Chambliss,Chris	.30	.20	.08
13 Randolph,Willie	.30	.20	.08
14 Nettles,Graig	.30	.20	.08
15 Dent,Bucky	.30	.20	.08
16 Spencer,Jim*	.30	.20	.08
17 Stanley,Fred	.21	.14	.06
18 Piniella,Lou	.30	.20	.08
19 White,Roy	.30	.20	.08
20 Rivers,Mickey	.30	.20	.08
21 Jackson,Reggie	.80	.55	.20
22 Blair,Paul	.21	.14	.06
Checklist card	.03	.02	.01

1979 BURGER KING PHILLIES (23)   2 1/2" X 3 1/2"

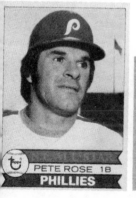

PETE ROSE 1B
PHILLIES

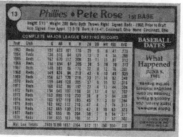

The 1979 Burger King Phillies set follows the regular format of 22 player cards and one unnumbered checklist card. The asterick indicates where the pose differs from the Topps card of that year.

	MINT	VG-E	F-G
COMPLETE SET	5.25	3.50	1.50
COMMON PLAYER(1-23)	.21	.14	.06
1 Ozark,Danny*	.30	.20	.08
2 Boone,Bob	.30	.20	.08
3 McCarver,Tim	.21	.14	.06
4 Carlton,Steve	.40	.26	.10
5 Christenson,Larry	.21	.14	.06
6 Ruthven,Dick	.21	.14	.06
7 Reed,Ron	.21	.14	.06
8 Lerch,Randy	.21	.14	.06
9 Brusstar,Warren	.21	.14	.06
10 McGraw,Tug	.30	.20	.08
11 Espinosa,Nino*	.30	.20	.08

	MINT	VG-E	F-G
12 Bird,Doug*	.30	.20	.08
13 Rose,Pete*	1.00	.65	.30
14 Trillo,Manny*	.30	.20	.08
15 Bowa,Larry	.40	.26	.10
16 Schmidt,Mike	.75	.50	.20
17 Mackanin,Pete*	.30	.20	.08
18 Cardenal,Jose	.21	.14	.06
19 Luzinski,Greg	.40	.26	.10
20 Maddox,Garry	.30	.20	.08
21 McBride,Bake	.30	.20	.08
22 Gross,Greg*	.30	.20	.08
Checklist	.03	.02	.01

1979 BURGER KING YANKEES (23)   2 1/2" X 3 1/2"

There are 22 numbered and one unnumbered c[..] list in the 1979 Burger Yankee set. The pose[..] Guidry, Tiant, John and [..] iquez, marked with a[..] terisk below, are dif[..] from those poses appe[..] in the regular topps [..] The team card has a p[..] of Lemon rather than M[..]

	MINT	VG-E	F-G
COMPLETE SET	5.25	3.50	1.50
COMMON PLAYER(1-23)	.21	.14	.06

	MINT	VG-E	F-G
1 Team Card - Lemon*	.40	.26	.10
2 Munson,Thurman	.75	.50	.20
3 Johnson,Cliff	.21	.14	.06
4 Guidry,Ron*	.40	.26	.10
5 Johnstone,Jay	.21	.14	.06
6 Hunter,Jim	.30	.20	.08
7 Beattie,Jim	.21	.14	.06
8 Tiant,Luis*	.30	.20	.08
9 John,Tommy*	.40	.26	.10
10 Gossage,Rich	.30	.20	.08
11 Figueroa,Ed	.21	.14	.06

	MINT	VG-E	F-G
12 Chambliss,Chris	.30	.20	.08
13 Randolph,Willie	.30	.20	.08
14 Dent,Bucky	.30	.20	.08
15 Nettles,Graig	.30	.20	.08
16 Stanley,Fred	.21	.14	.06
17 Spencer,Jim	.21	.14	.06
18 Piniella,Lou	.30	.20	.08
19 White,Roy	.30	.20	.08
20 Rivers,Mickey	.30	.20	.08
21 Jackson,Reggie	.75	.50	.20
22 Beniquez,Juan*	.30	.20	.08
Checklist	.03	.02	.01

1980 BURGER KING PHILLIES (23)   2 1/2" X 3 1/2"

The 1980 edition of B[..] King Phillies followed [..] established pattern o[..] numbered player cards [..] one unnumbered che[..] Cards marked with ast[..] contain poses different [..] those found in regular [..] Topps cards.

	MINT	VG-E	F-G
COMPLETE SET	3.75	2.50	1.00
COMMON PLAYER(1-23)	.15	.10	.04

	MINT	VG-E	F-G
1 Dallas Green	.25	.17	.07
2 Boone,Bob	.25	.17	.07
3 Moreland,Keith	.15	.10	.04
4 Rose,Pete	.75	.50	.20
5 Trillo,Manny	.25	.17	.07
6 Schmidt,Mike	.50	.35	.15
7 Bowa,Larry	.35	.24	.10
8 Vukovich,John	.15	.10	.04
9 McBride,Bake	.25	.17	.07
10 Maddox,Garry	.25	.17	.07
11 Luzinski,Greg	.35	.24	.10

	MINT	VG-E	F-G
12 Gross,Greg	.15	.10	.04
13 Unser,Del	.15	.10	.04
14 Smith,Lonnie	.15	.10	.04
15 Carlton,Steve	.50	.35	.15
16 Christenson,Larry	.15	.10	.04
17 Espinosa,Nino	.15	.10	.04
18 Lerch,Randy	.15	.10	.04
19 Ruthven,Dick	.15	.10	.04
20 McGraw,Tug	.25	.17	.07
21 Reed,Ron	.15	.10	.04
22 Saucier,Kevin	.15	.10	.04
Checklist	.03	.02	.01

1980 BURGER KING (34)
PITCH, HIT & RUN

2 1/2" X 3 1/2"

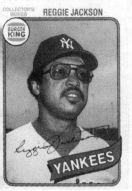

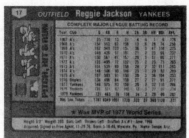

This Baltimore-area giveaway set was called "Pitch, Hit and Run," and featured a Burger King logo on the front. Those cards marked with an asterisk denote a different pose than found in the Topps regular issue. The unnumbered checklist card was given away with each group of three ballplayers, thus accounting for its wide availability with respect to the other cards.

	MINT	VG-E	F-G
COMPLETE SET	7.50	5.00	2.00
COMMON PLAYER(1-34)	.21	.14	.06
1 Blue,Vida*	.30	.20	.08
2 Carlton,Steve	.40	.26	.10
3 Fingers,Rollie	.30	.20	.08
4 Guidry,Ron*	.40	.26	.10
5 Koosman,Jerry*	.30	.20	.08
6 Niekro,Phil	.30	.20	.08
7 Palmer,Jim*	.40	.26	.10
8 Richard,J. R.	.30	.20	.08
9 Ryan,Nolan*	.40	.26	.10
10 Seaver,Tom*	.50	.35	.15
11 Sutter,Bruce	.30	.20	.08
12 Baylor,Don	.30	.20	.08
13 Brett,George	.75	.50	.20
14 Carew,Rod	.50	.35	.15
15 Foster,George	.40	.26	.10
16 Hernandez,Keith*	.40	.26	.10

	MINT	VG-E	F-G
17 Jackson,Reggie*	.50	.35	.15
18 Lynn,Fred*	.50	.35	.15
19 Parker,Dave	.40	.26	.10
20 Rice,Jim	.40	.26	.10
21 Rose,Pete	.75	.50	.20
22 Winfield,Dave*	.50	.35	.15
23 Bonds,Bobby*	.30	.20	.08
24 Cabell,Enos	.21	.14	.06
25 Cedeno,Cesar	.30	.20	.08
26 Cruz,Julio	.21	.14	.06
27 LeFlore,Ron*	.30	.20	.08
28 Lopes,Dave*.	.30	.20	.08
29 Moreno,Omar*	.30	.20	.08
30 Morgan,Joe*	.30	.20	.08
31 North,Bill	.21	.14	.06
32 Taveras,Frank	.21	.14	.06
33 Wilson,Willie	.30	.20	.08
Checklist	.03	.02	.01

1933 R306 BUTTER CREAM (29)

1 1/4" X 3 1/2"

The small, elongated cards of this set are unnumbered and highly valued by collectors. They are black & white in color and are found with or without the producer's name printed on the reverse. The ACC stated 25 to be the number of cards in the set, but new additions have pushed the known total to 29.

	MINT	VG-E	F-G
COMPLETE SET	2500.00	1700.00	700.00
COMMON PLAYER(1-29)	75.00	50.00	20.00
1 Averill,Earl	100.00	65.00	30.00
2 Brandt,Ed	75.00	50.00	20.00
3 Bush,Guy T.	75.00	50.00	20.00
4 Cochrane,Gordon	135.00	90.00	40.00
5 Cronin,Joe	135.00	90.00	40.00
6 Earnshaw,George	75.00	50.00	20.00
7 Ferrell,Wesley	75.00	50.00	20.00
8 Foxx,Jimmy E.	200.00	130.00	55.00
9 Frisch,Frank C.	135.00	90.00	40.00
10 Gelbert,Charles M.	75.00	50.00	20.00
11 Grove,"Lefty"	165.00	110.00	50.00
12 Hartnett,Leo	135.00	90.00	40.00
13 Herman,"Babe"	75.00	50.00	20.00

	MINT	VG-E	F-G
14 Klein,Charles	135.00	90.00	40.00
15 Kremer,Ray	75.00	50.00	20.00
16 Lindstrom,Fred C.	135.00	90.00	40.00
17 Lyons,Ted A.	135.00	90.00	40.00
18 Martin,"Pepper"	75.00	50.00	20.00
19 O'Farrell,Robert	75.00	50.00	20.00
20 Rommell,Ed A.	75.00	50.00	20.00
21 Root,Charles	75.00	50.00	20.00
22 Ruel,Harold	75.00	50.00	20.00
23 Simmons,"Al"	165.00	110.00	50.00
24 Terry,"Bill" N.	165.00	110.00	50.00
25 Uhle,George	75.00	50.00	20.00
26 Waner,Lloyd J.	135.00	90.00	40.00
27 Waner,Paul C.	165.00	110.00	50.00
28 Wilson,"Hack"	135.00	90.00	40.00
29 Wright,Glenn	75.00	50.00	20.00

1950–56 CALLAHAN (82)
HALL OF FAME

HONUS WAGNER 1936. Elected to the Hall of Fame, 1936. "The Flying Dutchman" shortstop and how!/ for Louisville (NL) 1897-99; for Pittsburgh, 1900-17. Born, Carnegie, Pennsylvania, February 24, 1874. Batted and threw righthanded. Height 5'11"; weight 200...

	MINT	VG-E	F-G
COMPLETE SET	100.00	70.00	30.00
COMMON PLAYER(1-82)	.80	.55	.20
1 Alexander,Grover	1.75	1.25	.50
2 Anson,Cap	1.75	1.25	.50
3 Baker,Frank (55)	1.75	1.25	.50
4 Barrow,Edward (54)	1.25	.90	.35
5 Bender,Chief (2)	1.25	.90	.35
6 Bresnahan,Roger	.80	.55	.20
7 Brouthers,Dan	.80	.55	.20
8 Brown,Mordecai	.80	.55	.20
9 Bulkeley,Morgan	.80	.55	.20
10 Burkett,Jesse	.80	.55	.20
11 Cartwright, Alexander	.80	.55	.20
12 Chadwick,Henry	.80	.55	.20
13 Chance,Frank	1.25	.90	.35
14 Chandler, Happy (52)	1.25	.90	.35
15 Chesbro,Jack	.80	.55	.20
16 Clarke,Fred	.80	.55	.20
17 Cobb,Ty	7.50	5.50	2.00
18A Cochran,Mickey	5.00	3.50	1.50
18B Cochrane,Mickey	1.75	1.25	.50
19 Collins,Eddie (2)	1.25	.90	.35
20 Collins,Jimmie	.80	.55	.20
21 Comiskey,Charles	.80	.55	.20
22 Connolly,Tom (54)	1.25	.90	.35
23 Cummings,Candy	.80	.55	.20
24 Dean,Dizzy (52)	3.50	2.50	1.00
25 Delahanty,Ed	.80	.55	.20
26 Dickey, Bill (54) (2)	2.50	1.75	.75
27 DiMaggio,Joe (55)	10.00	7.00	3.00
28 Duffy,Hugh	.80	.55	.20
29 Evers,Johnny	1.25	.90	.35
30 Ewing,Buck	.80	.55	.20
31 Foxx,Jimmie	2.50	1.75	.75
32 Frisch,Frank	1.75	1.25	.50
33 Gehrig,Lou	7.50	5.50	2.00
34 Gehringer,Charles	2.50	1.75	.75
35 Griffith,Clark	.80	.55	.20
36 Grove,Lefty	1.75	1.25	.50
37 Hartnett, Gabby (55)	1.75	1.25	.50
38 Heilmann, Harry (52)	1.25	.90	.35
39 Hornsby,Rogers	2.50	1.75	.75

1 3/4" X 2 1/2"

The 1950-56 Callahan Hall of Fame set was issued over a number of years at the Baseball Hall of Fame museum in Cooperstown, New York. New cards were added to the set each year when new members were inducted into the Hall of Fame. The cards with (2) in the checklist exist with two different biographies. The year of each card's first inclusion in the set is in ( ). The ACC designation is W576.

	MINT	VG-E	F-G
40 Hubbell,Carl	1.75	1.25	.50
41 Jennings,Hughy	.80	.55	.20
42 Johnson,Ban	.80	.55	.20
43 Johnson,Walter	2.50	1.75	.75
44 Keeler,Willie	.80	.55	.20
45 Kelly,Mike	1.25	.90	.35
46 Klem,Bill (54)	1.25	.90	.35
47 Lajoie,Napoleon	1.75	1.25	.50
48 Landis,Kenesaw	.80	.55	.20
49 Lyons,Ted (55)	1.75	1.25	.50
50 Mack,Connie	1.25	.90	.35
51 Maranville, Walter (54)	1.25	.90	.35
52 Mathewson,Christy	2.50	1.75	.75
53 McCarthy,Tommy	.80	.55	.20
54 McGinnity,Joe	.80	.55	.20
55 McGraw,John	1.75	1.25	.50
56 Nicholls,Charles	.80	.55	.20
57 O'Rourke,Jim	.80	.55	.20
58 Ott,Mel	1.75	1.25	.50
59 Pennock,Herb	.80	.55	.20
60 Plank,Eddie	1.25	.90	.35
61 Radbourne,Charles	.80	.55	.20
62 Robinson,Wilbert	.80	.55	.20
63 Ruth,Babe	10.00	7.00	3.00
64 Schalk,Ray (55)	1.25	.90	.35
65 Simmons,Al (52)	1.25	.90	.35
66 Sisler,George (2)	1.25	.90	.35
67 Spalding,A.G.	.80	.55	.20
68 Speaker,Tris	1.75	1.25	.50
69 Terry,Bill (54)	1.75	1.25	.50
70 Tinker,Joe	.80	.55	.20
71 Traynor,Pie	1.25	.90	.35
72 Vance,Dazzy (55)	1.25	.90	.35
73 Waddell,Rube	.80	.55	.20
74 Wagner,Hans	3.50	2.50	1.00
75 Wallace,Bobby (54)	1.25	.90	.35
76 Walsh,Ed	.80	.55	.20
77 Waner,Paul (52)	1.25	.90	.35
78 Wright,George	.80	.55	.20
79 Wright,Harry (54)	1.25	.90	.35
80 Young,Cy	.80	.55	.20
81 Museum Int. (54) (2)	1.25	.90	.35
82 Museum Ext. (54) (2)	1.25	.90	.35

UM8 BIG LEAGUE INC.

IRON CITY BEER CAN

1981 COCA-COLA TEAM SETS (132)   2 1/2" X 3 1/2"

In 1981 Topps produced 11 sets of 12 cards each for the Coca-Cola Company. Each set features 11 star players for a particular team plus an advertising card with the team name

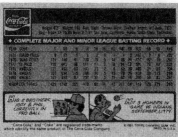

on the front. The player cards are quite similar to the 1981 Topps issue but feature a Coca-Cola logo on both the front and the back. The advertising card for each team features, on its back, an offer for obtaining an uncut sheet of 1981 Topps cards. These promotional item cards were actually issued by Coke in only a few of the cities, and most of these cards have reached collectors hands through dealers who have purchased the cards through suppliers.

COMPLETE SET	12.50	8.50	3.50
COMMON PLAYER	.05	.03	.01
Red Sox Checklist	.03	.02	.01
1 Tom Burgmeier	.05	.03	.01
2 Dennis Eckersley	.09	.06	.02
3 Dwight Evans	.09	.06	.02
4 Bob Stanley	.05	.03	.01
5 Glenn Hoffman	.09	.06	.02
6 Carney Lansford	.18	.12	.05
7 Frank Tanana	.09	.06	.02
8 Tony Perez	.09	.06	.02
9 Jim Rice	.30	.20	.08
10 Dave Stapleton	.09	.06	.02
11 Carl Yastrzemski	.50	.35	.15
Reds Checklist	.03	.02	.01
1 Johnny Bench	.30	.20	.08
2 Dave Collins	.09	.06	.02
3 Dave Concepcion	.09	.06	.02
4 Dan Driessen	.05	.03	.01
5 George Foster	.18	.12	.05
6 Ken.Griffey	.09	.06	.02
7 Tom Hume	.05	.03	.01
8 Ray Knight	.05	.03	.01
9 Ron Oester	.05	.03	.01
10 Tom Seaver	.30	.20	.08
11 Mario Soto	.05	.03	.01
Pirates Checklist	.03	.02	.01
1 Jim Bibby	.09	.06	.02
2 John Candelaria	.09	.06	.02
3 Mike Easler	.09	.06	.02
4 Tim Foli	.05	.03	.01
5 Phil Garner	.05	.03	.01
6 Bill Madlock	.09	.06	.02
7 Omar Moreno	.09	.06	.02
8 Ed Ott	.05	.03	.01
9 Dave Parker	.30	.20	.08
10 Willie Stargell	.30	.20	.08
11 Kent Tekulve	.09	.06	.02
Mets Checklist	.03	.02	.01
1 Neil Allen	.05	.03	.01
2 Doug Flynn	.05	.03	.01
3 Dave Kingman	.18	.12	.05
4 Randy Jones	.09	.06	.02
5 Pat Zachry	.05	.03	.01
6 Lee Mazzilli	.09	.06	.02
7 Rusty Staub	.09	.06	.02
8 Craig Swan	.09	.06	.02
9 Frank Taveras	.05	.03	.01
10 Alex Trevino	.05	.03	.01
11 Joel Youngblood	.05	.03	.01
Cardinals Checklist	.03	.02	.01
1 Bob Forsch	.05	.03	.01
2 George Hendrick	.09	.06	.02
3 Keith Hernandez	.30	.20	.08
4 Tom Herr	.05	.03	.01
5 Sixto Lezcano	.09	.06	.02
6 Ken Oberkfell	.09	.06	.02
7 Darrell Porter	.09	.06	.02
8 Tony Scott	.05	.03	.01
9 Lary Sorensen	.09	.06	.02
10 Bruce Sutter	.18	.12	.05
11 Garry Templeton	.18	.12	.05
Tigers Checklist	.03	.02	.01
1 Champ Summers	.05	.03	.01
2 Al Cowens	.05	.03	.01
3 Rich Hebner	.05	.03	.01
4 Steve Kemp	.18	.12	.05

5 Aurelio Lopez	.05	.03	.01
6 Jack Morris	.09	.06	.02
7 Lance Parrish	.09	.06	.02
8 Johnny Wockenfuss	.05	.03	.01
9 Alan Trammell	.09	.06	.02
10 Lou Whitaker	.09	.06	.02
11 Kirk Gibson	.30	.20	.08
Royals Checklist	.03	.02	.01
1 Willie Aikens	.12	.08	.03
2 George Brett	.75	.50	.20
3 Larry Gura	.12	.08	.03
4 Dennis Leonard	.12	.08	.03
5 Hal McRae	.06	.04	.01
6 Amos Otis	.12	.08	.03
7 Dan Quisenberry	.12	.08	.03
8 U.L. Washington	.06	.04	.01
9 John Wathan	.06	.04	.01
10 Frank White	.12	.08	.03
11 Willie Wilson	.40	.25	.10
Phillies Checklist	.03	.02	.01
1 Bob Boone	.09	.06	.02
2 Larry Bowa	.18	.12	.05
3 Steve Carlton	.30	.20	.08
4 Greg Luzinski	.09	.06	.02
5 Garry Maddox	.09	.06	.02
6 Bake McBride	.09	.06	.02
7 Tug McGraw	.09	.06	.02
8 Pete Rose	.50	.35	.15
9 Mike Schmidt	.30	.20	.08
10 Lonnie Smith	.05	.03	.01
11 Manny Trillo	.05	.03	.01
Cubs Checklist	.03	.02	.01
1 Tim Blackwell	.05	.03	.01
2 Bill Buckner	.09	.06	.02
3 Ivan DeJesus	.05	.03	.01
4 Leon Durham	.09	.06	.02
5 Steve Henderson	.05	.03	.01
6 Mike Krukow	.05	.03	.01
7 Ken Reitz	.05	.03	.01
8 Rick Reuschel	.09	.06	.02
9 Scot Thompson	.05	.03	.01
10 Dick Tidrow	.05	.03	.01
11 Mike Tyson	.05	.03	.01
White Sox Checklist	.03	.02	.01
1 Britt Burns	.09	.06	.02
2 Tod Cruz	.05	.03	.01
3 Rich Dotson	.05	.03	.01
4 Jim Essian	.05	.03	.01
5 Ed Farmer	.09	.06	.02
6 Lamar Johnson	.05	.03	.01
7 Ron LeFlore	.09	.06	.02
8 Chet Lemon	.09	.06	.02
9 Bob Molinaro	.05	.03	.01
10 Jim Morrison	.05	.03	.01
11 Wayne Nordhagen	.05	.03	.01
Astros Checklist	.03	.02	.01
1 Alan Ashby	.05	.03	.01
2 Cesar Cedeno	.18	.12	.05
3 Jose Cruz	.09	.06	.02
4 Art Howe	.05	.03	.01
5 Rafael Landestoy	.05	.03	.01
6 Joe Niekro	.09	.06	.02
7 Terry Puhl	.09	.06	.02
8 J.R. Richard	.18	.12	.05
9 Nolan Ryan	.30	.20	.08
10 Joe Sambito	.09	.06	.02
11 Don Sutton	.18	.12	.05

1914 CRACKER JACK 144 SERIES (144)   2 1/4 X 3"

135

William Killifer, catcher of the Philadelphia Nationals, was born at Paw Paw, Mich., April 13, 1886. In 1907 he began his playing career with Kalamazoo South Michigan League Club. He divided 1908 between Austin of Texas League, and San Francisco, of Pacific Coast. In 1909 he was with Houston Texas League club, and the following year received his first trial with St. Louis Americans. He was sent to Buffalo by St. Louis in 1911, from which team the Philadelphia Nationals secured him. At the close of 1913 he signed with the Chicago Federals, but came back to Philadelphia before the start of the 1914 season.

This is one of a series of colored pictures of famous Ball Players and Managers given Free with Cracker Jack, "The Famous Popcorn Confection," one card in each package. Our first issue is 15,000,000 pictures. Complete set has 144 pictures of Stars in the American, National and Federal Leagues.

RUECKHEIM BROS. & ECKSTEIN
Brooklyn, N.Y.   Chicago, Ill.

The 1914 Cracker Jacks set, called the Cracker Jacks series of 144, was issued in Cracker Jacks candies. Many or most of the cards have product residues (stains) on them. The series of 144 can be distinguished from the 1915 Cracker Jacks series of 176 by the fact that the tops of both the obverse and reverse of the card are at the same end of the card. This series is one of the few major card sets which includes Federal League players. The ACC designation is E145.

	MINT	VG-E	F-G
COMPLETE SET	4500.00	3000.00	1200.00
COMMON PLAYER(1-144)	30.00	20.00	8.00

		MINT	VG-E	F-G
1	Knabe	30.00	20.00	8.00
2	Baker	60.00	40.00	15.00
3	Tinker	60.00	40.00	15.00
4	Doyle	30.00	20.00	8.00
5	Miller,Wark	30.00	20.00	8.00
6	Plank (Phil. A.L.)	80.00	55.00	25.00
7	Collins (Phil. AL)	80.00	55.00	25.00
8	Oldring	30.00	20.00	8.00
9	Hoffman,Artie	30.00	20.00	8.00
10	McInnis	36.00	24.00	10.00
11	Stovall	30.00	20.00	8.00
12	Mack,Connie	100.00	65.00	25.00
13	Wilson	30.00	20.00	8.00
14	Crawford	60.00	40.00	15.00
15	Russell	30.00	20.00	8.00
16	Camnitz	30.00	20.00	8.00
17	Bresnahan(Catcher)	60.00	40.00	15.00
18	Evers	60.00	40.00	15.00
19	Bender (Phil. AL)	60.00	40.00	15.00
20	Falkenberg	30.00	20.00	8.00
21	Zimmerman	30.00	20.00	8.00
22	Wood	36.00	24.00	10.00
23	Comiskey	60.00	40.00	15.00
24	Mullen	30.00	20.00	8.00
25	Simon	30.00	20.00	8.00
26	Scott	30.00	20.00	8.00
27	Carrigan	30.00	20.00	8.00
28	Barry	30.00	20.00	8.00
29	Gregg (Clev.)	30.00	20.00	8.00
30	Cobb	225.00	150.00	60.00
31	Wagner	30.00	20.00	8.00
32	Brown,M.	60.00	40.00	15.00
33	Strunk	30.00	20.00	8.00
34	Thomas	30.00	20.00	8.00
35	Hooper	60.00	40.00	15.00
36	Walsh,Ed	60.00	40.00	15.00
37	Alexander	80.00	55.00	25.00
38	Dooin (Phil. N.L.)	30.00	20.00	8.00
39	Gandil	30.00	20.00	8.00
40	Auston (St. L.A.L.	30.00	20.00	8.00
41	Leach	30.00	20.00	8.00
42	Bridwell	30.00	20.00	8.00
43	Marquard (N.Y. Nat	60.00	40.00	15.00
44	Testeau	30.00	20.00	8.00
45	Luderus	30.00	20.00	8.00
46	Groom	30.00	20.00	8.00
47	Devore (Phi. N.L.)	30.00	20.00	8.00
48	Lord	80.00	55.00	25.00
49	Miller	30.00	20.00	8.00
50	Hummell	30.00	20.00	8.00
51	Rucker	30.00	20.00	8.00
52	Wheat	60.00	40.00	15.00
53	Miller,Otto	30.00	20.00	8.00
54	O'Toole	30.00	20.00	8.00
55	Hoblitzel (Cinn.)	30.00	20.00	8.00
56	Milan	30.00	20.00	8.00
57	Johnson	100.00	65.00	25.00
58	Schang	30.00	20.00	8.00
59	Gessler	30.00	20.00	8.00
60	Zeider	30.00	20.00	8.00

		MINT	VG-E	F-G
61	Schalk,Ray	60.00	40.00	15.00
62	Cashion	100.00	65.00	25.00
63	Adams	30.00	20.00	8.00
64	Archer,Jimmy	30.00	20.00	8.00
65	Speaker,Tris	100.00	65.00	25.00
66	Lajoie (Cleve.)	100.00	65.00	25.00
67	Crandall	30.00	20.00	8.00
68	Wagner,Honus	100.00	65.00	25.00
69	McGraw,John	80.00	55.00	25.00
70	Clarke,Fred	60.00	40.00	15.00
71	Meyers	30.00	20.00	8.00
72	Boehling	30.00	20.00	8.00
73	Carey,Max	60.00	40.00	15.00
74	Owens,Frank	30.00	20.00	8.00
75	Huggins,Miller	60.00	40.00	15.00
76	Hendrix,Claude	30.00	20.00	8.00
77	Jennings,Hugh	60.00	40.00	15.00
78	Merkle,Fred	36.00	24.00	10.00
79	Bodie,Ping	30.00	20.00	8.00
80	Ruelbach	30.00	20.00	8.00
81	Delehanty,J. C.	30.00	20.00	8.00
82	Cravath	30.00	20.00	8.00
83	Ford,Russ	30.00	20.00	8.00
84	Knetzer,E. E.	30.00	20.00	8.00
85	Herzog,Buck	30.00	20.00	8.00
86	Shotten	30.00	20.00	8.00
87	Casey	30.00	20.00	8.00
88	Mathewson (Pitchin	225.00	150.00	60.00
89	Cheney	30.00	20.00	8.00
90	Smith,Frank	30.00	20.00	8.00
91	Peckinpaugh,Roger	36.00	24.00	10.00
92	Demaree (N.Y. Nat)	30.00	20.00	8.00
93	Pratt (Throwing)	80.00	55.00	25.00
94	Cicotte,Eddie	30.00	20.00	8.00
95	Keating	30.00	20.00	8.00
96	Becker,Beals	30.00	20.00	8.00
97	Benton	30.00	20.00	8.00
98	LaPorte	30.00	20.00	8.00
99	Chance,Frank	150.00	100.00	40.00
100	Seaton	30.00	20.00	8.00
101	Schulte	30.00	20.00	8.00
102	Fisher	30.00	20.00	8.00
103	Jackson,Joe	100.00	65.00	25.00
104	Saier,Vic	30.00	20.00	8.00
105	Lavender,James	30.00	20.00	8.00
106	Birmingham	30.00	20.00	8.00
107	Downey	30.00	20.00	8.00
108	Magee (Phi. N.L.)	30.00	20.00	8.00
109	Blanding,Fred	30.00	20.00	8.00
110	Bescher	30.00	20.00	8.00
111	Callahan,Jim	100.00	65.00	25.00
112	Sweeney	30.00	20.00	8.00
113	Suggs	30.00	20.00	8.00
114	Moriarity,Geo. J.	30.00	20.00	8.00
115	Brennan,Addison	30.00	20.00	8.00
116	Zeider	30.00	20.00	8.00
117	Easterly	30.00	20.00	8.00
118	Konetchy (Pitts.NL	30.00	20.00	8.00
119	Peering	30.00	20.00	8.00
120	Doolan	30.00	20.00	8.00

		MINT	VG-E	F-G			MINT	VG-E	F-G
121	Perdue (Bos. N.L.)	30.00	20.00	8.00	133	Rickey,Branch	80.00	55.00	25.00
122	Bush	30.00	20.00	8.00	134	Marsans (Cin.)	30.00	20.00	8.00
123	Sallee	30.00	20.00	8.00	135	Killefer	30.00	20.00	8.00
124	Moore,Earl	30.00	20.00	8.00	136	Maranville,Rabbit	60.00	40.00	15.00
125	Niehoff	30.00	20.00	8.00	137	Raiden	30.00	20.00	8.00
126	Blair	30.00	20.00	8.00	138	Gowdy,Hank	36.00	24.00	10.00
127	Schmidt	30.00	20.00	8.00	139	Oakes	30.00	20.00	8.00
128	Evans	30.00	20.00	8.00	140	Murphy	30.00	20.00	8.00
129	Caldwell	30.00	20.00	8.00	141	Barger	30.00	20.00	8.00
130	Wingo,Ivy	30.00	20.00	8.00	142	Packard	30.00	20.00	8.00
131	Baumgardner	30.00	20.00	8.00	143	Daubert	36.00	24.00	10.00
132	Nunamaker	30.00	20.00	8.00	144	Walsh,James C.	30.00	20.00	8.00

1915 CRACKER JACK 176 SERIES (176)   2 1/4" X 3"

FRANK SMITH, BALTIMORE - FEDERALS

The 1915 Cracker Jacks set, called the Cracker Jacks series of 176, could be obtained from both boxes of Cracker Jacks and as a set directly from the company. An album could also be obtained for the set. The top of the obverse is at the same end of the card as the botton of the reverse in this series of 176. The ACC designation is E145.

		MINT	VG-E	F-G			MINT	VG-E	F-G
	COMPLETE SET	3600.00	2400.00	1000.00					
	COMMON PLAYER(1-176)	21.00	15.00	5.00					
1	Knabe,Otto	21.00	15.00	5.00	51	Rucker,Nap	21.00	15.00	5.00
2	Baker,Frank	45.00	30.00	12.00	52	Wheat,Zach	45.00	30.00	12.00
3	Tinker,Joe	45.00	30.00	12.00	53	Miller,Otto	21.00	15.00	5.00
4	Doyle,Larry	25.00	17.00	7.00	54	O'Toole,Marty	21.00	15.00	5.00
5	Miller,Ward	21.00	15.00	5.00	55	Hoblitzel(Bos. AL)	21.00	15.00	5.00
6	Plank(St. L. Fed.)	60.00	40.00	15.00	56	Milan,Clyde	21.00	15.00	5.00
7	Collins(Chic. AL)	60.00	40.00	15.00	57	Johnson,Walter	100.00	65.00	30.00
8	Oldring,Rube	21.00	15.00	5.00	58	Schang	21.00	15.00	5.00
9	Hoffman,Artie	21.00	15.00	5.00	59	Gessler	21.00	15.00	5.00
10	McInnis	25.00	17.00	7.00	60	Dugey	21.00	15.00	5.00
11	Stovall,George	21.00	15.00	5.00	61	Schalk,Ray	35.00	24.00	10.00
12	Mack,Connie	80.00	55.00	25.00	62	Mitchell	35.00	24.00	10.00
13	Wilson	21.00	15.00	5.00	63	Adams	21.00	15.00	5.00
14	Crawford,Sam	45.00	30.00	12.00	64	Archer,Jimmy	21.00	15.00	5.00
15	Russell	21.00	15.00	5.00	65	Speaker,Tris	80.00	55.00	25.00
16	Camnitz,Howie	21.00	15.00	5.00	66	Lajoie(Phi. A.L.)	100.00	65.00	30.00
17	Bresnahan,Roger	45.00	30.00	12.00	67	Crandall	21.00	15.00	5.00
18	Evers,Johnny	45.00	30.00	12.00	68	Wagner,Honus	100.00	65.00	30.00
19	Bender(Balt. Fed.)	45.00	30.00	12.00	69	McGraw,John	60.00	40.00	15.00
20	Falkenberg	21.00	15.00	5.00	70	Clarke,Fred	45.00	30.00	12.00
21	Zimmerman	21.00	15.00	5.00	71	Meyers	21.00	15.00	5.00
22	Wood,Joe	25.00	17.00	7.00	72	Boehling	21.00	15.00	5.00
23	Comiskey,Charles	45.00	30.00	12.00	73	Carey,Max	45.00	30.00	12.00
24	Mullen,George	21.00	15.00	5.00	74	Owens,Frank	21.00	15.00	5.00
25	Simon	21.00	15.00	5.00	75	Huggins,Miller	45.00	30.00	12.00
26	Scott	21.00	15.00	5.00	76	Hendrix,Claude	21.00	15.00	5.00
27	Carrigan,Bill	21.00	15.00	5.00	77	Jennings,Hugh	45.00	30.00	12.00
28	Barry,Jack	21.00	15.00	5.00	78	Merkle,Fred	25.00	17.00	7.00
29	Gregg(Bos. A.L.)	21.00	15.00	5.00	79	Bodie,Ping	21.00	15.00	5.00
30	Cobb,Ty	165.00	110.00	45.00	80	Ruelbach	21.00	15.00	5.00
31	Wagner,Heine	21.00	15.00	5.00	81	Delehanty,J. C.	21.00	15.00	5.00
32	Brown,M.	45.00	30.00	12.00	82	Cravath	21.00	15.00	5.00
33	Strunk,Amos	21.00	15.00	5.00	83	Ford,Russ	21.00	15.00	5.00
34	Thomas	21.00	15.00	5.00	84	Knetzer,E. E.	21.00	15.00	5.00
35	Hooper,Harry	45.00	30.00	12.00	85	Herzog,Buck	21.00	15.00	5.00
36	Walsh,Ed	45.00	30.00	12.00	86	Shotten	21.00	15.00	5.00
37	Alexander,Grover C	60.00	40.00	15.00	87	Casey	21.00	15.00	5.00
38	Dooin(Cincin.)	21.00	15.00	5.00	88	Mathewson(Portrait	100.00	65.00	30.00
39	Gandil,Chick	21.00	15.00	5.00	89	Cheney	21.00	15.00	5.00
40	Austin(Pit. Fed.)	21.00	15.00	5.00	90	Smith,Frank	21.00	15.00	5.00
41	Leach,Tommy	21.00	15.00	5.00	91	Peckinpaugh,Roger	25.00	17.00	7.00
42	Bridwell,Al	21.00	15.00	5.00	92	Demaree(Phi. N.L.)	21.00	15.00	5.00
43	Marquard(Bkn. Fed)	45.00	30.00	12.00	93	Pratt(Portrait)	35.00	24.00	10.00
44	Tesreau,Charles	21.00	15.00	5.00	94	Cicotte,Eddie	21.00	15.00	5.00
45	Luderus	21.00	15.00	5.00	95	Keating	21.00	15.00	5.00
46	Groom,Bob	21.00	15.00	5.00	96	Becker,Beals	21.00	15.00	5.00
47	Devore(Bos.N.L.)	21.00	15.00	5.00	97	Benton	21.00	15.00	5.00
48	O'Neill	35.00	24.00	10.00	98	LaPorte	21.00	15.00	5.00
49	Miller	21.00	15.00	5.00	99	Chase,Hal	45.00	30.00	12.00
50	Hummell,John	21.00	15.00	5.00	100	Seaton	21.00	15.00	5.00

	MINT	VG-E	F-G			MINT	VG-E	F-G
101 Schulte	21.00	15.00	5.00	139 Oakes	21.00	15.00	5.00
102 Fisher	21.00	15.00	5.00	140 Murphy	21.00	15.00	5.00
103 Jackson,Joe	100.00	65.00	30.00	141 Barger	21.00	15.00	5.00
104 Saier,Vic	21.00	15.00	5.00	142 Packard	21.00	15.00	5.00
105 Lavender,James	21.00	15.00	5.00	143 Daubert	25.00	17.00	7.00
106 Birmingham	21.00	15.00	5.00	144 Walsh,James C.	21.00	15.00	5.00
107 Downey	21.00	15.00	5.00	145 Cather	21.00	15.00	5.00
108 Magee(Bos. N.L.)	21.00	15.00	5.00	146 Tyler	21.00	15.00	5.00
109 Blanding,Fred	21.00	15.00	5.00	147 Magee,Lee	21.00	15.00	5.00
110 Bescher	21.00	15.00	5.00	148 Wilson	21.00	15.00	5.00
111 Moran	35.00	24.00	10.00	149 Janvrin	21.00	15.00	5.00
112 Sweeney	21.00	15.00	5.00	150 Johnston	21.00	15.00	5.00
113 Suggs	21.00	15.00	5.00	151 Whitted	21.00	15.00	5.00
114 Moriarity,Geo. J.	21.00	15.00	5.00	152 McQuillen	21.00	15.00	5.00
115 Brennan,Addison	21.00	15.00	5.00	153 James	21.00	15.00	5.00
116 Zeider	21.00	15.00	5.00	154 Rudolph	21.00	15.00	5.00
117 Easterly	21.00	15.00	5.00	155 Connolly	21.00	15.00	5.00
118 Konetchy(Pit. Fed)	21.00	15.00	5.00	156 Dubuc	21.00	15.00	5.00
119 Perring	21.00	15.00	5.00	157 Kaiserling	21.00	15.00	5.00
120 Doolan	21.00	15.00	5.00	158 Maisel	21.00	15.00	5.00
121 Perdue(St. L. NL)	21.00	15.00	5.00	159 Groh,Heine	21.00	15.00	5.00
122 Bush	21.00	15.00	5.00	160 Kauff	21.00	15.00	5.00
123 Sallee	21.00	15.00	5.00	161 Rousch,Ed	45.00	30.00	12.00
124 Moore,Earl	21.00	15.00	5.00	162 Stallings	21.00	15.00	5.00
125 Niehoff(Phi. N.L.)	21.00	15.00	5.00	163 Waling	21.00	15.00	5.00
126 Blair	21.00	15.00	5.00	164 Shawkey	21.00	15.00	5.00
127 Schmidt	21.00	15.00	5.00	165 Murphy	21.00	15.00	5.00
128 Evans	21.00	15.00	5.00	166 Bush	21.00	15.00	5.00
129 Caldwell	21.00	15.00	5.00	167 Griffith,Clark	45.00	30.00	12.00
130 Wingo,Ivy	21.00	15.00	5.00	168 Campbell	21.00	15.00	5.00
131 Baumgardner	21.00	15.00	5.00	169 Collins,Raymond	21.00	15.00	5.00
132 Nunamaker	21.00	15.00	5.00	170 Lobert	21.00	15.00	5.00
133 Branch,Rickey	45.00	30.00	12.00	171 Hamilton	21.00	15.00	5.00
134 Marsans(St. L. Fed	21.00	15.00	5.00	172 Mayer	21.00	15.00	5.00
135 Killefer	21.00	15.00	5.00	173 Walker	21.00	15.00	5.00
136 Maranville,Rabbit	45.00	30.00	12.00	174 Veach	21.00	15.00	5.00
137 Rariden	21.00	15.00	5.00	175 Benz	21.00	15.00	5.00
138 Gowdy,Hank	25.00	17.00	7.00	176 Vaughn	21.00	15.00	5.00

1954 DAN DEE (29)   2 1/2″ X 3 5/8″

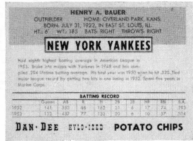

HANK BAUER
Hank Bauer

The 1954 Dan Dee P[otato] Chips set contains 29 [ ] blank backed cards. The[ ] Smith card and, to a [lesser] extent, the Walker C[ooper] card are quite difficul[t to] obtain. The poses on [many] of these cards are simil[ar to] other regional cards i[ssued] during the mid-1950's. [The] ACC designation is F342.

	MINT	VG-E	F-G			MINT	VG-E	F-G
COMPLETE SET	1400.00	900.00	400.00					
COMMON PLAYER(1-29)	28.00	20.00	8.00	15 Lemon,Bob		50.00	35.00	15.00
				16 Lopez,Al		40.00	28.00	12.00
1 Avila,Bobby	28.00	20.00	8.00	17 Mantle,Mickey		450.00	300.00	120.00
2 Bauer,Hank	35.00	25.00	10.00	18 Mitchell,Dale		28.00	20.00	8.00
3 Cooper,Walker	125.00	85.00	35.00	19 Rizzuto,Phil		40.00	28.00	12.00
4 Doby,Larry	35.00	25.00	10.00	20 Roberts,Curt		28.00	20.00	8.00
5 Easter,Luke	28.00	20.00	8.00	21 Rosen,Al		35.00	25.00	10.00
6 Feller,Bob	70.00	50.00	20.00	22 Schoendienst,Red		35.00	25.00	10.00
7 Friend,Bob	28.00	20.00	8.00	23 Smith,Paul		250.00	160.00	70.00
8 Garcia,Mike	35.00	25.00	10.00	24 Snider,Duke		70.00	50.00	20.00
9 Gordon,Sid	28.00	20.00	8.00	25 Strickland,George		28.00	20.00	8.00
10 Hegan,Jim	28.00	20.00	8.00	26 Surkont,Max		28.00	20.00	8.00
11 Hodges,Gil	50.00	35.00	15.00	27 Thomas,Frank		35.00	25.00	10.00
12 Houtteman,Art	28.00	20.00	8.00	28 Westlake,Wally		28.00	20.00	8.00
13 Irvin,Monte	40.00	28.00	12.00	29 Wynn,Early		50.00	35.00	15.00
14 LaPalme,Paul	28.00	20.00	8.00					

The 3rd NATIONAL CONVENTION IS IN ST. LOUIS IN AUGUST 1982—SEE INSIDE FRONT COVER FOR INFO.

1959 DARIGOLD FARMS (22)   2 1/2" X 2 3/8"

FRED HATFIELD, 3rd Base
Compliments of DARIGOLD FARMS

Featuring the Spokane Indians, this set of 22 unnumbered, black & white cards are found with yellow (1-8), red (9-16), and blue (17-22) backgrounds. The cards were attached to a milk carton by a tab. The SCB designation is F115-1.

	MINT	VG-E	F-G
COMPLETE SET	375.00	275.00	125.00
COMMON PLAYER(1-22)	18.00	13.00	5.00

	MINT	VG-E	F-G			MINT	VG-E	F-G
1 Barragan,Facundo	18.00	13.00	5.00	12 Miller,Larry	18.00	13.00	5.00
2 Bilko,Steve	21.00	15.00	6.00	13 Nicolosi,Chris	18.00	13.00	5.00
3 Bragan,Bobby	25.00	17.00	7.00	14 Norris,Allen	18.00	13.00	5.00
4 Churn,Chuck	18.00	13.00	5.00	15 Ortega,Phil	18.00	13.00	5.00
5 Davis,Tom	30.00	21.00	9.00	16 Paine,Phillips	18.00	13.00	5.00
6 Domenichelli,Dom	18.00	13.00	5.00	17 Parsons,Bill	18.00	13.00	5.00
7 Gaillombardo,Bob	18.00	13.00	5.00	18 Paterick,Hisel	18.00	13.00	5.00
8 Grob,Connie	18.00	13.00	5.00	19 Roig,Tony	18.00	13.00	5.00
9 Hatfield,Fred	18.00	13.00	5.00	20 Saffell,Tom	18.00	13.00	5.00
10 Lillis,Bob	21.00	15.00	6.00	21 Sherry,Norm	21.00	15.00	6.00
11 Merritt,Lloyd	18.00	13.00	5.00	22 Wade,Ben	18.00	13.00	5.00

1960 DARIGOLD FARMS (24)   2 3/8" X 2 9/16"

Compliments of DARIGOLD FARMS

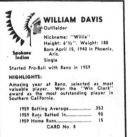

This set is very similar to the 1959 issue, with background colors of yellow (1-8), green (9-16), and red (17-24). The cards feature only players of the Spokane Indians (PCL).

	MINT	VG-E	F-G
COMPLETE SET	350.00	240.00	110.00
COMMON PLAYER(1-24)	16.00	11.00	5.00

	MINT	VG-E	F-G			MINT	VG-E	F-G
1 Nicolosi,Chris	16.00	11.00	5.00	13 Churn,Clarence	16.00	11.00	5.00
2 Pagliaroni,Jim	20.00	14.00	6.00	14 Conde,Ramon	16.00	11.00	5.00
3 Smalley,Roy	20.00	14.00	6.00	15 O'Donnell,George	16.00	11.00	5.00
4 Bethee,Bill	16.00	11.00	5.00	16 Roig,Tony	16.00	11.00	5.00
5 Liscio,Joe	16.00	11.00	5.00	17 Howard,Frank	30.00	21.00	9.00
6 Roberts,Curt	16.00	11.00	5.00	18 Harris,Billy	16.00	11.00	5.00
7 Palmquist,Ed	16.00	11.00	5.00	19 Brumley,Mike	16.00	11.00	5.00
8 Davis,William	30.00	21.00	9.00	20 Robinson,Earl	16.00	11.00	5.00
9 Gaillombardo,Bob	16.00	11.00	5.00	21 Fairly,Ron	25.00	17.00	7.00
10 Gomez,Pedro	16.00	11.00	5.00	22 Frazier,Joe	16.00	11.00	5.00
11 Nelson,Mel	16.00	11.00	5.00	23 Norris,Allen	16.00	11.00	5.00
12 Smith,Charlie	16.00	11.00	5.00	24 Young,Ford	16.00	11.00	5.00

1933 DELONG (24)

The 1933 Delong Gum set of 24 multi-colored cards was, along with the 1933 Goudey

No. 2, THE BATTING STANCE

Each boy must discover for himself the method of standing, swinging and striding that best suits his style. Try all the different methods until you hit on the one that fits your need, whether it be standing close to the plate or far away, feet together or spread apart, standing upright or crouched, swinging from the end of the handle or with hands "choked" halfway up the bat. Al Simmon's style is not like Rogers Hornsby's, yet both styles are very effective. Work out your own batting style by trying one thing and another until you hit the correct combination for your need.

—By Austen Lake,
Baseball Editor, Boston Transcript.

This is one of a continuing series of famous major league players. Each card with a different tip on inside baseball. More sport series to follow.

PLAY BALL GUM is as pure and as fine quality as any made—contains real chicle.

Copyright 1933   DELONG GUM COMPANY,
DeLong Gum Co.   Boston, Mass.

Big League series, one of the first baseball card sets issued with chewing gum. It was the only card set issued by this company. The reverse text was written by Austen Lake, who also wrote the sports tips found on the Diamond Stars series which began in 1934, leading to speculation that Delong was bought out by National Chicle. The ACC designation is R333.

	MINT	VG-E	F-G
COMPLETE SET	1650.00	1100.00	450.00
COMMON PLAYER(1-24)	50.00	35.00	15.00
1 McManus,Marty	50.00	35.00	15.00
2 Simmons,Al	60.00	40.00	15.00
3 Melillo,Oscar	50.00	35.00	15.00
4 Terry,W.	75.00	50.00	20.00
5 Gehringer,Charlie	75.00	50.00	20.00
6 Cochrane,Mickey	75.00	50.00	20.00
7 Gehrig,Lou	600.00	400.00	150.00
8 Cuyler,Kiki	60.00	40.00	15.00
9 Urbanski,Bill	50.00	35.00	15.00
10 O'Doul,Lefty	50.00	35.00	15.00
11 Lindstrom,Fred	60.00	40.00	15.00

	MINT	VG-E	F-G
12 Traynor,Pie	75.00	50.00	20.00
13 Maranville,Rabbit	60.00	40.00	15.00
14 Gomez,Lefty	75.00	50.00	20.00
15 Stephenson,Riggs	50.00	35.00	15.00
16 Warneke,Lon	50.00	35.00	15.00
17 Martin,Pepper	50.00	35.00	15.00
18 Dykes,Jim	50.00	35.00	15.00
19 Hafey,Chick	60.00	40.00	15.00
20 Vosmik,Joe	50.00	35.00	15.00
21 Foxx,Jimmie	165.00	110.00	50.00
22 Klein,Chuck	60.00	40.00	15.00
23 Grove,Lefty	90.00	60.00	25.00
24 Goslin,Goose	60.00	40.00	15.00

1934—36 DIAMOND STARS (108) 2 3/8" X 2 7/8"

The Diamond Stars set produced by National Chicle from 1934-1936 is also known as R-327 (ACC). The year of production can be determined by the statistics contained on the back of the card. There are 168 possible front-back combinations counting blue and green backs over all three years. The last twelve cards are repeat players and are quite scarce. A blank-backed proof sheet of 12 additional cards was recently discovered and has been reproduced from this original artwork and assigned numbers and text by Sport Americana.

ROGERS HORNSBY

	MINT	VG-E	F-G
COMPLETE SET	1500.00	1000.00	400.00
COMMON PLAYER(1-72)	7.00	5.00	2.00
COMMON PLAYER(73-96)	10.00	6.50	3.00
COMMON PLAYER(97-108)	36.00	24.00	10.00

		MINT	VG-E	F-G
1	Grove,Lefty	50.00	20.00	8.00
2	Simmons,Al	15.00	10.00	4.00
3	Maranville,Rabbit	12.50	8.50	3.50
4	Myer,Buddy	7.00	5.00	2.00
5	Bridges,Tommy	7.00	5.00	2.00
6	Bishop,Max	7.00	5.00	2.00
7	Fonseca,Lew	7.00	5.00	2.00
8	Vosmik,Joe	7.00	5.00	2.00
9	Cochrane,Mickey	18.00	12.00	5.00
10	Mahaffey,Leroy	7.00	5.00	2.00
11	Dickey,Bill	25.00	17.00	7.00
12	Walker,F.	7.00	5.00	2.00
13	Blaeholder,George	7.00	5.00	2.00
14	Terry,Bill	18.00	12.00	5.00
15	Bartell,Dick	7.00	5.00	2.00
16	Waner,L.	12.50	8.50	3.50
17	Frisch,Frank	18.00	12.00	5.00
18	Hafey,Chick	12.50	8.50	3.50
19	Mungo,Van Lingle	8.50	6.00	2.50
20	Hogan,Frank	7.00	5.00	2.00
21	Vergez,Johnny	7.00	5.00	2.00
22	Wilson,J.	7.00	5.00	2.00
23	Hallahan,Bill	7.00	5.00	2.00
24	Adams,Earl	7.00	5.00	2.00
25	Berger,Wally	7.00	5.00	2.00
26	Martin,Pepper	8.50	6.00	2.50
27	Traynor,Pie	15.00	10.00	4.00
28	Lopez,Al	12.50	8.50	3.50
29	Rolfe,Red	8.50	6.00	2.50
30	Manush,Heine	12.50	8.50	3.50
31	Cuyler,Kiki	12.50	8.50	3.50
32	Rice,Sam	12.50	8.50	3.50
33	Schoolboy,Rowe	8.50	6.00	2.50
34	Hack,Stan	8.50	6.00	2.50
35	Averill,Earl	12.50	8.50	3.50
36	Lombardi,Ernie	8.50	6.00	2.50
37	Urbanski,Billy	7.00	5.00	2.00
38	Chapman,B.	7.00	5.00	2.00
39	Hubbell,Carl	18.00	12.00	5.00
40	Ryan,Blondy	7.00	5.00	2.00
41	Hendrick,Harvey	7.00	5.00	2.00
42	Dykes,Jimmy	8.50	6.00	2.50
43	Lyons,Ted	12.50	8.50	3.50
44	Hornsby,Rogers	25.00	17.00	7.00
45	White,Jo-Jo	7.00	5.00	2.00
46	Lucas,Red	7.00	5.00	2.00
47	Bolton,Bob	7.00	5.00	2.00
48	Ferrell,Rick	7.00	5.00	2.00
49	Jordan,Buck	7.00	5.00	2.00
50	Ott,Mel	25.00	17.00	7.00
51	Whitehead,Burgess	7.00	5.00	2.00
52	Stainback,Tuck	7.00	5.00	2.00
53	Melillo,Oscar	7.00	5.00	2.00
54	Greenberg,Hank	18.00	12.00	5.00

		MINT	VG-E	F-G
55	Cuccinello,Tony	7.00	5.00	2.00
56	Suhr,Gus	7.00	5.00	2.00
57	Blanton,Cy	7.00	5.00	2.00
58	Myatt,Glenn	7.00	5.00	2.00
59	Bottomley,Jim	12.50	8.50	3.50
60	Ruffing,Red	12.50	8.50	3.50
61	Werber,Bill	7.00	5.00	2.00
62	Frankhouse,Fred	7.00	5.00	2.00
63	Frankhouse,Travis	7.00	5.00	2.00
64	Foxx,Jimmy	30.00	20.00	8.00
65	Bonura,Zeke	7.00	5.00	2.00
66	Medwick,Ducky	15.00	10.00	4.00
67	Owen,Mickey	8.50	6.00	2.50
68	Leslie,Sam	7.00	5.00	2.00
69	Grace,Earl	7.00	5.00	2.00
70	Trosky,Hal	7.00	5.00	2.00
71	Bluege,Ossie	7.00	5.00	2.00
72	Piet,Tony	7.00	5.00	2.00
73	Ostermueller,Fritz	10.00	6.50	3.00
74	Lazzeri,Tony	12.50	8.50	3.50
75	Burns,Jack	10.00	6.50	3.00
76	Rogell,Billy	10.00	6.50	3.00
77	Gehringer,Charlie	21.00	14.00	6.00
78	Kuhel,Joe	10.00	6.50	3.00
79	Hudlin,Willis	10.00	6.50	3.00
80	Chiozza,Lou	10.00	6.50	3.00
81	Delancey,Bill	10.00	6.50	3.00
82	Babich,Johnny	10.00	6.50	3.00
83	Waner,P.	21.00	14.00	6.00
84	Byrd,Sam	10.00	6.50	3.00
85	Solters,Moose	10.00	6.50	3.00
86	Crosetti,Frank	12.50	8.50	3.50
87	O'Neill,Steve	10.00	6.50	3.00
88	Selkirk,George	12.50	8.50	3.50
89	Stripp,Joe	10.00	6.50	3.00
90	Hayworth,Ray	10.00	6.50	3.00
91	Harris,Bucky	15.00	10.00	4.00
92	Allen,Ethan	10.00	6.50	3.00
93	Crowder,General	10.00	6.50	3.00
94	Ferrell,W.	12.50	8.50	3.50
95	Appling,Luke	18.00	12.00	5.00
96	Riggs,Lew	10.00	6.50	3.00
97	Lopez	55.00	37.50	17.00
98	Rowe,Schoolboy	45.00	30.00	12.00
99	Traynor	90.00	60.00	25.00
100	Averill	65.00	45.00	20.00
101	Bartell	36.00	24.00	10.00
102	Mungo	36.00	24.00	10.00
103	Dickey	100.00	65.00	30.00
104	Rolfe	36.00	24.00	10.00
105	Lombardi	45.00	30.00	12.00
106	Lucas	36.00	24.00	10.00
107	Hack	36.00	24.00	10.00
108	Berger	45.00	30.00	12.00

Produced under the auspices of Michael Schlecter Associates (MSA) in 1976, the ballplayer-on-disc format was distributed by a number of different advertisers - such as Crane's, Isaly's and Towne Club - and can be found in various regions of the country.

	MINT	VG-E	F-G
COMPLETE SET	7.50	5.00	2.00
COMMON PLAYER(1-70)	.06	.04	.02
1 Aaron,Hank	.70	.50	.20
2 Bench,Johnny	.50	.35	.15
3 Blue,Vida	.15	.11	.04
4 Bowa,Larry	.10	.07	.03
5 Brock,Lou	.40	.27	.12
6 Burroughs,Jeff	.10	.07	.03
7 Candelaria,John	.06	.04	.02
8 Cardenal,Jose	.06	.04	.02
9 Carew,Rod	.50	.35	.15
10 Carlton,Steve	.30	.20	.08
11 Cash,Dave	.06	.04	.02
12 Cedeno,Cesar	.10	.07	.03
13 Cey,Ron	.10	.07	.03
14 Fisk,Carlton	.15	.11	.04
15 Fuentes,Tito	.06	.04	.02
16 Garvey,Steve	.50	.35	.15
17 Griffey,Ken	.15	.11	.04
18 Gullett,Don	.06	.04	.02
19 Horton,Willie	.06	.04	.02
20 Hrabosky,Al	.10	.07	.03
21 Hunter,Catfish	.20	.14	.05
22 Jackson,Reggie	.50	.35	.15
23 Jones,Randy	.10	.07	.03
24 Kaat,Jim	.10	.07	.03
25 Kessinger,Don	.10	.07	.03
26 Kingman,Dave	.20	.14	.05
27 Koosman,Jerry	.10	.07	.03
28 Lolich,Mickey	.10	.07	.03
29 Luzinski,Greg	.20	.14	.05
30 Lynn,Fred	.50	.35	.15
31 Madlock,Bill	.10	.07	.03
32 May,Carlos	.06	.04	.02
33 Mayberry,John	.10	.07	.03
34 McBride,Bake	.10	.07	.03

	MINT	VG-E	F-G
35 Medich,Doc	.10	.07	.03
36 Messersmith,Andy	.10	.07	.03
37 Monday,Rick	.10	.07	.03
38 Montefusco,John	.10	.07	.03
39 Morales,Jerry	.06	.04	.02
40 Morgan,Joe	.20	.14	.05
41 Munson,Thurman	.50	.35	.15
42 Murcer,Bobby	.10	.07	.03
43 Oliver,Al	.20	.14	.05
44 Palmer,Jim	.40	.27	.12
45 Parker,Dave	.40	.27	.12
46 Perez,Tony	.15	.11	.04
47 Reuss,Jerry	.10	.07	.03
48 Robinson,Brooks	.40	.27	.12
49 Robinson,Frank	.40	.27	.12
50 Rogers,Steve	.10	.07	.03
51 Rose,Pete	.70	.50	.20
52 Ryan,Nolan	.30	.20	.08
53 Sanguillen,Manny	.06	.04	.02
54 Schmidt,Mike	.50	.35	.15
55 Seaver,Tom	.50	.35	.15
56 Simmons,Ted	.20	.14	.05
57 Smith,Reggie	.15	.11	.04
58 Stargell,Willie	.30	.20	.08
59 Staub,Rusty	.10	.07	.03
60 Stennett,Rennie	.06	.04	.02
61 Sutton,Don	.15	.11	.04
62 Thornton,Andy	.06	.04	.02
63 Tiant,Luis	.15	.11	.04
64 Torre,Joe	.15	.11	.04
65 Tyson,Mike	.06	.04	.02
66 Watson,Bob	.10	.07	.03
67 Wood,Wilbur	.06	.04	.02
68 Wynn,Jimmy	.06	.04	.02
69 Yastrzemski,Carl	.70	.50	.20
70 Zisk,Richie	.20	.14	.05

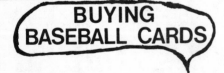

1981 DONRUSS (605)

2 1/2" X 3 1/2"

ROLLIE FINGERS PITCHER

In 1981 Donruss launched itself into the baseball card market with a set containing 600 numbered cards and five unnumbered checklists. The cards are printed on thin stock and more than one pose exists for several popular players. The numberous errors of the first run were later corrected by the company. These are marked p1 and p2 in the checklist and are fully explained in a special section following the checklist.

	MINT	VG-E	F-G
COMPLETE SET (P1)	21.00	14.00	6.00
COMPLETE SET (P2)	15.00	10.00	4.00
COMMON PLAYER(1-605)	.03	.02	.01

	MINT	VG-E	F-G
1 Smith,Ozzie	.07	.05	.02
2 Fingers,Rollie	.10	.07	.03
3 Wise,Rick	.05	.03	.01
4 Richards,Gene	.03	.02	.01
5 Trammel,Alan	.05	.03	.01
6 Brookens,Tom	.03	.02	.01
7A Dyer,Duffy (p1)	.10	.07	.03
7B Dyer,Duffy (p2)	.10	.07	.03
8 Fidrych,Mark	.05	.03	.01
9 Rozema,Dave	.03	.02	.01
10 Peters,Ricky	.05	.03	.01
11 Schmidt,Mike	.30	.20	.08
12 Stargell,Willie	.20	.13	.05
13 Foli,Tim	.03	.02	.01
14 Sanguillen,Manny	.03	.02	.01
15 Jackson,Grant	.03	.02	.01
16 Solomon,Eddie	.03	.02	.01
17 Moreno,Omar	.07	.05	.02
18 Morgan,Joe	.10	.07	.03
19 Landestoy,Rafael	.03	.02	.01
20 Bochy,Bruce	.03	.02	.01
21 Sambito,Joe	.05	.03	.01
22 Trillo,Manny	.05	.03	.01
23A Smith,Dave (p1)	.10	.07	.03
23B Smith,Dave (p2)	.10	.07	.03
24 Puhl,Terry	.05	.03	.01
25 Wills,Bump	.03	.02	.01
26A Ellis,John (p1)	.75	.50	.20
26B Ellis,John (p2)	.25	.17	.07
27 Kern,Jim	.05	.03	.01
28 Zisk,Richie	.07	.05	.02
29 Mayberry,John	.05	.03	.01
30 Davis,Bob	.03	.02	.01
31 Todd,Jackson	.03	.02	.01
32 Woods,Al	.03	.02	.01
33 Carlton,Steve	.25	.17	.07
34 Mazzilli,Lee	.07	.05	.02
35 Stearns,John	.03	.02	.01
36 Jackson,Roy	.03	.02	.01
37 Scott,Mike	.03	.02	.01
38 Johnson,Lamar	.03	.02	.01
39 Bell,Kevin	.03	.02	.01
40 Farmer,Ed	.05	.03	.01
41 Baumgarten,Ross	.03	.02	.01
42 Sutherland,Leo	.03	.02	.01
43 Meyer,Dan	.03	.02	.01
44 Reed,Ron	.03	.02	.01
45 Mendoza,Mario	.03	.02	.01
46 Honeycutt,Rick	.03	.02	.01
47 Abbott,Glen	.03	.02	.01
48 Roberts,Leon	.03	.02	.01
49 Carew,Rod	.25	.17	.07
50 Campaneris,Bert	.05	.03	.01
51A Donohue,Tom (p1)	.20	.13	.05
51B Donohue,Tom (p2)	.10	.07	.03
52 Frost,Dave	.03	.02	.01
53 Halicki,Ed	.03	.02	.01
54 Ford,Dan	.05	.03	.01
55 Maddox,Garry	.05	.03	.01
56A Garvey,Steve (p1)	.75	.50	.20
56B Garvey,Steve (p2)	.40	.25	.10
57 Russell,Bill	.03	.02	.01
58 Sutton,Don	.10	.07	.03
59 Smith,Reggie	.07	.05	.02
60 Monday,Rick	.05	.03	.01
61 Knight,Ray	.03	.02	.01
62 Bench,Johnny	.25	.17	.07

	MINT	VG-E	F-G
63 Soto,Mario	.03	.02	.01
64 Bair,Doug	.03	.02	.01
65 Foster,George	.15	.10	.04
66 Burroughs,Jeff	.05	.03	.01
67 Hernandez,Keith	.20	.13	.05
68 Herr,Tom	.03	.02	.01
69 Forsch,Bob	.03	.02	.01
70 Fulgham,John	.03	.02	.01
71A Bonds,Bobby (p1)	.30	.20	.08
71B Bonds,Bobby (p2)	.10	.07	.03
72A Stennett,Rennie (p1)	.10	.07	.03
72B Stennett,Rennie (p2)	.10	.07	.03
73 Strain,Joe	.03	.02	.01
74 Whitson,Ed	.03	.02	.01
75 Griffin,Tom	.03	.02	.01
76 North,Billy	.03	.02	.01
77 Garber,Gene	.03	.02	.01
78 Hargrove,Mike	.05	.03	.01
79 Rosello,Dave	.03	.02	.01
80 Hassey,Ron	.03	.02	.01
81 Monge,Sid	.03	.02	.01
82A Charboneau,Joe(pl	.45	.30	.12
82B Charboneau,Joe(p2	.25	.17	.07
83 Cooper,Cecil	.10	.07	.03
84 Bando,Sal	.05	.03	.01
85 Haas,Moose	.03	.02	.01
86 Caldwell,Mike	.05	.03	.01
87A Hisle,Larry (p1)	.20	.13	.05
87B Hisle,Larry (p2)	.10	.07	.03
88 Gomez,Luis	.03	.02	.01
89 Parrish,Larry	.05	.03	.01
90 Carter,Gary	.15	.10	.04
91 Gullickson,Bill	.05	.03	.01
92 Norman,Fred	.03	.02	.01
93 Hutton,Tommy	.03	.02	.01
94 Yastrzemski,Carl	.35	.24	.10
95 Hoffman,Glenn	.05	.03	.01
96 Eckersley,Dennis	.05	.03	.01
97A Burgmeier,Tom (p1	.10	.07	.03
97B Burgmeier,Tom (p2	.10	.07	.03
98 Remmerswaal,Win	.03	.02	.01
99 Horner,Bob	.25	.17	.07
100 Brett,George	.50	.35	.15
101 Chalk,Dave	.03	.02	.01
102 Leonard,Dennis	.07	.05	.02
103 Martin,Renie	.03	.02	.01
104 Otis,Amos	.05	.03	.01
105 Nettles,Graig	.10	.07	.03
106 Soderholm,Eric	.03	.02	.01
107 John,Tommy	.10	.07	.03
108 Underwood,Tom	.03	.02	.01
109 Piniella,Lou	.05	.03	.01
110 Klutts,Mickey	.03	.02	.01
111 Murcer,Bobby	.05	.03	.01
112 Murray,Eddie	.10	.07	.03
113 Dempsey,Rick	.03	.02	.01
114 McGregor,Scott	.05	.03	.01
115 Singleton,Ken	.10	.07	.03
116 Roenicke,Gary	.03	.02	.01
117 Revering,Dave	.03	.02	.01
118 Norris,Mike	.07	.05	.02
119 Henderson,Rickey	.15	.10	.04
120 Heath,Mike	.03	.02	.01
121 Cash,Dave	.03	.02	.01
122 Jones,Randy	.05	.03	.01

	MINT	VG-E	F-G		MINT	VG-E	F-G
123 Rasmussen,Eric	.03	.02	.01	215 Remy,Jerry	.03	.02	.01
124 Mumphrey,Jerry	.03	.02	.01	216 Torrez,Mike	.03	.02	.01
125 Hebner,Richie	.03	.02	.01	217 Lockwood,Skip	.03	.02	.01
126 Wagner,Mark	.03	.02	.01	218 Lynn,Fred	.25	.17	.07
127 Morris,Jack	.05	.03	.01	219 Chambliss,Chris	.05	.03	.01
128 Petry,Dan	.03	.02	.01	220 Aikens,Willie	.07	.05	.02
129 Robbins,Bruce	.03	.02	.01	221 Wathan,John	.03	.02	.01
130 Summers,Champ	.03	.02	.01	222 Quisenberry,Dan	.07	.05	.02
131A Rose,Pete (p1)	1.20	.80	.35	223 Wilson,Willie	.15	.10	.04
131B Rose,Pete (p2)	.60	.40	.15	224 Hurdle,Clint	.03	.02	.01
132 Stargell,Willie	.20	.13	.05	225 Watson,Bob	.05	.03	.01
133 Ott,Ed	.03	.02	.01	226 Spencer,Jim	.03	.02	.01
134 Bibby,Jim	.05	.03	.01	227 Guidry,Ron	.15	.10	.04
135 Blyleven,Bert	.07	.05	.02	228 Jackson,Reggie	.30	.20	.08
136 Parker,Dave	.25	.17	.07	229 Gamble,Oscar	.05	.03	.01
137 Robinson,Bill	.03	.02	.01	230 Cox,Jeff	.03	.02	.01
138 Cabell,Enos	.03	.02	.01	231 Tiant,Luis	.07	.05	.02
139 Bergman,Dave	.03	.02	.01	232 Dauer,Rich	.03	.02	.01
140 Richard,J. R.	.15	.10	.04	233 Graham,Dan	.03	.02	.01
141 Forsch,Ken	.03	.02	.01	234 Flanagan,Mike	.05	.03	.01
142 Bowa,Larry	.10	.07	.03	235 Lowenstein,John	.03	.02	.01
143 LaCorte,Frank	.03	.02	.01	236 Ayala,Benny	.03	.02	.01
144 Walling,Dennis	.03	.02	.01	237 Gross,Wayne	.03	.02	.01
145 Bell,Buddy	.07	.05	.02	238 Langford,Rick	.05	.03	.01
146 Jenkins,Ferguson	.07	.05	.02	239 Armas,Tony	.10	.07	.03
147 Darwin,Dannny	.05	.03	.01	240A Lacey,Bob (p1)	.20	.13	.05
148 Grubb,John	.03	.02	.01	240B Lacey,Bob (p2)	.10	.07	.03
149 Griffin,Alfredo	.03	.02	.01	241 Tenace,Gene	.03	.02	.01
150 Garvin,Jerry	.03	.02	.01	242 Shirley,Bob	.03	.02	.01
151 Mirabella,Paul	.03	.02	.01	243 Lucas,Gary	.03	.02	.01
152 Bosetti,Rick	.03	.02	.01	244 Turner,Jerry	.03	.02	.01
153 Ruthven,Dick	.03	.02	.01	245 Wockenfuss,John	.03	.02	.01
154 Taveras,Frank	.03	.02	.01	246 Papi,Stan	.03	.02	.01
155 Swan,Craig	.05	.03	.01	247 Wilcox,Milt	.03	.02	.01
156 Reardon,Jeff	.03	.02	.01	248 Schatzeder,Dan	.03	.02	.01
157 Henderson,Steve	.05	.03	.01	249 Kemp,Steve	.10	.07	.03
158 Morrison,Jim	.03	.02	.01	250 Lentine,Jim	.03	.02	.01
159 Borgmann,Glenn	.03	.02	.01	251 Rose,Pete	.50	.35	.15
160 Hoyt,Lamarr	.03	.02	.01	252 Madlock,Bill	.07	.05	.02
161 Wortham,Rich	.03	.02	.01	253 Berra,Dale	.05	.03	.01
162 Bosley,Thad	.03	.02	.01	254 Tekulve,Kent	.05	.03	.01
163 Cruz,Julio	.03	.02	.01	255 Romo,Enrique	.03	.02	.01
164A Unser,Del (p1)	.10	.07	.03	256 Easler,Mike	.05	.03	.01
164B Unser,Del (p2)	.10	.07	.03	257 Tanner,Chuck	.03	.02	.01
165 Anderson,Jim	.03	.02	.01	258 Howe,Art	.03	.02	.01
166 Beattie,Jim	.03	.02	.01	259 Ashby,Alan	.03	.02	.01
167 Rawley,Shane	.03	.02	.01	260 Ryan,Nolan	.20	.13	.05
168 Simpson,Joe	.03	.02	.01	261A Ruhle,Vern (p1)	.75	.50	.20
169 Carew,Rod	.25	.17	.07	261B Ruhle,Vern (p2)	.25	.17	.07
170 Patek,Fred	.03	.02	.01	262 Boone,Bob	.05	.03	.01
171 Tanana,Frank	.05	.03	.01	263 Cedeno,Cesar	.10	.07	.03
172 Martinez,Alfredo	.03	.02	.01	264 Leonard,Jeff	.03	.02	.01
173 Knapp,Chris	.03	.02	.01	265 Putnam,Pat	.03	.02	.01
174 Rudi,Joe	.05	.03	.01	266 Matlack,Jon	.05	.03	.01
175 Luzinski,Greg	.10	.07	.03	267 Rajsich,Dave	.03	.02	.01
176 Garvey,Steve	.30	.20	.08	268 Sample,Bill	.03	.02	.01
177 Ferguson,Joe	.03	.02	.01	269 Garcia,Damaso	.03	.02	.01
178 Welch,Bob	.05	.03	.01	270 Buskey,Tom	.03	.02	.01
179 Baker,Dusty	.07	.05	.02	271 McLaughlin,Joey	.03	.02	.01
180 Law,Rudy	.05	.03	.01	272 Bonnell,Barry	.03	.02	.01
181 Concepcion,Dave	.10	.07	.03	273 McGraw,Tug	.05	.03	.01
182 Bench,Johnny	.25	.17	.07	274 Jorgensen,Mike	.03	.02	.01
183 LaCoss,Mike	.03	.02	.01	275 Zachry,Pat	.03	.02	.01
184 Griffey,Ken	.07	.05	.02	276 Allen,Neil	.03	.02	.01
185 Collins,Dave	.05	.03	.01	277 Youngblood,Joel	.03	.02	.01
186 Asselstine,Brian	.03	.02	.01	278 Pryor,Greg	.03	.02	.01
187 Templeton,Garry	.15	.10	.04	279 Burns,Britt	.03	.02	.01
188 Phillips,Mike	.03	.02	.01	280 Dotson,Rich	.03	.02	.01
189 Vuckovich,Pete	.05	.03	.01	281 Lemon,Chet	.07	.05	.02
190 Urrea,John	.03	.02	.01	282 Kuntz,Rusty	.03	.02	.01
191 Scott,Tony	.03	.02	.01	283 Cox,Ted	.03	.02	.01
192 Evans,Darrell	.03	.02	.01	284 Lyle,Sparky	.07	.05	.02
193 May,Milt	.03	.02	.01	285 Cox,Larry	.03	.02	.01
194 Knepper,Bob	.05	.03	.01	286 Bannister,Floyd	.03	.02	.01
195 Moffitt,Randy	.03	.02	.01	287 McLaughlin,Byron	.03	.02	.01
196 Herndon,Larry	.03	.02	.01	288 Craig,Rodney	.03	.02	.01
197 Camp,Rick	.03	.02	.01	289 Grich,Bobby	.05	.03	.01
198 Thornton,Andre	.05	.03	.01	290 Thon,Dickie	.03	.02	.01
199 Veryzer,Tom	.03	.02	.01	291 Clear,Mark	.03	.02	.01
200 Alexander,Gary	.03	.02	.01	292 Lemanczyk,Dave	.03	.02	.01
201 Waits,Rick	.05	.03	.01	293 Thompson,Jason	.05	.03	.01
202 Manning,Rick	.03	.02	.01	294 Miller,Rick	.03	.02	.01
203 Molitor,Paul	.10	.07	.03	295 Smith,Lonnie	.05	.03	.01
204 Gantner,Jim	.03	.02	.01	296 Cey,Ron	.07	.05	.02
205 Mitchell,Paul	.03	.02	.01	297 Yeager,Steve	.03	.02	.01
206 Cleveland,Reggie	.03	.02	.01	298 Castillo,Bobby	.03	.02	.01
207 Lezcano,Sixto	.05	.03	.01	299 Mota,Manny	.05	.03	.01
208 Benedict,Bruce	.03	.02	.01	300 Johnstone,Jay	.03	.02	.01
209 Scott,Rodney	.03	.02	.01	301 Driessen,Dan	.05	.03	.01
210 Tamargo,John	.03	.02	.01	302 Nolan,Joe	.03	.02	.01
211 Lee,Bill	.03	.02	.01	303 Householder,Paul	.03	.02	.01
212 Dawson,Andre	.07	.05	.02	304 Spilman,Harry	.03	.02	.01
213 Office,Rowland	.03	.02	.01	305 Geronimo,Cesar	.03	.02	.01
214 Yastrzemski,Carl	.35	.24	.10	306A Matthews,Gary (pl	.30	.20	.08
				306B Matthews,Gary (p2	.15	.10	.04

	MINT	VG-E	F-G			MINT	VG-E	F-G
307 Reitz,Ken	.03	.02	.01		393 Walk,Bob	.03	.02	.01
308 Simmons,Ted	.10	.07	.03		394 Flynn,Doug	.03	.02	.01
309 Littlefield,John	.03	.02	.01		395 Falcone,Pete	.03	.02	.01
310 Frazier,George	.03	.02	.01		396 Hausman,Tom	.03	.02	.01
311 Iorg,Dane	.03	.02	.01		397 Maddox,Elliott	.03	.02	.01
312 Ivie,Mike	.03	.02	.01		398 Squires,Mike	.03	.02	.01
313 Littlejohn,Dennis	.03	.02	.01		399 Foley,Marvis	.03	.02	.01
314 Lavelle,Gary	.03	.02	.01		400 Trout,Steve	.03	.02	.01
315 Clark,Jack	.07	.05	.02		401 Nordhagen,Wayne	.03	.02	.01
316 Wohlford,Jim	.03	.02	.01		402 LaRussa,Tony	.03	.02	.01
317 Matula,Rick	.03	.02	.01		403 Bochte,Bruce	.05	.03	.01
318 Harrah,Toby	.03	.02	.01		404 McBride,Bake	.05	.03	.01
319A Kuiper,Duane (pl)	.20	.13	.05		405 Narron,Jerry	.03	.02	.01
319B Kuiper,Duane (p2)	.10	.07	.03		406 Dressler,Rob	.03	.02	.01
320 Barker,Len	.05	.03	.01		407 Heaverlo,Dave	.03	.02	.01
321 Cruz,Victor	.03	.02	.01		408 Paciorek,Tom	.05	.03	.01
322 Alston,Dell	.03	.02	.01		409 Lansford,Carney	.10	.07	.03
323 Yount,Robin	.07	.05	.02		410 Downing,Brian	.03	.02	.01
324 Moore,Charlie	.03	.02	.01		411 Aase,Don	.03	.02	.01
325 Sorensen,Lary	.05	.03	.01		412 Barr,Jim	.03	.02	.01
326A Thomas,Gorman (pl	.30	.20	.08		413 Baylor,Don	.10	.07	.03
326B Thomas,Gorman (p2	.15	.10	.04		414 Fregosi,Jim	.05	.03	.01
327 Rodgers,Bob	.03	.02	.01		415 Green,Dallas	.05	.03	.01
328 Niekro,Phil	.10	.07	.03		416 Lopes,Dave	.07	.05	.02
329 Speier,Chris	.03	.02	.01		417 Reuss,Jerry	.07	.05	.02
330A Rogers,Steve (pl)	.30	.20	.08		418 Sutcliffe,Rick	.03	.02	.01
330B Rogers,Steve (p2)	.15	.10	.04		419 Thomas,Derrel	.03	.02	.01
331 Fryman,Woodie	.03	.02	.01		420 Lasorda,Tommy	.05	.03	.01
332 Cromartie,Warren	.00	.00	.00		421 Leibrandt,Charles	.03	.02	.01
333 White,Jerry	.03	.02	.01		422 Seaver,Tom	.25	.17	.07
334 Perez,Tony	.10	.07	.03		423 Oester,Ron	.03	.02	.01
335 Fisk,Carlton	.15	.10	.04		424 Kennedy,Junior	.03	.02	.01
336 Drago,Dick	.03	.02	.01		425 Seaver,Tom	.25	.17	.07
337 Renko,Steve	.03	.02	.01		426 Cox,Bobby	.03	.02	.01
338 Rice,Jim	.25	.17	.07		427 Durham,Leon	.05	.03	.01
339 Royster,Jerry	.03	.02	.01		428 Kennedy,Terry	.03	.02	.01
340 White,Frank	.05	.03	.01		429 Martinez,Silvio	.03	.02	.01
341 Quirk,Jamie	.03	.02	.01		430 Hendrick,George	.07	.05	.02
342A Splittorff,Paul (pl)	.20	.13	.05		431 Schoendienst,Red	.05	.03	.01
342B Splittorff,Paul (p2)	.10	.07	.03		432 LeMaster,John	.03	.02	.01
343 Pattin,Marty	.03	.02	.01		433 Blue,Vida	.10	.07	.03
344 LaCock,Pete	.03	.02	.01		434 Montefusco,John	.03	.02	.01
345 Randolph,Willie	.07	.05	.02		435 Whitfield,Terry	.03	.02	.01
346 Cerone,Rick	.05	.03	.01		436 Bristol,Dave	.03	.02	.01
347 Gossage,Rich	.10	.07	.03		437 Murphy,Dale	.05	.03	.01
348 Jackson,Reggie	.30	.20	.08		438 Dybzinski,Jerry	.03	.02	.01
349 Jones,Ruppert	.03	.02	.01		439 Orta,Jorge	.03	.02	.01
350 McKay,Dave	.03	.02	.01		440 Garland,Wayne	.03	.02	.01
351 Berra,Yogi	.20	.13	.05		441 Dilone,Miguel	.05	.03	.01
352 Decinces,Doug	.05	.03	.01		442 Garcia,Dave.	.03	.02	.01
353 Palmer,Jim	.20	.13	.05		443 Money,Don	.05	.03	.01
354 Martinez,Tippy	.03	.02	.01		444A Martinez,Buck (pl	.20	.13	.05
355 Bumbry,Al	.03	.02	.01		444B Martinez,Buck (p2	.10	.07	.03
356 Weaver,Earl	.05	.03	.01		445 Augustine,Jerry	.03	.02	.01
357A Picciolo,Rob (pl)	.20	.13	.05		446 Oglivie,Ben	.05	.03	.01
357B Picciolo,Rob (p2)	.10	.07	.03		447 Slaton,Jim	.03	.02	.01
358 Keough,Matt	.05	.03	.01		448 Alexander,Doyle	.03	.02	.01
359 Murphy,Dwayne	.07	.05	.02		449 Bernazard,Tony	.03	.02	.01
360 Kingman,Brian	.05	.03	.01		450 Sanderson,Scott	.03	.02	.01
361 Fahey,Bill	.03	.02	.01		451 Palmer,Dave	.03	.02	.01
362 Mura,Steve	.03	.02	.01		452 Bahnsen,Stan	.03	.02	.01
363 Kinney,Dennis	.03	.02	.01		453 Williams,Dick	.03	.02	.01
364 Winfield,Dave	.30	.20	.08		454 Burleson,Rick	.07	.05	.02
365 Whitaker,Lou	.05	.03	.01		455 Allenson,Gary	.03	.02	.01
366 Parrish,Lance	.05	.03	.01		456 Stanley,Bob	.03	.02	.01
367 Corcoran,Tim	.03	.02	.01		457A Tudor,John (pl)	.10	.07	.03
368 Underwood,Pat	.03	.02	.01		457B Tudor,John (p2)	.10	.07	.03
369 Cowens,Al	.03	.02	.01		458 Evans,Dwight	.05	.03	.01
370 Anderson,Sparky	.05	.03	.01		459 Hubbard,Glenn	.05	.03	.01
371 Rose,Pete	.50	.35	.15		460 Washington,U. L.	.03	.02	.01
372 Garner,Phil	.05	.03	.01		461 Gura,Larry	.05	.03	.01
373 Nicosia,Steve	.03	.02	.01		462 Gale,Rich	.03	.02	.01
374 Candelaria,John	.05	.03	.01		463 McRae,Hal	.03	.02	.01
375 Robinson,Don	.03	.02	.01		464 Frey,Jim	.03	.02	.01
376 Lacy,Lee	.03	.02	.01		465 Dent,Bucky	.05	.03	.01
377 Milner,John	.03	.02	.01		466 Werth,Dennis	.03	.02	.01
378 Reynolds,Craig	.03	.02	.01		467 Davis,Ron	.03	.02	.01
379A Pujols,Luis (pl)	.20	.13	.05		468 Jackson,Reggie	.30	.20	.08
379B Pujols,Luis (p2)	.10	.07	.03		469 Brown,Bobby	.03	.02	.01
380 Niekro,Joe	.05	.03	.01		470 Davis,Mike	.03	.02	.01
381 Andujar,Joaquin	.03	.02	.01		471 Perry,Gaylord	.15	.10	.04
382 Moreland,Keith	.03	.02	.01		472 Belanger,Mark	.03	.02	.01
383 Cruz,Jose	.05	.03	.01		473 Palmer,Jim	.20	.13	.05
384 Virdon,Bill	.05	.03	.01		474 Stewart,Sammy	.03	.02	.01
385 Sundberg,Jim	.07	.05	.02		475 Stoddard,Tim	.03	.02	.01
386 Medich,Doc	.05	.03	.01		476 Stone,Steve	.05	.03	.01
387 Oliver,Al	.10	.07	.03		477 Newman,Jeff	.03	.02	.01
388 Norris,Jim	.03	.02	.01		478 McCatty,Steve	.05	.03	.01
389 Bailor,Bob	.03	.02	.01		479 Martin,Billy	.10	.07	.03
390 Whitt,Ernie	.03	.02	.01		480 Page,Mitchell	.03	.02	.01
391 Velez,Otto	.03	.02	.01		481 Young,Cy 1980 Carlton,Steve	.25	.17	.07
392 Howell,Roy	.03	.02	.01		482 Buckner,Bill	.07	.05	.02
					483A DeJesus,Ivan (pl)	.10	.07	.03
					483B DeJesus,Ivan (p2)	.10	.07	.03

	MINT	VG-E	F-G			MINT	VG-E	F-G
484 Johnson,Cliff	.03	.02	.01		549 Erickson,Roger	.03	.02	.01
485 Randle,Lenny	.03	.02	.01		550 Hrabosky,Al	.05	.03	.01
486 Milbourne,Larry	.03	.02	.01		551 Tidrow,Dick	.03	.02	.01
487 Smalley,Roy	.05	.03	.01		552 Ford,Dave	.03	.02	.01
488 Castino,John	.03	.02	.01		553 Kingman,Dave	.10	.07	.03
489 Jackson,Ron	.03	.02	.01		554A Vail,Mike (p1)	.10	.07	.03
490A Roberts,Dave (pl)	.10	.07	.03		554B Vail,Mike (p2)	.10	.07	.03
490B Roberts,Dave (p2)	.10	.07	.03		555A Martin,Jerry (pl)	.10	.07	.03
491 MVP AL 1980	.50	.35	.15		555B Martin,Jerry (p2)	.10	.07	.03
Brett,George					556A Figueroa,Jesus(pl	.10	.07	.03
492 Cubbage,Mike	.03	.02	.01		556B Figueroa,Jesus(p2	.10	.07	.03
493 Wilfong,Rob	.03	.02	.01		557 Stanhouse,Don	.03	.02	.01
494 Goodwin,Danny	.03	.02	.01		558 Foote,Barry	.03	.02	.01
495 Morales,Jose	.03	.02	.01		559 Blackwell,Tim	.03	.02	.01
496 Rivers,Mickey	.07	.05	.02		560 Sutter,Bruce	.15	.10	.04
497 Edwards,Mike	.03	.02	.01		561 Reuschel,Rick	.07	.05	.02
498 Sadek,Mike	.03	.02	.01		562 McGlothen,Lynn	.03	.02	.01
499 Sakata,Lenn	.03	.02	.01		563A Owchinko,Bob (pl)	.10	.07	.03
500 Michael,Gene	.05	.03	.01		563B Owchinko,Bob (p2)	.10	.07	.03
501 Roberts,Dave	.03	.02	.01		564 Verhoeven,John	.03	.02	.01
502 Dillard,Steve	.03	.02	.01		565 Landreaux,Ken	.05	.03	.01
503 Essian,Jim	.03	.02	.01		566A Adams,Glenn (pl)	.20	.13	.05
504 Mulliniks,Rance	.03	.02	.01		566B Adams,Glenn (p2)	.10	.07	.03
505 Porter,Darrell	.05	.03	.01		567 Powell,Hosken	.03	.02	.01
506 Torre,Joe	.05	.03	.01		568 Noles,Dick	.03	.02	.01
507 Crowley,Terry	.03	.02	.01		569 Ainge,Danny	.10	.07	.03
508 Travers,Bill	.03	.02	.01		570 Mattick,Bobby	.03	.02	.01
509 Norman,Nelson	.03	.02	.01		571 LeFebvre,Joe	.03	.02	.01
510 McClure,Bob	.03	.02	.01		572 Clark,Bobby	.03	.02	.01
511 Howe,Steve	.05	.03	.01		573 Lamp,Dennis	.03	.02	.01
512 Rader,Dave	.03	.02	.01		574 Lerch,Randy	.03	.02	.01
513 Kelleher,Mike	.03	.02	.01		575 Wilson,Mookie	.07	.05	.02
514 Garcia,Kiko	.03	.02	.01		576 LeFlore,Ron	.07	.05	.02
515 Biittner,Larry	.03	.02	.01		577 Dwyer,Jim	.03	.02	.01
516A Norwood,Willie(pl	.10	.07	.03		578 Castro,Bill	.03	.02	.01
516B Norwood,Willie(p2	.10	.07	.03		579 Minton,Greg	.03	.02	.01
517 Diaz,Bo	.03	.02	.01		580 Littell,Mark	.03	.02	.01
518 Beniquez,Juan	.03	.02	.01		581 Hassler,Andy	.03	.02	.01
519 Thompson,Scot	.03	.02	.01		582 Stieb,Dave	.03	.02	.01
520 Tracy,Jim	.03	.02	.01		583 Oberkfell,Ken	.03	.02	.01
521 Lezcano,Carlos	.03	.02	.01		584 Bradford,Larry	.03	.02	.01
522 Amalfitano,Joe	.03	.02	.01		585 Stanley,Fred	.03	.02	.01
523 Hanna,Preston	.03	.02	.01		586 Caudill,Bill	.03	.02	.01
524A Burris,Ray (pl)	.10	.07	.03		587 Capilla,Doug	.03	.02	.01
524B Burris,Ray (p2)	.10	.07	.03		588 Riley,George	.03	.02	.01
525 Perkins,Broderick	.03	.02	.01		589 Hernandez,Willie	.03	.02	.01
526 Hatcher,Mickey	.03	.02	.01		590 M.V.P. NL 1980	.30	.20	.08
527 Goryl,John	.03	.02	.01		Schmidt,Mike			
528 Davis,Dick	.03	.02	.01		591 Young,Cy 1980	.07	.05	.02
529 Wynegar,Butch	.03	.02	.01		Stone,Steve			
530 Butera,Sal	.03	.02	.01		592 Sofield,Rick	.03	.02	.01
531 Koosman,Jerry	.05	.03	.01		593 Rivera,Bombo	.03	.02	.01
532A Zahn,Geoff (pl)	.10	.07	.03		594 Ward,Gary	.03	.02	.01
532B Zahn,Geoff (p2)	.10	.07	.03		595A Edwards,Dave (pl)	.10	.07	.03
533 Martinez,Dennis	.05	.03	.01		595B Edwards,Dave (p2)	.10	.07	.03
534 Thomasson,Gary	.03	.02	.01		596 Proly,Mike	.03	.02	.01
535 Macko,Steve	.03	.02	.01		597 Boggs,Tommy	.03	.02	.01
536 Kaat,Jim	.10	.07	.03		598 Gross,Greg	.03	.02	.01
537 Best Hitters	.75	.50	.20		599 Sosa,Elias	.03	.02	.01
Brett & Carew					600 Kelly,Pat	.03	.02	.01
538 Raines,Tim	1.00	.65	.30		Checklist 1 (pl)	.07	.05	.02
539 Smith,Keith	.03	.02	.01		Checklist 1 (p2)	.07	.05	.02
540 Macha,Ken	.03	.02	.01		Checklist 2	.07	.05	.02
541 Hooton,Burt	.07	.05	.02		Checklist 3 (pl)	.07	.05	.02
542 Hobson,Butch	.05	.03	.01		Checklist 3 (p2)	.07	.05	.02
543 Stein,Bill	.03	.02	.01		Checklist 4 (pl)	.07	.05	.02
544 Stapleton,Dave	.07	.05	.02		Checklist 4 (p2)	.07	.05	.02
545 Pate,Bob	.03	.02	.01		Checklist 5 (pl)	.07	.05	.02
546 Corbett,Doug	.05	.03	.01		Checklist 5 (p2)	.07	.05	.02
547 Jackson,Darrell	.03	.02	.01					
548 Redfern,Pete	.03	.02	.01					

EXPLANATIONS OF ERRORS AND VARIATIONS IN 1981 DONRUSS CARDS

7A Duffy Dyer	1980 batting average on back has decimal point.
7B Duffy Dyer	1980 batting average on back has no decimal point.
23A Dave Smith	Line box around stats on back is not complete.
23B Dave Smith	Box totally encloses the stats at top.
26A John Ellis	Photo on front shows Danny Walton.
26B John Ellis	Photo on front is John Ellis,
51A Tom Donahue	Name on front misspelled "Donahue".
51B Tom Donohue	Name on front corrected to "Donohue".
56A Steve Garvey	On back, "Surpassed 25 HR for the 4th straight..."
56B Steve Garvey	On back, "Surpassed 21 HR for the 4th straight..."
71A Bobby Bonds	Record on back lists lifetime HR as "986".
71B Bobby Bonds	Record on back has correct lifetime HR total "326".
72A Rennie Stennett	On back under 1980, "breaking broke his leg in 1977"
72B Rennie Stennett	Word "broke" has been deleted
82A Joe Charboneau	On back, 1978 highlights, "For some reason..."
82B Joe Charboneau	On back, phrase "For some reason" has been deleted.
87A Larry Hisle	On back, '77 highlights, line ends with"... 28 RBI".
87B Larry Hisle	On back, '77 highlights, correct line "... 28 HR".
97A Tom Burgmeier	On back, "Bats: Left, Throws: Right".
97B Tom Burgmeier	On back, "Bats: Left, Throws:: Left:.
131A Pete Rose	On back, last line ends: "See card 251".
131B Pete Rose	On back, last line corrected to end, "see card 371".

```
164A Del Unser          Batting record on back has no "3B" heading.
164B Del Unser          Batting record on back corrected to show "3B" heading
240A Bob Lacy           Name on front misspelled Bob "Lacy".
240B Bob Lacey          Name on front corrected to Bob "Lacey".
261A Vern Ruhle         Photo on front is actually Ken Forsch.
261B Vern Ruhle         Photo on front corrected to show Vern Ruhle.
306A Gary Mathews       Name on front misspelled Gary "Mathews".
306B Gary Matthews      Name on front corrected to Gary "Matthews".
319A Dwane Kuiper       Name on front misspelled "Dwane" Kuiper.
319B Duane Kuiper       Name on front corrected to "Duane" Kuiper.
326A Gorman Thomas      On back, 2nd line reads: "30-HR mark 4th ..."
326B Gorman Thomas      On back, 2nd line corrected: "30-HR mark 3rd ..."
342A Paul Spittorff     Name on front misspelled Paul "Spittorf".
342B Paul Splittorff    Name on front corrected to Paul "Splittorff".
357A Bob Picciolo       Name on front misspelled "Bob" Picciolo.
357B Rob Picciolo       Name on front corrected to "Rob" Picciolo.
379A Luis Pujois        Name on front misspelled Luis "Pujois".
379B Luis Pujols        Name on front corrected to Luis "Pujols".
444A Buck Martinez      Picture negative reversed (Unif. number backwards).
444B Buck Martinez      Picture on front corrected.
457A John Tudor         On back, lifetime W-L reads: "9.7".
457B John Tudor         On back, pitching record corrected to read "9-7".
483A Ivan DeJesus       On back, lifetime hits reads: "702".
483B Ivan DeJesus       On back, lifetime hit record corrected to read "642".
490A Dave Roberts       Career Highlights, first line, "Showed pop in ..."
490B Dave Roberts       Career Highlights, first line, "Declared himself..."
516A Willie Norwood     Career Highlights, first line, "Spent most of ..."
516B Willie Norwood     Career Highlights, first line, "Traded to Seattle..."
524A Ray Burris         Career Highlights, first line, "Went on..."
524B Ray Burris         Career Highlights, first line, "Drafted by..."
532A Geoff Zahn         Career Highlights, first line, "Was 2nd in..."
532B Geoff Zahn         Career Highlights, first line, "Signed a 3 year..."
554A Mike Vail          Career Highlights, first line, "After two..."
554B Mike Vail          Career Highlights, first line, "Traded to..."
555A Jerry Martin       Career Highlights, first line, "Overcame a..."
555B Jerry Martin       Career Highlights, first line, "Traded to..."
556A Jesus Figueroa     Career Highlights, first line, "Had an..."
556B Jesus Figueroa     Career Highlights, first line, "Traded to..."
563A Bob Owchinko       Career Highlights, first line, "Traded to..."
563B Bob Owchinko       Career Highlights, first line, "Involved in a..."
566A Glen Adams         Name on front misspelled "Glen" Adams.
566B Glenn Adams        Name on front corrected to "Glenn" Adams.
595A Dave Edwards       Career Highlights, first line, "Sidelined the..."
595B Dave Edwards       Career Highlights, first line, "Traded to..."
Checklist 1-120 A       Card No. 51 is misspelled "Donahue"
Checklist 1-120 B       Card No. 51 has been corrected to read "Donohue"
Checklist 241-360 A     Number 306 Gary Matthews misspelled Gary "Mathews".
Checklist 241-360 B     No. 306 Gary Matthews corrected.
Checklist 361-480 A     Card No. 379 misspelled Luis "Pujois".
Checklist 361-480 B     Card No. 379 corrected to Luis "Pujols".
Checklist 481-600 A     Card No. 566 Glenn Adams misspelled "Glen" Adams.
Checklist 481-600 B     Card No. 566 Glen Adams corrected.
```

1982 DONRUSS (660) 2 1/2" X 3 1/2"

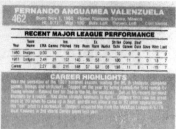

The 1982 Donruss set contains 660 cards of which 653 are numbered and the remaining seven are unnumbered check-lists. The first 26 cards of set are entitled "Don Diamond Kings" and fea paintings by Dick Perez Perez-Steele Galleries. The was marketed with a pu piece rather than bubble g There are 63 pieces to puzzle, which when put gether make a collage of E Ruth entitled "Hall of F Diamond King." The stock in this year's Don cards is considerably thi than that of the 1981 cards

	MINT	VG-E	F-G
COMPLETE SET	14.50	10.00	4.00
COMMON PLAYER	.03	.02	.01

1 Pete Rose	.40	.25	.10
2 Gary Carter	.15	.10	.04
3 Steve Garvey	.25	.17	.07
4 Vida Blue	.11	.07	.03
5 Alan Trammel	.05	.03	.01
6 Len Barker	.05	.03	.01
7 Dwight Evans	.05	.03	.01
8 Rod Carew	.25	.17	.07
9 George Hendrick	.07	.05	.02
10 Phil Niekro	.07	.05	.02
11 Richie Zisk	.07	.05	.02
12 Dave Parker	.15	.10	.04
13 Nolan Ryan	.20	.13	.05
14 Ivan DeJesus	.05	.03	.01
15 George Brett	.40	.25	.10
16 Tom Seaver	.25	.17	.07
17 Dave Kingman	.15	.10	.04
18 Dave Winfield	.25	.17	.07
19 Mike Norris	.11	.07	.03
20 Carlton Fisk	.11	.07	.03
21 Ozzie Smith	.07	.05	.02
22 Roy Smalley	.05	.03	.01
23 Buddy Bell	.07	.05	.02
24 Ken Singleton	.07	.05	.02
25 John Mayberry	.05	.03	.01
26 Gorman Thomas	.11	.07	.03
27 Earl Weaver	.05	.03	.01
28 Rollie Fingers	.15	.10	.04
29 Sparky Anderson	.05	.03	.01
30 Dennis Eckersley	.05	.03	.01
31 Dave Winfield	.25	.17	.07
32 Burt Hooton	.07	.05	.02
33 Rick Waits	.05	.03	.01
34 George Brett	.40	.25	.10
35 Steve McCatty	.11	.07	.03
36 Steve Rogers	.07	.05	.02
37 Bill Stein	.03	.02	.01
38 Steve Renko	.03	.02	.01
39 Mike Squires	.03	.02	.01
40 George Hendrick	.05	.03	.01
41 Bob Knepper	.05	.03	.01
42 Steve Carlton	.20	.13	.05
43 Larry Biittner	.03	.02	.01
44 Chris Welsh	.03	.02	.01
45 Steve Nicosia	.03	.02	.01
46 Jack Clark	.11	.07	.03
47 Chris Chambliss	.05	.03	.01
48 Ivan De Jesus	.03	.02	.01
49 Lee Mazzilli	.07	.05	.02
50 Julio Cruz	.03	.02	.01
51 Pete Redfern	.03	.02	.01
52 Dave Stieb	.03	.02	.01
53 Doug Corbett	.05	.03	.01
54 Jorge Bell	.03	.02	.01
55 Joe Simpson	.03	.02	.01
56 Rusty Staub	.07	.05	.02
57 Hector Cruz	.03	.02	.01
58 Claudell Washington	.03	.02	.01
59 Enrique Romo	.03	.02	.01
60 Gary Lavelle	.03	.02	.01
61 Tim Flannery	.03	.02	.01
62 Joe Nolan	.03	.02	.01
63 Larry Bowa	.11	.07	.03
64 Sixto Lezcano	.05	.03	.01

65 Joe Sambito	.05	.03	.01
66 Bruce Kison	.03	.02	.01
67 Wayne Nordhagen	.03	.02	.01
68 Woodie Fryman	.03	.02	.01
69 Billy Sample	.03	.02	.01
70 Amos Otis	.07	.05	.02
71 Matt Keough	.07	.05	.02
72 Toby Harrah	.03	.02	.01
73 Dave Righetti	.05	.03	.01
74 Carl Yastrzemski	.30	.20	.08
75 Bob Welch	.05	.03	.01
76 Alan Trammel	.05	.03	.01
77 Rick Dempsey	.03	.02	.01
78 Paul Molitor	.11	.07	.03
79 Dennis Martinez	.05	.03	.01
80 Jim Slaton	.03	.02	.01
81 Champ Summers	.03	.02	.01
82 Carney Lansford	.15	.10	.04
83 Barry Foote	.03	.02	.01
84 Steve Garvey	.25	.17	.07
85 Rick Manning	.03	.02	.01
86 John Wathan	.03	.02	.01
87 Brian Kingman	.03	.02	.01
88 Andre Dawson	.11	.07	.03
89 Jim Kern	.05	.03	.01
90 Bobby Grich	.05	.03	.01
91 Bob Forsch	.03	.02	.01
92 Art Howe	.03	.02	.01
93 Marty Bystrom	.03	.02	.01
94 Ozzie Smith	.07	.05	.02
95 Dave Parker	.15	.10	.04
96 Doyle Alexander	.03	.02	.01
97 Al Hrabosky	.05	.03	.01
98 Frank Taveras	.03	.02	.01
99 Tim Blackwell	.03	.02	.01
100 Floyd Bannister	.03	.02	.01
101 Alfredo Griffin	.03	.02	.01
102 Dave Engle	.03	.02	.01
103 Mario Soto	.03	.02	.01
104 Ross Baumgarten	.03	.02	.01
105 Ken Singleton	.07	.05	.02
106 Ted Simmons	.11	.07	.03
107 Jack Morris	.07	.05	.02
108 Bob Watson	.05	.03	.01
109 Dwight Evans	.05	.03	.01
110 Tom LaSorda	.05	.03	.01
111 Bert Blyleven	.05	.03	.01
112 Dan Quisenberry	.05	.03	.01
113 Rickey Henderson	.15	.10	.04
114 Gary Carter	.15	.10	.04
115 Brian Downing	.05	.03	.01
116 Al Oliver	.11	.07	.03
117 Lamarr Hoyt	.03	.02	.01
118 Cesar Cedeno	.11	.07	.03
119 Keith Moreland	.05	.03	.01
120 Bob Shirley	.03	.02	.01
121 Terry Kennedy	.03	.02	.01
122 Frank Pastore	.03	.02	.01
123 Gene Garber	.03	.02	.01
124 Tony Pena	.03	.02	.01
125 Allen Ripley	.03	.02	.01
126 Randy Martz	.03	.02	.01
127 Richie Zisk	.07	.05	.02
128 Mike Scott	.03	.02	.01
129 Lloyd Moseby	.03	.02	.01
130 Rob Wilfong	.03	.02	.01

131 Tim Stoddard	.03	.02	.01
132 Gorman Thomas	.11	.07	.03
133 Dan Petry	.03	.02	.01
134 Bob Stanley	.03	.02	.01
135 Lou Piniella	.05	.03	.01
136 Pedro Guerrero	.11	.07	.03
137 Len Barker	.05	.03	.01
138 Rich Gale	.03	.02	.01
139 Wayne Gross	.03	.02	.01
140 Tim Wallach	.03	.02	.01
141 Gene Mauch	.05	.03	.01
142 Doc Medich	.05	.03	.01
143 Tony Bernazard	.03	.02	.01
144 Bill Virdon	.07	.05	.02
145 John Littlefield	.03	.02	.01
146 Dave Bergman	.03	.02	.01
147 Dick Davis	.03	.02	.01
148 Tom Seaver	.20	.13	.05
149 Matt Sinatro	.03	.02	.01
150 Chuck Tanner	.05	.03	.01
151 Leon Durham	.07	.05	.02
152 Gene Tenace	.03	.02	.01
153 Al Bumbry	.03	.02	.01
154 Mark Brouhard	.03	.02	.01
155 Rick Peters	.05	.03	.01
156 Jerry Remy	.03	.02	.01
157 Rick Reuschel	.05	.03	.01
158 Steve Howe	.05	.03	.01
159 Alan Bannister	.03	.02	.01
160 U.L. Washington	.03	.02	.01
161 Rick Langford	.05	.03	.01
162 Bill Gullickson	.05	.03	.01
163 Mark Wagner	.03	.02	.01
164 Geoff Zahn	.03	.02	.01
165 Ron Leflore	.07	.05	.02
166 Dane Iorg	.03	.02	.01
167 Joe Niekro	.05	.03	.01
168 Pete Rose	.40	.25	.10
169 Dave Collins	.07	.05	.02
170 Rick Wise	.05	.03	.01
171 Jim Bibby	.05	.03	.01
172 Larry Herndon	.03	.02	.01
173 Bob Horner	.25	.17	.07
174 Steve Dillard	.03	.02	.01
175 Mookie Wilson	.07	.05	.02
176 Dan Meyer	.03	.02	.01
177 Fernando Arroyo	.03	.02	.01
178 Jackson Todd	.03	.02	.01
179 Darrell Jackson	.03	.02	.01
180 Al Woods	.03	.02	.01
181 Jim Anderson	.03	.02	.01
182 Dave Kingman	.15	.10	.04
183 Steve Henderson	.05	.03	.01
184 Brian Asselstine	.03	.02	.01
185 Rod Scurry	.03	.02	.01
186 Fred Breining	.03	.02	.01
187 Danny Boone	.03	.02	.01
188 Junior Kennedy	.03	.02	.01
189 Sparky Lyle	.07	.05	.02
190 Whitey Herzog	.05	.03	.01
191 Dave Smith	.05	.03	.01
192 Ed Ott	.03	.02	.01
193 Greg Luzinski	.11	.07	.03
194 Bill Lee	.03	.02	.01
195 Don Zimmer	.05	.03	.01
196 Hal McRae	.03	.02	.01
197 Mike Norris	.11	.07	.03
198 Duane Kuiper	.03	.02	.01
199 Rick Cerone	.05	.03	.01
200 Jim Rice	.20	.13	.05
201 Steve Yeager	.03	.02	.01
202 Tom Brookens	.03	.02	.01
203 Jose Morales	.03	.02	.01
204 Roy Howell	.03	.02	.01
205 Tippy Martinez	.03	.02	.01
206 Moose Haas	.03	.02	.01
207 Al Cowens	.03	.02	.01
208 Dave Stapleton	.05	.03	.01
209 Bucky Dent	.05	.03	.01
210 Ron Cey	.11	.07	.03
211 Jorge Orta	.03	.02	.01
212 Jamie Quirk	.03	.02	.01
213 Jeff Jones	.03	.02	.01
214 Tim Raines	.25	.17	.07
215 Jon Matlack	.05	.03	.01
216 Rod Carew	.25	.17	.07
217 Jim Kaat	.11	.07	.03
218 Joe Pittman	.03	.02	.01
219 Larry Christenson	.03	.02	.01
220 Juan Bonilla	.03	.02	.01
221 Mike Easler	.05	.03	.01
222 Vida Blue	.11	.07	.03
223 Rick Camp	.03	.02	.01
224 Mike Jorgensen	.03	.02	.01
225 Jody Davis	.03	.02	.01
226 Mike Parrott	.03	.02	.01
227 Jim Clancy	.03	.02	.01
228 Hosken Powell	.03	.02	.01
229 Tom Hume	.03	.02	.01
230 Britt Burns	.05	.03	.01
231 Jim Palmer	.20	.13	.05
232 Bob Rodgers	.03	.02	.01
233 Milt Wilcox	.03	.02	.01
234 Dave Revering	.03	.02	.01
235 Mike Torrez	.05	.03	.01
236 Robert Castillo	.03	.02	.01
237 Von Hayes	.03	.02	.01
238 Renie Martin	.05	.03	.01
239 Dwayne Murphy	.11	.07	.03
240 Rodney Scott	.03	.02	.01
241 Fred Patek	.03	.02	.01
242 Mickey Rivers	.07	.05	.02
243 Steve Trout	.03	.02	.01
244 Jose Cruz	.05	.03	.01
245 Manny Trillo	.05	.03	.01
246 Lary Sorensen	.05	.03	.01
247 Dave Edwards	.03	.02	.01
248 Dan Driessen	.03	.02	.01
249 Tommy Boggs	.03	.02	.01
250 Dale Berra	.05	.03	.01
251 Ed Whitson	.03	.02	.01
252 Lee Smith	.03	.02	.01
253 Tom Paciorek	.05	.03	.01
254 Pat Zachry	.03	.02	.01
255 Luis Leal	.03	.02	.01
256 John Castino	.05	.03	.01
256 Rich Dauer	.03	.02	.01
258 Cecil Cooper	.11	.07	.03
259 Dave Rozema	.03	.02	.01
260 John Tudor	.03	.02	.01
261 Jerry Mumphrey	.05	.03	.01
262 Jay Johnstone	.03	.02	.01
263 Bo Diaz	.03	.02	.01
264 Dennis Leonard	.07	.05	.02
265 Jim Spencer	.03	.02	.01
266 John Milner	.03	.02	.01
267 Don Aase	.03	.02	.01
268 Jim Sundberg	.07	.05	.02
269 Lamar Johnson	.03	.02	.01
270 Frank LaCorte	.03	.02	.01
271 Barry Evans	.03	.02	.01
272 Enos Cabell	.03	.02	.01
273 Del Unser	.03	.02	.01
274 George Foster	.15	.10	.04
275 Brett Butler	.03	.02	.01
276 Lee Lacy	.03	.02	.01
277 Ken Reitz	.03	.02	.01
278 Keith Hernandez	.15	.10	.04
279 Doug Decinces	.05	.03	.01
280 Charlie Moore	.03	.02	.01
281 Lance Parrish	.05	.03	.01
282 Ralph Houk	.05	.03	.01
283 Rich Gossage	.11	.07	.03
284 Jerry Reuss	.07	.05	.02
285 Mike Stanton	.03	.02	.01
286 Frank White	.05	.03	.01
287 Bob Owchinko	.03	.02	.01
288 Scott Sanderson	.03	.02	.01
289 Bump Wills	.03	.02	.01
290 Dave Frost	.03	.02	.01
291 Chet Lemon	.05	.03	.01
292 Tito Landrum	.03	.02	.01
293 Von Ruhle	.03	.02	.01
294 Mike Schmidt	.25	.17	.07
295 Sam Mejias	.03	.02	.01
296 Gary Lucas	.03	.02	.01
297 John Candelaria	.03	.02	.01
298 Jerry Martin	.03	.02	.01
299 Dale Murphy	.05	.03	.01
300 Mike Lum	.03	.02	.01
301 Tom Hausman	.03	.02	.01
302 Glenn Abbott	.03	.02	.01
303 Roger Erickson	.03	.02	.01
304 Otto Velez	.03	.02	.01
305 Danny Goodwin	.03	.02	.01
306 John Mayberry	.05	.03	.01
307 Lenny Randle	.03	.02	.01
308 Bob Bailor	.03	.02	.01
309 Jerry Morales	.03	.02	.01
310 Rufino Linares	.03	.02	.01
311 Kent Tekulve	.05	.03	.01
312 Joe Morgan	.11	.07	.03
313 John Urrea	.03	.02	.01
314 Paul Householder	.03	.02	.01
315 Garry Maddox	.05	.03	.01
316 Mike Ramsey	.03	.02	.01
317 Alan Ashby	.03	.02	.01
318 Bob Clark	.03	.02	.01
319 Tony Larussa	.05	.03	.01
320 Charlie Lea	.05	.03	.01
321 Danny Darwin	.05	.03	.01
322 Cesar Geronimo	.03	.02	.01

323	Tom Underwood	.03	.02	.01
324	Andre Thornton	.05	.03	.01
325	Rudy May	.03	.02	.01
326	Frank Tanana	.05	.03	.01
327	Davey Lopes	.07	.05	.02
328	Richie Hebner	.03	.02	.01
329	Mike Flanagan	.05	.03	.01
330	Mike Caldwell	.03	.02	.01
331	Scott McGregor	.05	.03	.01
332	Jerry Augustine	.03	.02	.01
333	Stan Papi	.03	.02	.01
334	Rick Miller	.03	.02	.01
335	Graig Nettles	.07	.05	.02
336	Dusty Baker	.07	.05	.02
337	Dave Garcia	.03	.02	.01
338	Larry Gura	.05	.03	.01
339	Cliff Johnson	.03	.02	.01
340	Warren Cromartie	.03	.02	.01
341	Steve Comer	.03	.02	.01
342	Rick Burleson	.07	.05	.02
343	John Martin	.03	.02	.01
344	Craig Reynolds	.03	.02	.01
345	Mike Proly	.03	.02	.01
346	Ruppert Jones	.03	.02	.01
347	Omar Moreno	.05	.03	.01
348	Greg Minton	.03	.02	.01
349	Rick Mahler	.03	.02	.01
350	Alex Trevino	.03	.02	.01
351	Mike Krukow	.03	.02	.01
352	Shane Rawley	.03	.02	.01
353	Garth Iorg	.03	.02	.01
354	Pete Mackanin	.03	.02	.01
355	Paul Moskau	.03	.02	.01
356	Richard Dotson	.03	.02	.01
357	Steve Stone	.05	.03	.01
358	Larry Hisle	.07	.05	.02
359	Aurelio Lopez	.03	.02	.01
360	Oscar Gamble	.05	.03	.01
361	Tom Burgmeier	.03	.02	.01
362	Terry Forster	.05	.03	.01
363	Joe Charboneau	.07	.05	.02
364	Ken Brett	.03	.02	.01
365	Tony Armas	.15	.10	.04
366	Chris Speier	.03	.02	.01
367	Fred Lynn	.20	.13	.05
368	Buddy Bell	.07	.05	.02
369	Jim Essian	.03	.02	.01
370	Terry Puhl	.05	.03	.01
371	Greg Gross	.03	.02	.01
372	Bruce Sutter	.15	.10	.04
373	Joe Lefebvre	.03	.02	.01
374	Ray Knight	.03	.02	.01
375	Bruce Benedict	.03	.02	.01
376	Tim Foli	.03	.02	.01
377	Al Holland	.03	.02	.01
378	Ken Kravec	.03	.02	.01
379	Jeff Burroughs	.05	.03	.01
380	Pete Falcone	.03	.02	.01
381	Ernie Whitt	.03	.02	.01
382	Brad Havens	.03	.02	.01
383	Terry Crowley	.03	.02	.01
384	Don Money	.05	.03	.01
385	Dan Schatzeder	.03	.02	.01
386	Gary Allenson	.03	.02	.01
387	Yogi Berra	.15	.10	.04
388	Ken Landreaux	.05	.03	.01
389	Mike Hargrove	.03	.02	.01
390	Darryl Motley	.03	.02	.01
391	Dave McKay	.03	.02	.01
392	Stan Bahnsen	.03	.02	.01
393	Ken Forsch	.03	.02	.01
394	Mario Mendoza	.03	.02	.01
395	Jim Morrison	.03	.02	.01
396	Mike Ivie	.03	.02	.01
397	Broderick Perkins	.03	.02	.01
398	Darrell Evans	.03	.02	.01
399	Ron Reed	.03	.02	.01
400	Johnny Bench	.20	.13	.05
401	Steve Bedrosian	.03	.02	.01
402	Bill Robinson	.03	.02	.01
403	Bill Buckner	.07	.05	.02
404	Ken Oberkfell	.03	.02	.01
405	Cal Ripken Jr.	.05	.03	.01
406	Jim Gantner	.03	.02	.01
407	Kirk Gibson	.15	.10	.04
408	Tony Perez	.11	.07	.03
409	Tommy John	.11	.07	.03
410	Dave Stewart	.03	.02	.01
411	Dan Spillner	.03	.02	.01
412	Willie Aikens	.07	.05	.02
413	Mike Heath	.03	.02	.01
414	Ray Burris	.03	.02	.01
415	Leon Roberts	.03	.02	.01
416	Mike Witt	.03	.02	.01
417	Bob Molinaro	.03	.02	.01
418	Steve Braun	.03	.02	.01

419	Nolan Ryan	.20	.13	.05
420	Tug McGraw	.07	.05	.02
421	Dave Concepcion	.11	.07	.03
422	Juan Eichelberger	.03	.02	.01
423	Rick Rhoden	.03	.02	.01
424	Frank Robinson	.15	.10	.04
425	Eddie Miller	.03	.02	.01
426	Bill Caudill	.03	.02	.01
427	Doug Flynn	.03	.02	.01
428	Larry Andersen	.03	.02	.01
429	Al Williams	.03	.02	.01
430	Jerry Garvin	.03	.02	.01
431	Glenn Adams	.03	.02	.01
432	Barry Bonnell	.03	.02	.01
433	Jerry Narron	.03	.02	.01
434	John Stearns	.03	.02	.01
435	Mike Tyson	.03	.02	.01
436	Glenn Hubbard	.03	.02	.01
437	Eddie Solomon	.03	.02	.01
438	Jeff Leonard	.03	.02	.01
439	Randy Bass	.03	.02	.01
440	Mike LaCoss	.03	.02	.01
441	Gary Matthews	.05	.03	.01
442	Mark Littell	.03	.02	.01
443	Don Sutton	.07	.05	.02
444	John Harris	.03	.02	.01
445	Vada Pinson	.05	.03	.01
446	Elias Sosa	.03	.02	.01
447	Charlie Hough	.03	.02	.01
448	Willie Wilson	.15	.10	.04
449	Fred Stanley	.03	.02	.01
450	Tom Veryzer	.03	.02	.01
451	Ron Davis	.05	.03	.01
452	Mark Clear	.05	.03	.01
453	Bill Russell	.03	.02	.01
454	Lou Whitaker	.05	.03	.01
455	Dan Graham	.03	.02	.01
456	Reggie Cleveland	.03	.02	.01
457	Sammy Stewart	.03	.02	.01
458	Pete Vuckovich	.05	.03	.01
459	John Wockenfuss	.03	.02	.01
460	Glen Hoffman	.05	.03	.01
461	Willie Randolph	.05	.03	.01
462	Fernando Valenzuela	.30	.20	.08
463	Ron Hassey	.03	.02	.01
464	Paul Splittorff	.03	.02	.01
465	Rob Picciolo	.03	.02	.01
466	Larry Parrish	.05	.03	.01
467	Johnny Grubb	.03	.02	.01
468	Dan Ford	.05	.03	.01
469	Silvio Martinez	.03	.02	.01
470	Kiko Garcia	.03	.02	.01
471	Bob Boone	.05	.03	.01
472	Luis Salazar	.03	.02	.01
473	Randy Niemann	.03	.02	.01
474	Tom Griffin	.03	.02	.01
475	Phil Niekro	.07	.05	.02
476	Hubie Brooks	.07	.05	.02
477	Dick Tidrow	.03	.02	.01
478	Jim Beattie	.03	.02	.01
479	Damaso Garcia	.03	.02	.01
480	Mickey Hatcher	.05	.03	.01
481	Joe Price	.03	.02	.01
482	Ed Farmer	.05	.03	.01
483	Eddie Murray	.15	.10	.04
484	Ben Oglivie	.07	.05	.02
485	Kevin Saucier	.03	.02	.01
486	Bobby Murcer	.07	.05	.02
487	Bill Campbell	.05	.03	.01
488	Reggie Smith	.07	.05	.02
489	Wayne Garland	.03	.02	.01
490	Jim Wright	.03	.02	.01
491	Billy Martin	.15	.10	.04
492	Jim Fanning	.03	.02	.01
493	Don Baylor	.11	.07	.03
494	Rick Honeycutt	.05	.03	.01
495	Carlton Fisk	.11	.07	.03
496	Denny Walling	.03	.02	.01
497	Bake McBride	.05	.03	.01
498	Darrell Porter	.05	.03	.01
499	Gene Richards	.03	.02	.01
500	Ron Oester	.03	.02	.01
501	Ken Dayley	.03	.02	.01
502	Jason Thompson	.05	.03	.01
503	Milt May	.03	.02	.01
504	Doug Bird	.03	.02	.01
505	Bruce Bochte	.03	.02	.01
506	Neil Allen	.05	.03	.01
507	Joey McLaughlin	.03	.02	.01
508	Butch Wynegar	.03	.02	.01
509	Gary Roenicke	.03	.02	.01
510	Robin Yount	.07	.05	.02
511	Dave Tobik	.03	.02	.01
512	Rich Gedman	.03	.02	.01
513	Gene Nelson	.03	.02	.01
514	Rick Monday	.05	.03	.01

515 Miguel Dilone	.05	.03	.01
516 Clint Hurdle	.03	.02	.01
517 Jeff Newman	.03	.02	.01
518 Grant Jackson	.03	.02	.01
519 Andy Hassler	.03	.02	.01
520 Pat Putnam	.03	.02	.01
521 Greg Pryor	.03	.02	.01
522 Tony Scott	.03	.02	.01
523 Steve Mura	.03	.02	.01
524 Johnnie LeMaster	.03	.02	.01
525 Dick Ruthven	.03	.02	.01
526 John McNamara	.03	.02	.01
527 Larry McWilliams	.03	.02	.01
528 Johnny Ray	.03	.02	.01
529 Pat Tabler	.03	.02	.01
530 Tom Herr	.03	.02	.01
531 San Diego Chicken	.05	.03	.01
532 Sal Butera	.03	.02	.01
533 Mike Griffin	.03	.02	.01
534 Kelvin Moore	.03	.02	.01
535 Reggie Jackson	.25	.17	.07
536 Ed Romero	.03	.02	.01
537 Derrel Thomas	.03	.02	.01
538 Mike O'Berry	.03	.02	.01
539 Jack O'Connor	.03	.02	.01
540 Bob Ojeda	.03	.02	.01
541 Roy Lee Jackson	.03	.02	.01
542 Lynn Jones	.03	.02	.01
543 Gaylord Perry	.15	.10	.04
544 Phil Garner	.05	.03	.01
545 Garry Templeton	.15	.10	.04
546 Rafael Ramirez	.03	.02	.01
547 Jeff Reardon	.03	.02	.01
548 Ron Guidry	.11	.07	.03
549 Tim Laudner	.03	.02	.01
550 John Henry Johnson	.03	.02	.01
551 Chris Bando	.05	.03	.01
552 Bobby Brown	.03	.02	.01
553 Larry Bradford	.03	.02	.01
554 Scot Fletcher	.03	.02	.01
555 Jerry Royster	.03	.02	.01
556 Shooty Babitt	.03	.02	.01
557 Ken Hrbek	.03	.02	.01
558 Guidry & John	.11	.07	.03
559 Mark Bomback	.03	.02	.01
560 Julio Valdez	.03	.02	.01
561 Buck Martinez	.03	.02	.01
562 Mike Marshall	.05	.03	.01
563 Rennie Stennett	.03	.02	.01
564 Steve Crawford	.03	.02	.01
565 Bob Babcock	.03	.02	.01
566 Johnny Podres	.05	.03	.01
567 Paul Serna	.03	.02	.01
568 Harold Baines	.07	.05	.02
569 Dave LaRoche	.03	.02	.01
570 Lee May	.05	.03	.01
571 Gary Ward	.03	.02	.01
572 John Denny	.03	.02	.01
573 Roy Smalley	.05	.03	.01
574 Bob Brenly	.03	.02	.01
575 Jackson & Winfield	.20	.13	.05
576 Luis Pujols	.03	.02	.01
577 Butch Hobson	.03	.02	.01
578 Harvey Kuenn	.05	.03	.01
579 Cal Ripken	.03	.02	.01
580 Juan Berenguer	.03	.02	.01
581 Benny Ayala	.03	.02	.01
582 Vance Law	.03	.02	.01
583 Rick Leach	.05	.03	.01
584 George Frazier	.03	.02	.01
585 Rose & Schmidt	.20	.13	.05
586 Joe Rudi	.05	.03	.01
587 Juan Beniquez	.03	.02	.01
588 Luis De Leon	.03	.02	.01
589 Craig Swan	.03	.02	.01
590 Dave Chalk	.03	.02	.01
591 Billy Gardner	.03	.02	.01
592 Sal Bando	.05	.03	.01
593 Bert Campaneris	.05	.03	.01
594 Steve Kemp	.11	.07	.03
595 Randy Lerch	.03	.02	.01
596 Bryan Clark	.03	.02	.01
597 David Ford	.03	.02	.01
598 Mike Scioscia	.03	.02	.01
599 John Lowenstein	.03	.02	.01
600 Rene Lachmann	.03	.02	.01
601 Mick Kelleher	.03	.02	.01
602 Ron Jackson	.03	.02	.01
603 Jerry Koosman	.05	.03	.01
604 Dave Goltz	.03	.02	.01
605 Ellis Valentine	.05	.03	.01
606 Lonnie Smith	.05	.03	.01
607 Joaquin Andujar	.05	.03	.01
608 Garry Hancock	.03	.02	.01
609 Jerry Turner	.03	.02	.01
610 Bob Bonner	.03	.02	.01
611 Jim Dwyer	.03	.02	.01
612 Terry Bulling	.03	.02	.01
613 Joel Youngblood	.03	.02	.01
614 Larry Milbourne	.03	.02	.01
615 Gene Roof	.03	.02	.01
616 Keith Drumright	.03	.02	.01
617 Dave Rosello	.03	.02	.01
618 Rickey Keeton	.03	.02	.01
619 Dennis Lamp	.03	.02	.01
620 Sid Monge	.03	.02	.01
621 Jerry White	.03	.02	.01
622 Luis Aguayo	.03	.02	.01
623 Jamie Easterly	.03	.02	.01
624 Steve Sax	.03	.02	.01
625 Dave Roberts	.03	.02	.01
626 Rick Bosetti	.03	.02	.01
627 Terry Francona	.03	.02	.01
628 Seaver & Bench	.20	.13	.05
629 Paul Mirabella	.03	.02	.01
630 Rance Mulliniks	.03	.02	.01
631 Kevin Hickey	.03	.02	.01
632 Reid Nichols	.03	.02	.01
633 Dave Geisel	.03	.02	.01
634 Ken Griffey	.11	.07	.03
635 Bob Lemon	.07	.05	.02
636 Orlando Sanchez	.03	.02	.01
637 Bill Almon	.03	.02	.01
638 Danny Ainge	.11	.07	.03
639 Willie Stargell	.15	.10	.04
640 Bob Sykes	.03	.02	.01
641 Ed Lynch	.03	.02	.01
642 John Ellis	.03	.02	.01
643 Ferguson Jenkins	.07	.05	.02
644 Lenn Sakata	.03	.02	.01
645 Juilo Gonzalez	.03	.02	.01
646 Jesse Orosco	.03	.02	.01
647 Jerry Dybzinski	.03	.02	.01
648 Tommy Davis	.05	.03	.01
649 Ron Gardenhire	.03	.02	.01
650 Felipe Alou	.05	.03	.01
651 Harvey Haddix	.05	.03	.01
652 Willie Upshaw	.03	.02	.01
653 Bill Madlock	.07	.05	.02
Checklist Diamond Kings	.05	.03	.01
Checklist 1	.03	.02	.01
Checklist 2	.03	.02	.01
Checklist 3	.03	.02	.01
Checklist 4	.03	.02	.01
Checklist 5	.03	.02	.01
Checklist 6	.03	.02	.01

1941 DOUBLE PLAY (75) SEPIA   2 1/2" X 3 1/8"

FRANK McCORMICK
CINCINNATI REDS. First baseman. Born June 9, 1913. Bats
right. Throws right. Height 6
ft. 4 in. Wt. 200 lbs. Batted .309.
No. 9 Double Play

BILL WERBER
CINCINNATI REDS. Third baseman. Born June 20, 1908. Bats
right. Throws right. Ht. 5 ft.
10 in. Wt. 170 lbs. Batted .277.
No. 10 Double Play

STANLEY HACK
CHICAGO CUBS. Third
baseman. Born Dec. 6,
1909. Bats left. Throws
right. Height 5 ft. 11½
in. Weight 171 lbs.
Batted .317.
No. 97 Double Play

BOB KLINGER
PITTSBURGH PIRATES.
Pitcher. Born June 4,
1910. Bats and throws
right. Height 6 feet.
Weight 180 lbs. Won 8.
Lost 13.
No. 98 Double Play

The 1941 Double Play se
R-330 (ACC), is a blank-bac
issue from Gum Products cor
taining 75 two-player card
Card nos. 81-100 are vertica
action pictures of players is
ued elsewhere in the se
Cards cut in half have great
reduced value.

	MINT	VG-E	F-G
COMPLETE SET	600.00	450.00	200.00
COMMON PAIRS (1-100)	6.00	4.50	2.00
COMMON PAIRS (101-150)	7.50	5.50	2.50
CUT HALVES	1.00	.65	.25

No.	Players	MINT	VG-E	F-G
1-2	French-Page	6.00	4.50	2.00
3-4	Herman-Hack	7.50	5.50	2.50
5-6	Lonnie Frey-J. VanderMeer	7.50	5.50	2.50
7-8	Derringer-Bucky Walters	7.50	5.50	2.50
9-10	McCormick-Bill Werber	6.00	4.50	2.00
11-12	Ripple-Lombardi	7.50	5.50	2.50
13-14	Kampouris-Wyatt	6.00	4.50	2.00
15-16	Owen-Paul Waner	9.00	6.50	3.00
17-18	C. Lavagetto-Pete Reiser	7.50	5.50	2.50
19-20	Wasdell-Camilli	6.00	4.50	2.00
21-22	Walker-Medwick	9.00	6.50	3.00
23-24	Reese-Higbe	11.00	7.50	3.50
25-26	Danning-Melton	6.00	4.50	2.00
27-28	Gumbert-B. Whitehead	6.00	4.50	2.00
29-30	Orengo-Moore	6.00	4.50	2.00
31-32	Mel Ott-Young	13.50	9.00	4.00
33-34	Handley-Vaughn	7.50	5.50	2.50
35-36	Klinger-Brown	6.00	4.50	2.00
37-38	Moore-Mancuso	6.00	4.50	2.00
39-40	Mize-Slaughter	15.00	10.00	4.50
41-42	Cooney-Sisti	6.00	4.50	2.00
43-44	West-Rowell	6.00	4.50	2.00
45-46	Litwhiler-May	6.00	4.50	2.00
47-48	Hayes-Brancato	6.00	4.50	2.00
49-50	Johnson-Nagel	6.00	4.50	2.00
51-52	Newsom-H. Greenberg	11.00	7.50	3.50
53-54	McCoskey-C. Gehringer	11.00	7.50	3.50
55-56	Higgins-Bartell	6.00	4.50	2.00
57-58	Ted Williams-J. Tabor	50.00	35.00	15.00
59-60	Cronin-Foxx	20.00	13.00	6.00
61-62	Gomez-Rizzuto	15.00	10.00	4.50
63-64	Joe DiMaggio-Keller	65.00	45.00	20.00
65-66	Rolfe-Dickey	13.50	9.00	4.00
67-68	Gordon-Ruffing	9.00	6.50	3.00
69-70	Tresh-Appling	9.00	6.50	3.00
71-72	Solters-Rigney	6.00	4.50	2.00
73-74	Meyer-Chapman	6.00	4.50	2.00
75-76	Travis-Case	6.00	4.50	2.00
77-78	J. Krakauskas-Bob Feller	15.00	10.00	4.50
79-80	Keltner-Trosky	6.00	4.50	2.00
81-82	Ted Williams-Joe Cronin	60.00	40.00	18.00
83-84	Gordon-Keller	7.50	5.50	2.50
85-86	H. Greenberg-Red Ruffing	15.00	10.00	4.50
87-88	Trosky-Case	6.00	4.50	2.00
89-90	Ott-Whitehead	13.50	9.00	4.00
91-92	Danning-Gumbert	6.00	4.50	2.00
93-94	Young-Melton	6.00	4.50	2.00
95-96	Ripple-Walters	6.00	4.50	2.00
97-98	Jack-Klinger	6.00	4.50	2.00
99-100	Mize-Litwhiler	9.00	6.50	3.00
101-102	D. Dallessandro-Augie Galan	7.50	5.50	2.50
103-104	Lee-Cavaretta	7.50	5.50	2.50
105-106	Grove-Doerr	11.00	7.50	3.50
107-108	Pytlak-Dom DiMaggio	9.00	6.50	3.00
109-110	Priddy-Murphy	7.50	5.50	2.50
111-112	Henrich-Russo	9.00	6.50	3.00
113-114	Crosetti-Sturm	9.00	6.50	3.00
115-116	I. Goodman-McCormick	7.50	5.50	2.50
117-118	Joost-Koy	7.50	5.50	2.50
119-120	Lloyd Waner-Majeski	9.00	6.50	3.00
121-122	Hassett-Moore	7.50	5.50	2.50
123-124	Etten-Rizzo	7.50	5.50	2.50
125-126	Chapman-Moses	7.50	5.50	2.50
127-128	Babich-Siebert	7.50	5.50	2.50
129-130	Potter-McCoy	7.50	5.50	2.50
131-132	Campbell-Lou Boudreau	11.00	7.50	3.50
133-134	Hemsley-Harder	7.50	5.50	2.50
135-136	Walker-Heving	7.50	5.50	2.50
137-138	Rucker-Adams	7.50	5.50	2.50
139-140	M. Arnovich-Carl Hubbell	11.00	7.50	3.50
141-142	Riggs-Durocher	9.00	6.50	3.00
143-144	F. Fitzsimmons-Joe Vosmik	7.50	5.50	2.50
145-146	Crespi-Brown	7.50	5.50	2.50
147-148	Heffner-Clift	7.50	5.50	2.50
149-150	Garms-Fletcher	7.50	5.50	2.50

ATTEND A SPORTS MEMORABILIA SHOW OR CON—
VENTION IN YOUR AREA SOMETIME THIS YEAR.
THEY ARE BOTH INTERESTING AND ENJOYABLE TO
ALL MEMBERS OF THE FAMILY.

1950 DRAKES (36)

2 1/2" X 2 1/2"

BOBBY THOMSON Outfield, New York Giants
Born: Glasgow, Scotland, October 25, 1923
Ht. 6-2½; Wt: 185 Eyes: Brown Hair: Brown
Bats: Right — Throws: Right

One of the few European ball players in baseball,
Bob was brought to this country by his parents
when he was two years old. They settled in Staten
Island where he grew up. The Giants signed him
out of high school and he was sent to their Rocky
Mount farm team for 1942. He played 29 games
at third base and then entered the service. He won
his wings in the Air Force. He returned to baseball in 1946 with Jersey City, batting .310 and
hitting 26 homers, a record for the JC ball park.
He joined the Giants at the end of that campaign.
The next season he spent mainly in the outfield,
and was a rookie sensation batting .283, hitting
29 homers and driving in 85 runs. He slumped
the next season, but came back strong in 1949
batting .309, driving in 109 runs and numbering
27 homers among his 198 hits.

TV BASEBALL STAR PICTURES
Save 'em — Trade 'em. For a limited time only in
DRAKE'S OATMEAL **COOKIES**
OR JUMBLE
© 1950 by Drake Bakeries, Inc.
9

The 1950 Drake Cookies set contains 36 numbered black & white cards. The players are pictures inside a simulated television screen and the caption "TV Baseball Series" appears on the cards. The ACC designation is D358.

	MINT	VG-E	F-G
COMPLETE SET	1200.00	800.00	350.00
COMMON PLAYER(1-36)	33.00	22.00	9.00
1 Roe,Preacher	36.00	24.00	10.00
2 Hartung,Clint	33.00	22.00	9.00
3 Torgeson,Earl	33.00	22.00	9.00
4 Brissie,Lou	33.00	22.00	9.00
5 Snider,Duke	75.00	50.00	20.00
6 Campanella,Roy	90.00	60.00	25.00
7 Jones,Sheldon	33.00	22.00	9.00
8 Lockman,Whitey	33.00	22.00	9.00
9 Thomson,Bobby	36.00	24.00	10.00
10 Sisler,Dick	33.00	22.00	9.00
11 Hodges,Gil	50.00	35.00	14.00
12 Waitkus,Eddie	33.00	22.00	9.00
13 Kerr,Bobby	33.00	22.00	9.00
14 Spahn,Warren	60.00	40.00	15.00
15 Kerr,Buddy	33.00	22.00	9.00
16 Gordon,Sid	33.00	22.00	9.00
17 Marshall,Willard	33.00	22.00	9.00
18 Furillo,Carl	36.00	24.00	10.00
19 Reese,Peewee	50.00	35.00	14.00
20 Dark,Alvin	36.00	24.00	10.00
21 Ennis,Del	33.00	22.00	9.00
22 Stanky,Ed	36.00	24.00	10.00
23 Henrich,Tom	36.00	24.00	10.00
24 Berra,Yogi	75.00	50.00	20.00
25 Rizzuto,Phil	50.00	35.00	14.00
26 Coleman,Jerry	33.00	22.00	9.00
27 Page,Joe	33.00	22.00	9.00
28 Reynolds,Allie	36.00	24.00	10.00
29 Scarborough,Ray	33.00	22.00	9.00
30 Tebbetts,Birdie	33.00	22.00	9.00
31 McDermott,Maurice	33.00	22.00	9.00
32 Pesky,Johnny	33.00	22.00	9.00
33 DiMaggio,Dom	42.00	28.00	12.00
34 Stephens,Vern	33.00	22.00	9.00
35 Elliott,Bob	33.00	22.00	9.00
36 Slaughter,Enos	42.00	28.00	12.00

1981 DRAKES (33)

2 1/2" X 3 1/2"

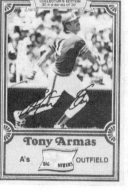

Tony led A's in Homers & RBI's in 1980.

The 1981 Drakes Bakeries set contains 33 cards of National and American League stars. Produced in conjunction with Topps and released to the public in Drake's Cakes, this set features red frames for American League players and blue frames for National League players. A Drake's Cakes logo with the words "Big Hitters" appears on the lower front of each card. The backs are quite similar to the 1981 Topps backs but contain the Drake's logo, a different card number, and a short paragraph entitled "What Makes a Big Hitter?"— all at the top of the card.

	MINT	VG-E	F-G
COMPLETE SET	7.50	5.00	2.00
COMMON PLAYER	.15	.10	.04
1 Carl Yastrzemski	.75	.50	.20
2 Rod Carew	.50	.35	.14
3 Pete Rose	.75	.50	.20
4 Dave Parker	.30	.20	.08
5 George Brett	.75	.50	.20
6 Eddie Murray	.30	.20	.08
7 Mike Schmidt	.50	.35	.14
8 Jim Rice	.50	.35	.14
9 Fred Lynn	.50	.35	.14
10 Reggie Jackson	.50	.35	.14
11 Steve Garvey	.50	.35	.14
12 Ken Singleton	.21	.14	.06
13 Bill Buckner	.15	.10	.04
14 Dave Winfield	.30	.20	.08
15 Jack Clark	.21	.14	.06
16 Cecil Cooper	.21	.14	.06
17 Bob Horner	.30	.20	.08
18 George Foster	.30	.20	.08
19 Dave Kingman	.21	.14	.06
20 Cesar Cedeno	.21	.14	.06
21 Joe Charboneau	.15	.10	.04
22 George Hendrick	.15	.10	.04
23 Gary Carter	.30	.20	.08
24 Al Oliver	.21	.14	.06
25 Bruce Bochte	.15	.10	.04
26 Jerry Mumphrey	.15	.10	.04
27 Steve Kemp	.21	.14	.06
28 Bob Watson	.21	.14	.06
29 John Castino	.15	.10	.04
30 Tony Armas	.21	.14	.06
31 John Mayberry	.21	.14	.06
32 Carlton Fisk	.30	.20	.08
33 Lee Mazzilli	.21	.14	.06

1966 EAST HILLS PIRATES (25)   3 1/4'' X 4 1/4''

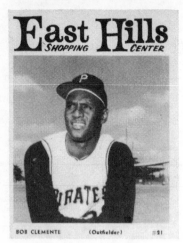

The 1966 East Hills Pirates set contains 25 full color, numbered (by uniform number) cards and features Pittsburgh Pirates only. The SCB designation is F 405.

	MINT	VG-E	F-G
COMPLETE SET	4.50	3.00	1.20
COMMON PLAYER(1-45)	.15	.10	.04
3 Walker,Harry	.15	.10	.04
7 Bailey,Bob	.15	.10	.04
8 Stargell,Willie	.75	.50	.20
9 Mazeroski,Bill	.30	.20	.08
10 Pagliaroni,Jim	.15	.10	.04
11 Pagan,Jose	.15	.10	.04
12 May,Jerry	.15	.10	.04
14 Alley,Gene	.15	.10	.04
15 Mota,Manny	.20	.13	.05
16 Rodgers,Andy	.15	.10	.04
17 Clendenon,Donn	.15	.10	.04
18 Alou,Matty	.20	.13	.05

	MINT	VG-E	F-
19 Mikkelsen,Pete	.15	.10	.04
20 Gonder,Jess	.15	.10	.04
21 Clemente,Bob	1.35	.90	.40
22 Fryman,Woody	.15	.10	.04
24 Lynch,Jerry	.15	.10	.04
25 Sisk,Tommie	.15	.10	.04
26 Face,Roy	.30	.20	.08
28 Blass,Steve	.20	.13	.05
32 Law,Vernon	.20	.13	.05
34 McBean,Al	.15	.10	.04
39 Veale,Bob	.15	.10	.04
43 Cardwell,Don	.15	.10	.04
45 Michael,Gene	.30	.20	.08

1954 ESSKAY (36)

DARRELL JOHNSON, Catcher
Born August 25, 1927
Hometown, Richmond, Calif.
Throws Right — Bats Right

The 1954 Esskay Meats set contains 36 color, unnumbered cards featuring Baltimore Orioles only. The cards were issued in panels of two on boxes of Esskay hot dogs; consequently, many have grease stains on the cards and are quite difficult to obtain in mint condition. The 1954 Esskay set can be distinguished from the 1955 Esskay set supposedly by the white or off-white (the 1955 set) backs of the cards. The backs of the 1954 cards are also supposedly "waxed" to a greater degree than the 1955 cards. The ACC designation is F181.

2 1/4" X 3 1/2"

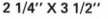

	MINT	VG-E	F-G
COMPLETE SET	2400.00	1600.00	700.00
COMMON PLAYER(1-36)	75.00	50.00	20.00
1 Abrams,Cal	75.00	50.00	20.00
2 Berry,Neil	90.00	60.00	25.00
3 Blyzka,Michael	75.00	50.00	20.00
4 Brecheen,Harry	90.00	60.00	25.00
5 Coan,Gil	75.00	50.00	20.00
6 Coleman,Joe	75.00	50.00	20.00
7 Courtney,Clint	90.00	60.00	25.00
8 Diering,Charles E.	75.00	50.00	20.00
9 Dykes,Jimmie	90.00	60.00	25.00
10 Fanovich,Frank	75.00	50.00	20.00
11 Fox,Howard	75.00	50.00	20.00
12 Fridley,Jim	75.00	50.00	20.00
13 Garcia,Chico	75.00	50.00	20.00
14 Heard,Jehosie	75.00	50.00	20.00
15 Johnson,Darrel	90.00	60.00	25.00
16 Kennedy,Robert D.	90.00	60.00	25.00
17 Kokos,Dick	75.00	50.00	20.00
18 Koslo,Dave	75.00	50.00	20.00

	MINT	VG-E	F-G
19 Kretlow,Lou	75.00	50.00	20.00
20 Kryhoski,Richard D	75.00	50.00	20.00
21 Kuzava,Robert	75.00	50.00	20.00
22 Larsen,Don	120.00	80.00	35.00
23 Lenhardt,Don	75.00	50.00	20.00
24 Littlefield,Dick	75.00	50.00	20.00
25 Mele,Sam	75.00	50.00	20.00
26 Moss,John Lester	75.00	50.00	20.00
27 Murray,Ray L.	75.00	50.00	20.00
28 Newsom,Bobo	90.00	60.00	25.00
29 Oliver,Tom	75.00	50.00	20.00
30 Pillette,Duane	75.00	50.00	20.00
31 Skaff,Francis M.	75.00	50.00	20.00
32 Stuart,Marlin	75.00	50.00	20.00
33 Turley,Robert L.	120.00	80.00	35.00
34 Waitkus,Eddie	90.00	60.00	25.00
35 Wertz,Vic	90.00	60.00	25.00
36 Young,Robert G.	75.00	50.00	20.00

1955 ESSKAY (27)

2 1/4" X 3 1/2"

CHARLES E. DIERING, Outfielder
Born, February 5, 1922
Hometown, St. Louis, Mo.
Throws Right — Bats Right

The 1955 Esskay Meats set was issued in panels of two on boxes of Esskay hot dogs. This set of 27 full color, blank back, unnumbered cards features Baltimore Orioles only. Many of the players in the 1954 Esskay set were also issued in this set. The ACC designation is F181.

	MINT	VG-E	F-G
COMPLETE SET	2100.00	1400.00	600.00
COMMON PLAYER(1-27)	75.00	50.00	20.00
1 Abrams,Cal	75.00	50.00	20.00
2 Alexander,Robert	75.00	50.00	20.00
3 Brecheen,Harry	90.00	60.00	25.00
4 Byrd,Harry	75.00	50.00	20.00
5 Coan,Gil	75.00	50.00	20.00
6 Coleman,Joe	75.00	50.00	20.00
7 Cox,William	90.00	60.00	25.00
8 Diering,Charles E.	75.00	50.00	20.00
9 Evers,Walter	90.00	60.00	25.00
10 Johnson,Don	75.00	50.00	20.00
11 Kennedy,Robert D.	90.00	60.00	25.00
12 Kretlow,Lou	75.00	50.00	20.00
13 Kuzava,Robert	75.00	50.00	20.00

	MINT	VG-E	F-G
14 Marsh,Fred	75.00	50.00	20.00
15 Maxwell,Charles	75.00	50.00	20.00
16 McDonald,Jim	75.00	50.00	20.00
17 Miller,Bill	75.00	50.00	20.00
18 Miranda,Willie	90.00	60.00	25.00
19 Moore,Raymond L.	75.00	50.00	20.00
20 Moss,John Lester	75.00	50.00	20.00
21 Newsom,Bobo	90.00	60.00	25.00
22 Pillette,Duane	75.00	50.00	20.00
23 Smith,Harold W.	75.00	50.00	20.00
24 Triandos,Gus	105.00	70.00	30.00
25 Waitkus,Eddie	90.00	60.00	25.00
26 Woodling,Gene	90.00	60.00	25.00
27 Young,Robert G.	75.00	50.00	20.00

1908 E90—1 (120)

1 1/2" X 2 3/4"

The 1908 E90-1 set contains 120 unnumbered cards. In order, the Mitchell-Cincinnati, Sweeney-Boston, Graham, Walsh, Stahl and Speaker cards are more difficult to obtain than other cards in the set. Several players exist in more than one pose. These cards are noted in the checklist.

	MINT	VG-E	F-G
COMPLETE SET	1350.00	900.00	400.00
COMMON PLAYER(1-120)	6.50	4.50	2.00

		MINT	VG-E	F-G
1	Bailey,William	6.50	4.50	2.00
2	Baker,Frank	12.00	8.00	3.50
3	Barry,Jack	6.50	4.50	2.00
4	Bell,George	6.50	4.50	2.00
5	Bemis,Harry	6.50	4.50	2.00
6	Bender,Chief	12.00	8.00	3.50
7	Bescher,Bob	6.50	4.50	2.00
8	Blankenship,C	6.50	4.50	2.00
9	Bliss,John	6.50	4.50	2.00
10	Bradley,William J	6.50	4.50	2.00
11	Bransfield-blue bkgd	9.00	6.00	2.50
12	Bransfield-pink bkgd	12.00	8.00	3.50
13	Bresnahan,Roger	12.00	8.00	3.50
14	Bridwell,Al	6.50	4.50	2.00
15	Brown,Bost NL	6.50	4.50	2.00
16	Brown,Chic NL	25.00	17.00	7.00
17	Bush,Donie	6.50	4.50	2.00
18	Butler,John A	9.00	6.00	2.50
19	Camnitz,Howie	6.50	4.50	2.00
20	Chance,Frank	18.00	12.00	5.00
21	Chase,Hal	7.50	5.00	2.00
22	Clarke,Phi NL	12.00	8.00	3.50
23	Clarke,Pit	40.00	26.00	10.00
24	Clement,Wallace O	12.00	8.00	3.50
25	Cobb,"Ty"	75.00	50.00	20.00
26	Collins,Eddie	12.00	8.00	3.50
27	Corridon,Frank	6.50	4.50	2.00
28	Crawford,Sam	12.00	8.00	3.50
29	Criger,Lou	6.50	4.50	2.00
30	Davis,H "Jasper"	6.50	4.50	2.00
31	Davis,George	6.50	4.50	2.00
32	Demmitt,Ray	12.00	8.00	3.50
33	Donlin,Mike	6.50	4.50	2.00
34	Donovan,Wild Bill	6.50	4.50	2.00
35	Dooin,Red	6.50	4.50	2.00
36	Dougherty,Patsy	6.50	4.50	2.00
37	Duffy,Hugh	75.00	50.00	20.00
38	Dygert,Jimmy	6.50	4.50	2.00
39	Ellis,Rube	6.50	4.50	2.00
40	Engle,Clyde	6.50	4.50	2.00
41	Fromme,Art	12.00	8.00	3.50
42	Gibson-back view	25.00	17.00	7.00
43	Gibson-front view	7.50	5.00	2.00
44	Graham,George	75.00	50.00	20.00
45	Grant,Eddie	6.50	4.50	2.00
46	Gray,Dolly	6.50	4.50	2.00
47	Groom,Bob	6.50	4.50	2.00
48	Hall,Charles	6.50	4.50	2.00
49	Hartzell-green bkgd	7.50	5.00	2.00
50	Hartzell-pink bkgd	7.50	5.00	2.00
51	Heitmuller,William	6.50	4.50	2.00
52	Howell-follow thru	7.50	5.00	2.00
53	Howell-windup	12.00	8.00	3.50
54	Irwin	6.50	4.50	2.00
55	Isbell,Frank	6.50	4.50	2.00
56	Jackson,Joe	40.00	26.00	10.00
57	Jennings,Hugh	12.00	8.00	3.50
58	Jordan,Buck	6.50	4.50	2.00
59	Joss-portrait	18.00	12.00	5.00
60	Joss-horizontal pitching	40.00	26.00	10.00
61	Karger,Ed	25.00	17.00	7.00
62	Keeler-por pink bkgd	18.00	12.00	5.00
63	Keeler-por red bkgd	25.00	17.00	7.00

		MINT	VG-E	F-G
64	Keeler-horizontal throwing	40.00	26.00	10.00
65	Knight,John	18.00	12.00	5.00
66	Krause,Harry	6.50	4.50	2.00
67	Lajoie,Napolean	25.00	17.00	7.00
68	Leach-batting	7.50	5.00	2.00
69	Leach-throwing	7.50	5.00	2.00
70	Leever,Sam	6.50	4.50	2.00
71	Lobert,Hans	18.00	12.00	5.00
72	Lumley,Harry	6.50	4.50	2.00
73	Marquard,Rube	12.00	8.00	3.50
74	Mathewson,Christy	40.00	26.00	10.00
75	McInnes,J "Stuffy"	7.50	5.00	2.00
76	McIntyre,Matty	6.50	4.50	2.00
77	McLean,Larry	18.00	12.00	5.00
78	McQuillan,George	6.50	4.50	2.00
79	Miller,John "Dots"	6.50	4.50	2.00
80	Mitchell,Cin	200.00	130.00	55.00
81	Mitchell,N Y AL	6.50	4.50	2.00
82	Mullin,George	6.50	4.50	2.00
83	Oakes,Rebel	6.50	4.50	2.00
84	O'Connor,Patrick	6.50	4.50	2.00
85	O'Leary,Charley	6.50	4.50	2.00
86	Overall,Orval	18.00	12.00	5.00
87	Pastorius,Jim	6.50	4.50	2.00
88	Phelps,Ed	6.50	4.50	2.00
89	Plank,Eddie	18.00	12.00	5.00
90	Richie,Lew	6.50	4.50	2.00
91	Schaefer,Germany	6.50	4.50	2.00
92	Schlitzer,Victor	18.00	12.00	5.00
93	Seigle	18.00	12.00	5.00
94	Shean,Dave	12.00	8.00	3.50
95	Sheckard,Jimmy	12.00	8.00	3.50
96	Speaker,Tris	75.00	50.00	20.00
97	Stahl,Jake	40.00	26.00	10.00
98	Stanage,Oscar	6.50	4.50	2.00
99	Stone-green bkgd	7.50	5.00	2.00
100	Stone-sky bkgd	7.50	5.00	2.00
101	Stovall,George	6.50	4.50	2.00
102	Summers,Ed	6.50	4.50	2.00
103	Sweeney,Bos	135.00	90.00	40.00
104	Sweeney,N Y	6.50	4.50	2.00
105	Tannehill-Chi Amer	7.50	5.00	2.00
106	Tannehill-Chi Nat	7.50	5.00	2.00
107	Tenney,Fred	6.50	4.50	2.00
108	Thomas-Phila Amer	7.50	5.00	2.00
109	Thomas-Boston Nat	7.50	5.00	2.00
110	Tinker,Joe	12.00	8.00	3.50
111	Unglaub,Bob	6.50	4.50	2.00
112	Upp,Jerry	12.00	8.00	3.50
113	Wagner-batting	40.00	26.00	10.00
114	Wagner-throwing	40.00	26.00	10.00
115	Wallace,Bobby	12.00	8.00	3.50
116	Walsh,Ed	75.00	50.00	20.00
117	Willis,Vic	6.50	4.50	2.00
118	Wiltse,Hooks	18.00	12.00	5.00
119	Young-Boston Amer	18.00	12.00	5.00
120	Young-Cleveland	25.00	17.00	7.00

1910 E90—2 (11)

1 1/2" X 2 3/4"

The 1910 E90-2 American Caramels Baseball Star set contains 11 unnumbered cards featuring players from the 1909 Pittsburgh Pirates. The backs of these cards are exactly like the E90-1 cards; however, blue print is used for the names of the players and the teams on the fronts of the cards.

	MINT	VG-E	F-G
COMPLETE SET	210.00	140.00	60.00
COMMON PLAYER(1-11)	16.50	11.00	5.00
1 Adams,Charles "Babe"	16.50	11.00	5.00
2 Clarke,Fred	27.00	18.00	8.00
3 Gibson,George	16.50	11.00	5.00
4 Hyatt,Ham	16.50	11.00	5.00

	MINT	VG-E	F-G
5 Leach,Tommy	16.50	11.00	5.00
6 Leever,Sam	16.50	11.00	5.00
7 Maddox,Nick	16.50	11.00	5.00
8 Miller,John "Dots"	16.50	11.00	5.00
9 Phillippe,Deacon	20.00	13.00	5.50
10 Wagner,Honus	75.00	50.00	20.00
11 Wilson,John "Chief"	16.50	11.00	5.00

1910 E90—3 (20)

1 1/2" X 2 3/4"

The E90-3 American Caramels "All the Star Players" set contains 20 unnumbered cards featuring the Chicago White Sox and Chicago Cubs. The Cubs are listed in the checklist below with the prefix letter C while the White Sox are designated by the prefix letters WS. The backs are slightly different from E90-1 cards and the fronts differ in the use of the team nicknames.

	MINT	VG-E	F-G
COMPLETE SET	330.00	220.00	90.00
COMMON PLAYER(1-20)	16.50	11.00	5.00
C1 Archer,Jimmy	16.50	11.00	5.00
C2 Brown,Mordecai	27.00	18.00	8.00
C3 Chance,Frank	36.00	24.00	10.00
C4 Cole,King	16.50	11.00	5.00
C5 Evers,Johnny	27.00	18.00	8.00
C6 Hoffman,Solly	16.50	11.00	5.00
C7 Overall,Orval	16.50	11.00	5.00
C8 Schulte,Frank	16.50	11.00	5.00
C9 Scheckard,Jimmy	16.50	11.00	5.00

	MINT	VG-E	F-G
C10 Steinfeldt,Harry	20.00	13.00	5.50
C11 Tinker,Joe	27.00	18.00	8.00
WS1 Blackburne,Lena	16.50	11.00	5.00
WS2 Dougherty,Patsy	16.50	11.00	5.00
WS3 Gandil,Chick	16.50	11.00	5.00
WS4 Hahn,Ed	16.50	11.00	5.00
WS5 Payne,Fred	20.00	13.00	5.50
WS6 Purtell,Billy	20.00	13.00	5.50
WS7 Smith,Frank "Nig"	16.50	11.00	5.00
WS8 Walsh,Ed	27.00	18.00	8.00
WS9 Zeider,Rollie	16.50	11.00	5.00

E91 BASE BALL CARAMELS (99) 1 1/2" X 2 3/4"

E91 encompasses three separate sets of color cards issued in 1908 and 1910. The 33 ballplayer drawings of the 1908 set were also used in the two 1910 sets. Eleven players were dropped and 11 added in set 2 (the first 1910 set), and all new players were added for set 3. Although there are 99 cards in E91, there are only 75 different players, so that, for example, there are two cards of Bender with identical fronts, but a different player is "named" in the same pose in set 3. Likewise, there can be three different players assigned to the same pose—one from each set. The set 1 checklist lists "Athletics" first; set 2 lists "Chicago" first; set 3 "Pittsburgh" first.

	MINT	VG-E	F-G
COMPLETE SET	525.00	350.00	150.00
COMMON PLAYER(1-99)	5.25	3.50	1.50

		MINT	VG-E	F-G
1	Bender,Chief	7.50	5.00	2.00
2	Bresnahan,Roger	7.50	5.00	2.00
3	Bridwell,Al	5.25	3.50	1.50
4	Brown,Mordecai	7.50	5.00	2.00
5	Chance,Frank	9.00	6.00	2.50
6	Collins,James	5.25	3.50	1.50
7	Davis,Harry	5.25	3.50	1.50
8	Devlin,Art	5.25	3.50	1.50
9	Donlin,Mike	5.25	3.50	1.50
10	Evers,Johnny	7.50	5.00	2.00
11	Hartzell,Fred	5.25	3.50	1.50
12	Kling,Johnny	5.25	3.50	1.50
13	Mathewson,Christy	13.50	9.00	4.00
14	McGinnity,Joe	9.00	6.00	2.50
15	McGraw,John	9.00	6.00	2.50
16	Murphy,Danny	5.25	3.50	1.50
17	Nichols,Simon	5.25	3.50	1.50
18	Oldring,Rube	5.25	3.50	1.50
19	Overal,Orval	5.25	3.50	1.50
20	Plank,Eddie	9.00	6.00	2.50
21	Reulbach,Ed	5.25	3.50	1.50
22	Scheckard,Jimmy	5.25	3.50	1.50
23	Schreckengost,Osee	5.25	3.50	1.50
24	Shulte,Frank	5.25	3.50	1.50
25	Seybold,Ralph	5.25	3.50	1.50
26	Seymore,J. B.	5.25	3.50	1.50
27	Shay,Daniel	5.25	3.50	1.50
28	Slagle,James	5.25	3.50	1.50
29	Steinfeldt,Harry	6.00	4.00	1.50
30	Taylor,Luther	5.25	3.50	1.50
31	Tenney,Fred	5.25	3.50	1.50
32	Tinker,Joe	7.50	5.00	2.00
33	Waddell,Rube	7.50	5.00	2.00
34	Archer,Jimmy	5.25	3.50	1.50
35	Baker,J. Frank	7.50	5.00	2.00
36	Barry,Jack	5.25	3.50	1.50
37	Bender,Chief	7.50	5.00	2.00
38	Bridwell,Al	5.25	3.50	1.50
39	Brown,Mordecai	7.50	5.00	2.00
40	Chance,Frank	9.00	6.00	2.50
41	Collins,Eddie	7.50	5.00	2.00
42	Davis,Harry	5.25	3.50	1.50
43	Devlin,Art	5.25	3.50	1.50
44	Donlin,Mike	5.25	3.50	1.50
45	Doyle,Larry	5.25	3.50	1.50
46	Evers,Johnny	7.50	5.00	2.00
47	Ganley,Bob	5.25	3.50	1.50
48	Hartzell,Fred	5.25	3.50	1.50
49	Hoffman,Solly	5.25	3.50	1.50
50	Krause,Harry	5.25	3.50	1.50
51	Marquard,Rube	7.50	5.00	2.00
52	Mathewson,Christy	13.50	9.00	4.00
53	McGraw,John	9.00	6.00	2.50
54	Meyers,Chief	5.25	3.50	1.50
55	Murphy,Danny	5.25	3.50	1.50
56	Murray,Red	5.25	3.50	1.50
57	Overall,Orval	5.25	3.50	1.50
58	Plank,Eddie	9.00	6.00	2.50
59	Reulbach,Ed	5.25	3.50	1.50
60	Scheckard,Jimmy	5.25	3.50	1.50
61	Schulte,Frank	5.25	3.50	1.50
62	Seymore,J. B.	5.25	3.50	1.50
63	Steinfeldt,Harry	6.00	4.00	1.50
64	Tenney,Fred	5.25	3.50	1.50
65	Thomas,Ira	5.25	3.50	1.50
66	Tinker,Joe	7.50	5.00	2.00
67	Barbeau,Jap	5.25	3.50	1.50
68	Browne,George	5.25	3.50	1.50
69	Carger,Ed	5.25	3.50	1.50
70	Chech,Robert	5.25	3.50	1.50
71	Clarke,Fred	7.50	5.00	2.00
72	Conroy,Wid	5.25	3.50	1.50
73	Delehanty,Jim	5.25	3.50	1.50
74	Donahue,Jiggs	5.25	3.50	1.50
75	Donohue,J. A.	5.25	3.50	1.50
76	Gibson,George	5.25	3.50	1.50
77	Groom,Bob	5.25	3.50	1.50
78	Hooper,Harry	7.50	5.00	2.00
79	Hughes,Tom	5.25	3.50	1.50
80	Johnson,Walter	13.50	9.00	4.00
81	Leach,Tommy	5.25	3.50	1.50
82	Leever,Sam	5.25	3.50	1.50
83	Lord,Harry	5.25	3.50	1.50
84	McBride,George	5.25	3.50	1.50
85	McConnell,Amby	5.25	3.50	1.50
86	Milan,Clyde	5.25	3.50	1.50
87	Miller,J. B.	5.25	3.50	1.50
88	Niles,Harry	5.25	3.50	1.50
89	Phillippe,Deacon	6.00	4.00	1.50
90	Speaker,Tris	11.00	7.00	3.00
91	Stahl,Jack	6.00	4.00	1.50
92	Storke,Allen	5.25	3.50	1.50
93	Street,Gabby	5.25	3.50	1.50
94	Unglaub,Bob	5.25	3.50	1.50
95	Wagner,C.	5.25	3.50	1.50
96	Wagner,Hans	13.50	9.00	4.00
97	Willis,Vic	5.25	3.50	1.50
98	Wilson,Owen	5.25	3.50	1.50
99	Wood,Joe	6.00	4.00	1.50

E92 50 BASE BALL PLAYERS (55)   1 1/2" X 2 3/4"

re are 55 cards in this set ed about 1910 by Dock-, Nadja, and Croft and n. There are four known rses, with the "Base Ball Gum" (Dockman) back the most common, and the "Nadja" back the most difficult (Nadja backs with blue printing on the obverse belong to E104). The set contains poses identical to those in E101, E102 and E105.

Base Ball Gum.

THIS CARD IS ONE OF A SET OF 50 Base Ball Players PROMINENT MEMBERS OF NATIONAL AND AMERICAN LEAGUES, ONE OF WHICH IS WRAPPED WITH EVERY PACKAGE OF BASE BALL GUM.

Manufactured only by JOHN H. DOCKMAN & SONS

Play Ball! AND EAT

Nadja Caramels

The Winners

CANDY CROFTS

CROFT AND ALLEN CO. Philadelphia, Pa.

CROFT'S SWISS MILK COCOA

Served Hot at Our Fountain 11 South 15th St. Montague & Co. Philadelphia, Pa.

Bridwell, s.s. N. Y., Nat'l

	MINT	VG-E	F-G
PLETE SET	850.00	600.00	250.00
MON PLAYER(1-55)	7.50	5.00	2.00
Bailey,Bill	7.50	5.00	2.00
Barry,Jack	12.00	8.00	3.00
Bemis,Harry	7.50	5.00	2.00
Bender,Chief (striped cap)	30.00	20.00	8.00
Bender,Chief (white cap)	12.00	8.00	3.00
Bergen,Bill	7.50	5.00	2.00
Bescher,Bob	7.50	5.00	2.00
Bridwell,Al	7.50	5.00	2.00
Casey	7.50	5.00	2.00
Chance,Frank	12.00	8.00	3.00
Chase,Hal	9.00	6.00	2.50
Cobb,Ty	90.00	60.00	25.00
Collins,Eddie	40.00	26.00	10.00
Crawford,Sam	12.00	8.00	3.00
Davis,Harry	7.50	5.00	2.00
Devlin,Art	7.50	5.00	2.00
Donovan,Wild Bill	7.50	5.00	2.00
Dooin,Red	12.00	8.00	3.00
Doolan,Mickey	7.50	5.00	2.00
Dougherty,Patsy	7.50	5.00	2.00
Doyle,Larry (batting)	9.00	6.00	2.50
Doyle,Larry (throwing)	9.00	6.00	2.50
Evers,Johnny	65.00	45.00	20.00
Gibson,George	7.50	5.00	2.00

		MINT	VG-E	F-G
23	Hartsel,Topsy	7.50	5.00	2.00
24	Hartzell,Fred	65.00	45.00	20.00
25	Howell,Harry	65.00	45.00	20.00
26	Jacklitsch,Fred	12.00	8.00	3.00
27	Jennings,Hugh	12.00	8.00	3.00
28	Kleinow,Red	7.50	5.00	2.00
29	Knabe,Otto	12.00	8.00	3.00
30	Knight,John	12.00	8.00	3.00
31	LaJoie,Napoleon	20.00	13.00	5.00
32	Lobert,Hans	7.50	5.00	2.00
33	Magee,Sherry	7.50	5.00	2.00
34	Mathewson,Christy	30.00	20.00	8.00
35	McGraw,John	20.00	13.00	5.00
36	McLean,Larry	7.50	5.00	2.00
37A	Miller,J. B. (batting)	9.00	6.00	2.50
37B	Miller,J. B. (fielding)	12.00	8.00	3.00
38	Murphy,Danny	7.50	5.00	2.00
39	O'Hara,Bill	7.50	5.00	2.00
40	Schaefer,Germany	7.50	5.00	2.00
41	Schlei,Admiral	7.50	5.00	2.00
42	Schmidt,Boss	7.50	5.00	2.00
43	Seigle	7.50	5.00	2.00
44	Shean,Dave	7.50	5.00	2.00
45	Smith	7.50	5.00	2.00
46	Stone,George	65.00	45.00	20.00
47	Tinker,Joe	12.00	8.00	3.00
48A	Wagner,Honus (batting)	40.00	26.00	10.00
48B	Wagner,Honus (throw)	40.00	26.00	10.00
49	Wallace,Bobby	65.00	45.00	20.00
50	Young,Cy	20.00	13.00	5.00
51	Zimmerman,Heinie	7.50	5.00	2.00

E93 BASE BALL STARS (30)   1 1/2" X 2 3/4"

The E93 set was distributed by Standard Caramel in 1910. It consists of black & white player photos which were tinted and placed against solid color backgrounds. A checklist, starting with "Ames," is printed in brown ink on the reverse. Some blank backs are known and all poses also appear in W555.

BASE BALL STARS
This card is one of a set of 30 stars from original photographs
1. AMES, New York National
2. BENDER, Phila. American
3. BROWN, Chicago National
4. COLLINS, Phila. American
5. CHANCE, Chicago National
6. COVELESKIE, Cincinnati Nat'l
7. CHASE, New York American
8. COBB, Detroit American
9. CLARKE, Pittsburg National
10. DELEHANTY, Detroit American
11. DONOVAN, Philadelphia National
12. DOOIN, Philadelphia National
13. EVERS, Chicago National
14. GIBSON, Pittsburg National
15. GRIFFITH, Cincinnati National
16. JENNINGS, Detroit American
17. JONES, Detroit American
18. JOSS, Cleveland American
19. LAJOIE, Cleveland American
20. LEACH, Pittsburg National
21. MATHEWSON, N. Y. National
22. McGRAW, New York National
23. PHILLIPPI, Pittsburg National
24. PLANK, Philadelphia American
25. PASTORIOUS, Brooklyn Nat'l
26. TINKER, Chicago National
27. WADDELL, St. Louis American
28. WAGNER, Pittsburg National
29. WILTSE, New York National
30. CY, YOUNG, Cleveland Amer.
Manufactured only by
Standard Caramel Co., Lancaster, Pa.

TINKER, Chicago Nat'l.

	MINT	VG-E	F-G
PLETE SET	450.00	300.00	120.00
MON PLAYER(1-30)	9.00	6.00	2.50
Ames,Red	9.00	6.00	2.50
Bender,Chief	15.00	10.00	4.00
Brown,Mordecai	15.00	10.00	4.00
Chance,Frank	20.00	13.00	5.50
Chase,Hal	10.00	6.50	3.00
Cobb,Ty	90.00	60.00	25.00
Collins,Eddie	15.00	10.00	4.00
Coveleskie,Stan	15.00	10.00	4.00
Clarke,Fred	15.00	10.00	4.00
Delehanty	10.00	6.50	3.00
Donovan,Wild Bill	9.00	6.00	2.50
Dooin,Red	9.00	6.00	2.50
Evers,Johnny	15.00	10.00	4.00
Gibson,George	9.00	6.00	2.50
Griffith,Clarke	15.00	10.00	4.00

		MINT	VG-E	F-G
16	Jennings,Hugh	15.00	10.00	4.00
17	Jones	9.00	6.00	2.50
18	Joss,Addie	20.00	13.00	5.50
19	LaJoie,Napoleon	27.00	18.00	8.00
20	Leach,Tommy	9.00	6.00	2.50
21	Mathewson,Christy	36.00	24.00	10.00
22	McGraw,John	20.00	13.00	5.50
23	Pastorius,Jim	9.00	6.00	2.50
24	Phillippe,Deacon	10.00	6.50	3.00
25	Plank,Eddie	15.00	10.00	4.00
26	Tinker,Joe	15.00	10.00	4.00
27	Waddel,Rube	15.00	10.00	4.00
28	Wagner,Honus	36.00	24.00	10.00
29	Wiltse,Hooks	9.00	6.00	2.50
30	Young,Cy	20.00	13.00	5.50

E94 STAR BASE BALL PLAYERS (30)   1 1/2" X 2 3/4"

DOOLAN, Phila. Natl.

	This card is one of a set of Star Base Ball Players' Cards as follows :
	MOORE, Philadelphia National
	GRANT, Cincinnati National
	MURRAY, New York National
	BYRNE, Pittsburg National
	CRAWFORD, Detroit American
	AUSTIN, New York American
	JOE LAKE, St. Louis National
	LOBERT, Philadelphia National
	MAGEE, Philadelphia National
	HUGH JENNINGS, Det. American
	DOOLAN, Philadelphia National
	OLD CY YOUNG, Cleveland Amer.
	HARRY DAVIS, Phila. American
	McGRAW, New York National
	TY COBB, Detroit American
	TOMMY LEACH, Pittsburg Natl.
	LORD, Chicago American
	DOUGHERTY, New York American
	LAJOIE, Cleveland American
	DEVORE, New York National
	CHANCE, Chicago National
	CICOTTE, Boston American
	BATES, Philadelphia National
	HANS WAGNER, Pittsburg Natl.
	SPEAKER, Boston American
	KLEINOW, New York American
	BESCHER, Cincinnati National
	TURNER, Cleveland American
	EVERS, Chicago National
	DEVLIN, New York National

The E94 format, like that of E93, consists of tinted, black & white photos on solid color backgrounds (seven colors seen; each player seen in more than one color). Issued in 1911, cards from this set may be found with advertising overstamps covering the gray-print checklist on the back (begins with "Moore"). Some blank backs have been found, and the set is identical to M131.

	MINT	VG-E	F-G
COMPLETE SET	450.00	300.00	120.00
COMMON PLAYER(1-30)	11.00	7.00	3.00

		MINT	VG-E	F-G
1	Austin,Jimmy	11.00	7.00	3.00
2	Bates,Johnny	11.00	7.00	3.00
3	Bescher,Bob	11.00	7.00	3.00
4	Byrne,Bobby	11.00	7.00	3.00
5	Chance,Frank	27.00	18.00	8.00
6	Cicotte,Eddie	11.00	7.00	3.00
7	Cobb,Ty	90.00	60.00	25.00
8	Crawford,Sam	20.00	13.00	5.50
9	Davis,Harry	11.00	7.00	3.00
10	Devlin,Art	11.00	7.00	3.00
11	Devore,Josh	11.00	7.00	3.00
12	Doolan,Mickey	11.00	7.00	3.00
13	Dougherty,Patsy	11.00	7.00	3.00
14	Evers,Johnny	20.00	13.00	5.50
15	Grant,Eddie	11.00	7.00	3.00

		MINT	VG-E	F-G
16	Jennings,Hugh	20.00	13.00	5.50
17	Keinow,Red	11.00	7.00	3.00
18	Lajoie,Napoleon	36.00	24.00	10.00
19	Lake,Joe	11.00	7.00	3.00
20	Leach,Tommy	11.00	7.00	3.00
21	Lobert,Hans	11.00	7.00	3.00
22	Lord,Harry	11.00	7.00	3.00
23	Magee,Sherry	11.00	7.00	3.00
24	McGraw,John	27.00	18.00	8.00
25	Moore,Earl	11.00	7.00	3.00
26	Murray,Red	11.00	7.00	3.00
27	Speaker,Tris	27.00	18.00	8.00
28	Turner,Terry	11.00	7.00	3.00
29	Wagner,Hans	50.00	35.00	15.00
30	Young,Old Cy	36.00	24.00	10.00

E95 25 BALL PLAYERS (25)   1 1/2" X 2 3/4"

WAGNER, PITTSBURG NAT'L.

	This card is one of a set of 25 BALL PLAYERS Cards, as follows :
	1. WAGNER, Pittsburg National
	2. MADDOX, Pittsburg National
	3. MERKLE, New York National
	4. MORGAN, Athletics American
	5. BENDER, Athletics American
	6. KRAUSE, Athletics American
	7. DEVLIN, New York National
	8. McINTYRE, Detroit American
	9. COBB, Detroit American
	10. WILLETTS, Detroit American
	11. CRAWFORD, Detroit Amer.
	12. MATTHEWSON, N. Y. Nat'l
	13. WILTSE, New York National
	14. DOYLE, New York National
	15. LEACH, Pittsburg National
	16. LORD, Boston American
	17. CICOTTE, Boston American
	18. CARRIGAN, Boston American
	19. WILLIS, Pittsburg National
	20. EVERS, Chicago National
	21. CHANCE, Chicago National
	22. HOFFMAN, Chicago National
	23. PLANK, Athletics American
	24. COLLINS, Athletics American
	25. REULBACH, Chicago Nat'l
	Made by
	PHILADELPHIA CARAMEL CO.
	Camden, New Jersey

This set of color drawings was issued by the Philadelphia Caramel Company about 1909. The back is checklisted with its own numbering system (begins with 1. Wagner), but has been alphabetized for convenience in this listing. Blank backs found in this set are probably cut from advertising panels and should not be considered as proof cards.

	MINT	VG-E	F-G
COMPLETE SET	300.00	200.00	80.00
COMMON PLAYER(1-25)	7.50	5.00	2.00

		MINT	VG-E	F-G
1	Bender,Chief	12.00	8.00	3.50
2	Carrigan,Bill	7.50	5.00	2.00
3	Chance,Frank	18.00	12.00	5.00
4	Cicotte,Eddie	7.50	5.00	2.00
5	Cobb,Ty	75.00	50.00	20.00
6	Collins,Eddie	12.00	8.00	3.50
7	Crawford,Sam	12.00	8.00	3.50
8	Devlin,Art	7.50	5.00	2.00
9	Doyle,Larry	7.50	5.00	2.00
10	Evers,Johnny	12.00	8.00	3.50
11	Hoffman,Solly	7.50	5.00	2.00
12	Krause,Harry	7.50	5.00	2.00
13	Leach,Tommy	7.50	5.00	2.00

		MINT	VG-E	F-G
14	Lord,Harry	7.50	5.00	2.00
15	Maddox,Nick	7.50	5.00	2.00
16	Mathewson,Christy	27.00	18.00	8.00
17	McIntyre,Matty	7.50	5.00	2.00
18	Merkle,Fred	8.50	6.00	2.50
19	Morgan,Harry (Cy)	7.50	5.00	2.00
20	Plank,Eddie	18.00	12.00	5.00
21	Reulbach,Ed	7.50	5.00	2.00
22	Wagner,Honus	36.00	24.00	10.00
23	Willett,Ed	7.50	5.00	2.00
24	Willis,Vic	7.50	5.00	2.00
25	Wiltse,Hooks	7.50	5.00	2.00

E96 30 BALL PLAYERS (30)　　　　1 1/2" X 2 3/4"

> This Card is one of a New Set of
> **30 BALL PLAYERS**
> 1. DAVIS, Athletics
> 2. CONNIE MACK, Athletics
> 3. THOMAS, Athletics
> 4. BAKER, Athletics
> 5. DOOIN, Phila. Natl.
> 6. McQUILLAN, Phila. Natl.
> 7. KONETCHY, St. Louis Natl
> 8. KARGER, St. Louis Natl.
> 9. MOWRAY, St. Louis Natl.
> 10. MURRAY, St. Louis Natl.
> 11. LAJOIE, Cleveland
> 12. ROSSMAN, Cleveland
> 13. RUCKER, Brooklyn
> 14. JENNINGS, Detroit
> 15. DONOVAN, Detroit
> 16. DELAHANTY, Detroit
> 17. MULLIN, Detroit
> 18. ARRELANES, Boston Am
> 19. SPENCER, Boston Am.
> 20. KLING, Chicago
> 21. PFISTER, Chicago
> 22. BROWN, Chicago
> 23. TINKER, Chicago
> 24. CLARK, Pittsburg
> 25. GIBSON, Pittsburg
> 26. ADAMS, Pittsburg
> 27. AMES, N. Y. Natl.
> 28. MARQUARD, N. Y. Natl.
> 29. HERZOG, N. Y. Natl.
> 30. MYERS, N. Y. Natl.
> Previous Series 25, making total issue 55 Cards
> **PHILADELPHIA CARAMEL CO.**
> Camden, N. J.

The red-printed backs in this set carry the statement "Previous Series 25, making total issue 55 cards," and for this reason it is often referred to as the second series of E95. Issued about 1912, the numbering of the original checklist (starts with 1. Davis) has been rearranged alphabetically below. Some blank backs are known.

	MINT	VG-E	F-G
COMPLETE SET	270.00	180.00	80.00
COMMON PLAYER(1-30)	8.00	5.50	2.25

		MINT	VG-E	F-G				MINT	VG-E	F-G
1	Adams,Bert	8.00	5.50	2.25		16	Konetchy,Ed	8.00	5.50	2.25
2	Ames,Red	8.00	5.50	2.25		17	Lajoie,Napoleon	22.50	15.00	6.00
3	Arrelanes	8.00	5.50	2.25		18	Mack,Connie	22.50	15.00	6.00
4	Baker,J. Frank	12.50	8.50	3.50		19	Marquard,Rube	12.50	8.50	3.50
5	Brown,Mordecai	12.50	8.50	3.50		20	McQuillan,George	8.00	5.50	2.25
6	Clark,Fred (sic)	12.50	8.50	3.50		21	Meyers,Chief	8.00	5.50	2.25
7	Davis,Harry	8.00	5.50	2.25		22	Mowrey,Mike	8.00	5.50	2.25
8	Delahanty,Jim	9.00	6.00	2.50		23	Mullin,George	8.00	5.50	2.25
9	Donovan,Wild Bill	8.00	5.50	2.25		24	Murray,Red	8.00	5.50	2.25
10	Dooin,Red	8.00	5.50	2.25		25	Pfeister,Jack	8.00	5.50	2.25
11	Gibson,George	8.00	5.50	2.25		26	Rossman,Claude	8.00	5.50	2.25
12	Herzog,Buck	8.00	5.50	2.25		27	Rucker,Nap	8.00	5.50	2.25
13	Jennings,Hugh	12.50	8.50	3.50		28	Spencer,Tubby	8.00	5.50	2.25
14	Karger,Ed	8.00	5.50	2.25		29	Thomas,Ira	8.00	5.50	2.25
15	Kling,Johnny	8.00	5.50	2.25		30	Tinker,Joe	12.50	8.50	3.50

E97 30 BALL PLAYERS (32)　　　　1 1/2" X 2 3/4"

> This card is one of a set of
> **30 BALL PLAYERS**
> Cards, as follows:
> AUSTIN, New York American
> BRADLEY, Cleveland American
> BIRMINGHAM, Cleveland American
> BRANSFIELD, Philadelphia National
> CARRIGAN, Boston American
> CAMNITZ, Pittsburg National
> DURHAM, New York American
> DYGERT, Philadelphia American
> DOOLAN, Philadelphia National
> DEVORE, Philadelphia American
> DAVIS, Philadelphia American
> HEMPHILL, New York American
> HEINCHMAN, Cleveland American
> HARTSEL, Philadelphia American
> KROH, Chicago National
> KLEINOW, New York American
> KELLY, Boston National
> KEELER, New York National
> McINTYRE, Detroit American
> McCONNELL, Boston American
> MOORE, Philadelphia National
> MULLIN, Detroit American
> MURRAY, New York National
> MEYERS, New York National
> NICHOLS, Cleveland American
> ROSSMAN, Detroit American
> SULLIVAN, Chicago American
> STEINFELDT, Chicago National
> SCHLEI, New York National
> CY. YOUNG, Cleveland American
> **C.A.BRIGGS CO.**, Lozenge Makers
> Boston, Mass.

The C.A. Briggs Company distributed this set in 1909, and it is one of the most highly prized of caramel issues. The cards come in two distinct varieties: one group in color with a brown-print checklist on back; the other with identical player poses in black & white with blank backs. A comparison of team and name variations suggests that the black & white set pre-dates the color issue.

	MINT	VG-E	F-G
COMPLETE SET	700.00	500.00	200.00
COMMON PLAYER(1-32)	20.00	13.00	6.00

	MINT	VG-E	F-G			MINT	VG-E	F-G
Austin,Jimmy	20.00	13.00	6.00		18 Kroh,Rube	20.00	13.00	6.00
Birmingham,Joe	20.00	13.00	6.00		19 McConnell,Amby	20.00	13.00	6.00
Bradley,William J.	20.00	13.00	6.00		20 McIntyre,Matty	20.00	13.00	6.00
Bransfield,Kitty	20.00	13.00	6.00		21 Meyers,Chief	20.00	13.00	6.00
Camnitz,Howie	20.00	13.00	6.00		22 Moore,Earl	20.00	13.00	6.00
Carrigan,Bill	20.00	13.00	6.00		23 Mullin,George	20.00	13.00	6.00
Davis,Harry	20.00	13.00	6.00		24 Murray,Red	20.00	13.00	6.00
Devore,Josh	20.00	13.00	6.00		25 Nichols,Simon(sic)	20.00	13.00	6.00
Doolan,Mickey	20.00	13.00	6.00		26 Rossman,Claude	20.00	13.00	6.00
Durham,Bull	20.00	13.00	6.00		27 Schlei,Admiral	20.00	13.00	6.00
Dygert,Jimmy	20.00	13.00	6.00		28 Steinfeldt,Harry	22.50	15.00	6.50
Hartsel,Topsy	20.00	13.00	6.00		29A Sullivan,W. J.	22.50	15.00	6.50
Hemphill,Charlie	20.00	13.00	6.00		29B Sullivan,W. J. (Boston)	90.00	60.00	25.00
Hinchman,Bill	20.00	13.00	6.00		30A Young,Cy (Boston)	90.00	60.00	25.00
Keeler,Willie	45.00	30.00	12.00		30B Young,Cy (Cleve.)	36.00	24.00	10.00
Kelly,Joseph J.	36.00	24.00	10.00					
Kleinow,Red	20.00	13.00	6.00					

> Most serious collectors subscribe to at least one of the hobby papers. Read the ads in this Guide for The Trader Speaks (for advanced collectors), Sports Collectors Digest, and Baseball Hobby News to determine which one or more appeal to you.

E98 30 BALL PLAYERS (30)   1 1/2" X 2 3/4"

E98 is an anonymous set with more similarities to Standard Caramel issues than to Briggs. Most players are found with four different background colors and the brown-print checklist (starts with 1. "Christy" Mathewson) has been alphabetized below. The set was issued in 1910.

	MINT	VG-E	F-G
COMPLETE SET	550.00	375.00	160.00
COMMON PLAYER(1-30)	14.00	10.00	4.00

	MINT	VG-E	F-G
1 Bender,Chief	21.00	14.00	6.00
2 Bresnahan,Roger	21.00	14.00	6.00
3 Bridwell,Al	14.00	10.00	4.00
4 Brown,Miner	21.00	14.00	6.00
5 Chance,Frank	24.00	16.00	7.00
6 Chase,Hal	16.00	11.00	4.50
7 Clarke,Fred	21.00	14.00	6.00
8 Cobb,Ty	90.00	60.00	25.00
9 Collins,Eddie	21.00	14.00	6.00
10 Coombs,Jack	16.00	11.00	4.50
11 Dahlen,Bill	14.00	10.00	4.00
12 Davis,Harry	14.00	10.00	4.00
13 Dooin,Red	14.00	10.00	4.00
14 Evers,Johnny	21.00	14.00	6.00
15 Ford,Russ	14.00	10.00	4.00

	MINT	VG-E	F-G
16 Jennings,Hughey	21.00	14.00	6.00
17 Kling,Johnny	14.00	10.00	4.00
18 Lajoie,Napoleon	45.00	30.00	12.00
19 Mack,Connie	36.00	24.00	10.00
20 Mathewson,Christy	45.00	30.00	12.00
21 McGraw,John	24.00	16.00	7.00
22 McLean,Larry	14.00	10.00	4.00
23 Meyers,Chief	14.00	10.00	4.00
24 Mullin,George	14.00	10.00	4.00
25 Tenney,Fred	14.00	10.00	4.00
26 Tinker,Joe	21.00	14.00	6.00
27 Vaughn,Hippo	14.00	10.00	4.00
28 Wagner,Hans	45.00	30.00	12.00
29 Walsh,Ed	21.00	14.00	6.00
30 Young,Cy	24.00	16.00	7.00

E99 30 COAST LEAGUE PLAYERS (30)   1 1/2" X 2 3/4"

Although there is no manufacturer's name to be found on the cards of this series, the similarities to set E100 almost certainly mark it as a product of Bishop & Co. The 30 subjects are Coast League players, portrayed in black and white photos on solid color backgrounds. The cards are unnumbered but are back listed (starting with "Knapp"). The set was issued about 1910, and some players are found with more than one background color. The cards have been alphabetized and assigned numbers in the checklist below.

	MINT	VG-E	F-G
COMPLETE SET	1000.00	650.00	250.00
COMMON PLAYER	36.00	24.00	10.00

	MINT	VG-E	F-G
1 Bodie	36.00	24.00	10.00
2 N. Brashear	36.00	24.00	10.00
3 Briggs	36.00	24.00	10.00
4 Byones	36.00	24.00	10.00
5 Cameron	36.00	24.00	10.00
6 Casey	36.00	24.00	10.00
7 Cutshaw	36.00	24.00	10.00
8 Delmas	36.00	24.00	10.00
9 Dillon	36.00	24.00	10.00
10 Hasty	36.00	24.00	10.00
11 Hitt	36.00	24.00	10.00
12 Hap. Hogan	36.00	24.00	10.00
13 Hunt	36.00	24.00	10.00
14 Krapp	36.00	24.00	10.00
15 Lindsay	36.00	24.00	10.00

	MINT	VG-E	F-G
16 Maggert	36.00	24.00	10.0
17 McArdle	36.00	24.00	10.0
18 McCredie	36.00	24.00	10.0
19 Melchoir	36.00	24.00	10.0
20 Mohler	36.00	24.00	10.0
21 Nagle	36.00	24.00	10.0
22 Nelson	36.00	24.00	10.0
23 Nourse	36.00	24.00	10.0
24 Olsen	36.00	24.00	10.0
25 Raymer	36.00	24.00	10.0
26 Smith	36.00	24.00	10.0
27 Tennent	36.00	24.00	10.0
28 Thorsen	36.00	24.00	10.0
29 Van Buren	36.00	24.00	10.0
30 Wolverton	36.00	24.00	10.0

DON'T MISS OUT ON THE SPORT AMERICANA 1982 BASEBALL CARD SUMMARY. DETAILS ARE LOCATED IN THE 1982 TOPPS SECTION OF THIS PRICE GUIDE.

E100 BISHOP 30 COAST LEAGUE (30)   1 1/2" X 2 3/4"
BALLPLAYERS

Each of the 30 cards of this Coast League set have the inscription "Bishop & Co." printed on the reverse at the bottom. Otherwise, the style of the cards is similar to set E99: they have black and white photos set on solid color backgrounds, they are backlisted (starts with "Seaton"), and they are unnumbered. There are color variations for many players, and subjects marked by an asterisk are found only in a blank-backed, slightly larger card with a green background. The cards have been alphabetized and numbered in the checklist below.

	MINT	VG-E	F-G
COMPLETE SET	1000.00	650.00	250.00
COMMON PLAYER	36.00	24.00	10.00

	MINT	VG-E	F-G			MINT	VG-E	F-G
Baum	36.00	24.00	10.00	16 O'Rourke		36.00	24.00	10.00
Burrell *	36.00	24.00	10.00	17 Patterson		36.00	24.00	10.00
Carlisle	36.00	24.00	10.00	18 Pearce *		36.00	24.00	10.00
Cutshaw	36.00	24.00	10.00	19 Peckinpaugh		40.00	27.00	12.00
Daley	36.00	24.00	10.00	20 Pfyle *		36.00	24.00	10.00
Danzig *	36.00	24.00	10.00	21 Powell		36.00	24.00	10.00
Delhi	36.00	24.00	10.00	22 Rapps		36.00	24.00	10.00
Delmas	36.00	24.00	10.00	23 Seaton *		36.00	24.00	10.00
Hitt *	36.00	24.00	10.00	24 Steen		36.00	24.00	10.00
Hogan	36.00	24.00	10.00	25 Suter		36.00	24.00	10.00
Lerchen	36.00	24.00	10.00	26 Tennant		36.00	24.00	10.00
McCreedie	36.00	24.00	10.00	27 Thomas		36.00	24.00	10.00
Mohler	36.00	24.00	10.00	28 Tozer		36.00	24.00	10.00
Moore	36.00	24.00	10.00	29 Wares		36.00	24.00	10.00
Nelson	36.00	24.00	10.00	30 Weaver		36.00	24.00	10.00

E101 50 BASE BALL PLAYERS (50)   1 1/2" X 2 3/4"

The "Prominent Members of National and American Leagues" portrayed in E101 are identical to the line drawings of E92 and E105. The set was distributed about 1910.

	MINT	VG-E	F-G
COMPLETE SET	600.00	400.00	150.00
COMMON PLAYER(1-50)	11.00	7.00	3.00

	MINT	VG-E	F-G			MINT	VG-E	F-G
Barry,Jack	11.00	7.00	3.00	26 Knabe,Otto		11.00	7.00	3.00
Bemis,Harry	15.00	10.00	4.00	27 Knight,John		11.00	7.00	3.00
Bender,Chief (2)	15.00	10.00	4.00	28 Lajoie,Napoleon		25.00	17.00	7.00
Bergen,Bill	11.00	7.00	3.00	29 Lobert,Hans		11.00	7.00	3.00
Bescher,Bob	11.00	7.00	3.00	30 Magee,Sherry		11.00	7.00	3.00
Bridwell,Al	11.00	7.00	3.00	31 Mathewson,Christy		36.00	24.00	10.00
Casey,Doc	11.00	7.00	3.00	32 McGraw,John		18.00	12.00	5.00
Chance,Frank	18.00	12.00	5.00	33 McLean,Larry		11.00	7.00	3.00
Chase,Hal	12.00	8.00	3.50	34A Miller,J. B.		12.00	8.00	3.50
Cobb,Ty	90.00	60.00	25.00		(batting)			
Collins,Eddie	15.00	10.00	4.00	34B Miller,J. B.		12.00	8.00	3.50
Crawford,Sam	15.00	10.00	4.00		(fielding)			
Davis,Harry	11.00	7.00	3.00	35 Murphy,Danny		11.00	7.00	3.00
Devlin,Art	11.00	7.00	3.00	36 O'Harra,Bill		11.00	7.00	3.00
Donovan,Wild Bill	11.00	7.00	3.00	37 Schaefer,Germany		11.00	7.00	3.00
Dooin,Red	11.00	7.00	3.00	38 Schlei,Admiral		11.00	7.00	3.00
Doolan,Mickey	11.00	7.00	3.00	39 Schmidt,Boss		11.00	7.00	3.00
Dougherty,Patsy	11.00	7.00	3.00	40 Seigle		11.00	7.00	3.00
A Doyle,Larry	12.00	8.00	3.50	41 Shean,Dave		11.00	7.00	3.00
(batting)				42 Smith		11.00	7.00	3.00
B Doyle,Larry(throw	12.00	8.00	3.50	43 Tinker,Joe		15.00	10.00	4.00
Evers,Johnny	11.00	7.00	3.00	44A Wagner,Honus		50.00	35.00	15.00
Gibson,George	11.00	7.00	3.00		(batting)			
Harsel,Topsy	11.00	7.00	3.00	44B Wagner,Honus		50.00	35.00	15.00
Jacklitsch,Fred	11.00	7.00	3.00		(throwing)			
Jennings,Hugh	15.00	10.00	4.00	45 Young,Cy		18.00	12.00	5.00
Kleinow,Red	11.00	7.00	3.00	46 Zimmerman,Heine		11.00	7.00	3.00

N173-2 DOG'S HEAD

N173-1 OLD JUDGE

N566 NEWSBOY

**19th CENTURY
ADVERTISING PIECE**

**M117 SPORTING TIMES
INSERT**

**19th CENTURY
CIGAR AD**

**JOSEPH HALL
STUDIO CABINET**

1888 POLICE GAZETTE

N693 KALAMAZOO BAT

**LARGE 19th CENTURY
CABINETS & AD CARDS**